Wreckers

Wreckers

Disaster in the Age of Discovery

SIMON PARK

PENGUIN
VIKING

VIKING

UK | USA | Canada | Ireland | Australia
India | New Zealand | South Africa

Viking is part of the Penguin Random House group of companies
whose addresses can be found at global.penguinrandomhouse.com

Penguin Random House UK,
One Embassy Gardens, 8 Viaduct Gardens, London sw11 7bw

penguin.co.uk

Penguin
Random House
UK

First published 2025

001

Set in 12/14.75pt Bembo Book MT Pro
Typeset by Jouve (UK), Milton Keynes
Printed and bound in Great Britain by Clays Ltd, Elcograf S.p.A.

The authorized representative in the EEA is Penguin Random House Ireland,
Morrison Chambers, 32 Nassau Street, Dublin D02 YH68

A CIP catalogue record for this book is available from the British Library

ISBN: 978–0–241–74132–0

To Mum, Dad, Richard, Oliver and Alice

Contents

List of Illustrations

List of Maps

Introduction: A Disasterful View of History

At the end of the fifteenth century, men in ships set off from the ports of Europe into the unknown. Tenacious, intrepid, they crossed oceans never before traversed and found lands they had never dreamed of.

But that's far from the full story. When it comes to the first century of European transcontinental voyages by sea and the empires that were built on the back of them, we are too addicted to an action-hero version of history: triumphant beginnings with swashbuckling protagonists. Even recent books that challenge the history of empire struggle to avoid casting European captains as heroes who pushed forward the boundaries of knowledge. Yet building and maintaining an empire was not just a matter of reaching a faraway destination. It was, instead, a violent, messy, improvised process that took place over a long period of time. Disaster frequently struck early colonizers, and when it did, the foundations of empire trembled, even if the edifice did not immediately fall. Individuals, rulers and communities across the world rejected explorers, laughed at them and often set the rules of engagement in trade and territorial expansion despite European attempts to determine the world agenda with their weapons and their arrogance.

In his searing exposition of the history of European colonization and its after-effects in Latin America, the Uruguayan writer Eduardo Galeano provocatively concluded that 'development is a voyage with more shipwrecks than navigators'.[1] In the original Spanish, however, the word given as 'shipwreck' in the translation is *náufrago*, which refers more to the person wrecked than the vessel smashed apart. The slippage in the translation is slight, but important: Galeano is more interested in people than in ships. And so too is this book. *Wreckers* is about people who are wrecked, but also people who might be involved in the act of wrecking (and not just ships). The cast of characters in the chapters that follow occupy both these roles, wrecker and wrecked, hostage-taker and hostage to fortune. The central premise of this book is to underline that both these facets of voyaging were at play during the age of so-called 'discovery' and that during the sixteenth century itself, tales of disaster, failure, resistance and comeuppance circulated widely and were as integral to comprehending empire as any bloated propaganda.

Overall, this book offers an alternative timeline of the hundred years after Columbus first crossed the Atlantic and reached the Caribbean in 1492, one that brings out the fractures and fault lines that accompanied the increasing geographical range of European ships. I have gathered stories from across languages and continents which entangle us in the allegiances and rivalries, fighting and fighting back, short tempers and blunders that were part and parcel of imperial advances. These stories show that the tide was often set against Europeans, not to lionize their efforts further by suggesting they succeeded 'against the odds', but to put them back into proper perspective. As we follow Europeans on their voyages, we learn that they did not just depart out of insatiable curiosity and the spirit of adventure. Europeans knew that West Africa, China and India abounded in goods and gold, so they set their course to these places, seeking a slice of their riches. They left, then, with a sense of lack and of envy usually concealed by noisy arrogance. They hoped that their risky ventures would change their countries' fortunes. But the wreckers' green eyes often led to sinking ships: they stacked them too high with merchandise or bankrupted investors by mistaking worthless rocks for treasure. They killed, abducted and enslaved.

Christopher Columbus, Vasco da Gama, Gonzalo Guerrero, Ferdinand Magellan, Jean-François de la Rocque, Marguerite de Roberval, Hans Staden, Manuel and Leonor de Sousa de Sepúlveda, Martin Frobisher: my cast of Spaniards, Portuguese, French, Germans, English get kidnapped, stranded, abandoned and betrayed. Most wash up on the coasts of the Americas, Asia or Africa not as triumphant conquistadores but as castaways clinging to the splintered timbers of wrecks, resisted by communities everywhere from Brazil to Southeast Africa, from India to the Philippines. The weather does weird and dangerous things in these stories, flings ships in unwanted directions, leaves them stranded, or hacks at their timbers until the ship splits apart, turned inside out. We are used, perhaps, to thinking about shipwreck – the leitmotif of this book – as an ending: the premature, destructive culmination of a journey. But in these stories it is often just the prelude: the long and difficult part often comes next. After careering across the world's oceans, these stories end up traipsing through jungle, over sands, up mountains, across plains.

In the first fifty years of the sixteenth century, around 12 per cent of the Portuguese ships on the route between Lisbon and India were wrecked, and this rose to 16–18 per cent between 1550 and 1650.[2] Some 20 per cent of voyages travelling across the Pacific on the route between the Philippines and Mexico failed, either because of shipwreck or because the ships were forced to turn back.[3] The figures are lower for the Spanish Atlantic route, but researchers in Spain have, nonetheless, catalogued some 700 different wrecks of Spanish ships off the coast of the Bahamas and the United States dating between 1492 and 1898.[4] Estimates suggest around 7.5 per cent of English ships trading with the Indies during the Jacobean period were lost.[5] Shipwreck was a fact of life and a persistent worry for seafarers' families, merchants and bureaucrats alike, not just for their frequency but for the high toll of lives and financial loss involved when a ship did sink.[6]

Even when shipwrecks did not occur, many early attempts at colonization failed, with numerous places constantly embattled. In contrast to Spain's rapid expansion in parts of Mexico and Peru, all seven of Spain's attempts to colonize Florida during the sixteenth century failed.[7] So, too, did Diego de Nicuesa's attempt to colonize Panama in 1510 and Pedro Sarmiento de Gamboa's attempt to establish a colony near the Strait of Magellan in 1584.[8] Further struggles in Panama and Yucatán are detailed in Part Two. All French attempts to establish colonies in the sixteenth century, in both North and South America, were eventually abandoned. Marguerite de Roberval's story, encountered in Part Four, encompasses some of these struggles. While the later French empire developed differently, the early decades were not marked by easy imperial triumph. The Portuguese empire also faced constant challenges. For instance, it lost control of Aden in 1548, was expelled from Bahrain in 1602 and driven out of Hormuz by the Persians and English in 1622. It lost Mombasa by 1698 and was forced to leave Muscat in 1650 after continuous attacks, including significant assaults in 1552 and 1581 by Ottoman forces. In India, the Portuguese struggled to maintain control over key locations such as Goa, Daman and Diu. Diu, in particular, faced repeated conflicts, including major sieges in 1538 and 1546 by Gujarati and Ottoman forces. In Morocco, the Portuguese established several forts from the fifteenth century onwards but were eventually driven out, including from Agadir in 1541, Ceuta in 1578 and Tangier in 1661.[9] Elsewhere, Lucas Vázquez de Ayllón's colony in South Carolina in 1526 succumbed to disease and food shortages, while João Álvares Fagundes's Newfoundland and Nova Scotia settlements in the 1520s were abandoned due to severe weather and conflicts with local peoples. Similarly, Sir Walter Raleigh's 'Lost Colony' of Roanoke in 1587 probably vanished due to drought and local conflicts.[10] Part Seven details how the English fared around Baffin Island. European expansion must be seen in tandem with these more challenging stories. Resistance, adverse weather, disease and misjudgements hindered, even if they did not halt, colonial ambitions across the globe.

Depending on where you are reading this book and with what experience, different characters may be more or less familiar to you: some are emblems of resistance or sources of (sometimes ambiguous) pride in different places around the world. But rarely do these individuals meet each other in the pages of a single book, meaning that comparisons and connections lie overlooked. Often narratives about empire limit themselves to national or linguistic boundaries, despite the fact that, as you'll see, Europeans were constantly measuring themselves against each other and trying to occupy the same regions, and European individuals constantly kept shifting their allegiances. All their stories have had interesting afterlives. They have been translated and retold, had illustrations added or removed, been turned into theatrical spectacles or memorialized with statues (some of which have provoked protests). But the people and events in the chapters that follow have always been the subject of widespread debate. Many people of the past didn't accept simplistic hero-worship any more easily than we do, and recovering that sense of continual contestation is crucial.

One important aspect of this book comes from my own scholarly upbringing and experience, and that is the inclusion of Portuguese materials. Documents and books written in Portuguese seldom appear more than fleetingly in historical studies of empire or of Renaissance Europe in general. Yet Portugal transported more slaves across the Atlantic than any other nation, and Portuguese is one of the most spoken languages of the southern hemisphere because of the country's long and violent colonial history. As you'll see, Portuguese pilots and ships end up appearing in several chapters of this book that are not ostensibly about Portugal at all. Those Portuguese materials are key to understanding the global picture of the past, and it is in Portuguese-speaking countries that some of the most compelling new ideas are emerging to redress that past.

To see what I mean by the dual dimensions of maritime history – catastrophe alongside transcontinental crossings – you only have to glance over the contents of a manuscript preserved today in the Morgan Library of New York. This set of images, produced in Goa in western India, between 1558 and 1565, catalogues the Portuguese

The second fleet of Pedro Álvares Cabral in 1500 and its fate

Shipwreck of one of Fernão Soares
de Albergaria's fleet in 1552

Shipwreck of a Portuguese
ship on the way to India in 1547

armadas dispatched from Lisbon to Asia since Vasco da Gama's first voyage to Calicut (Kozhikode) in 1497/8.

You would expect these hand-drawn pages of caravels and carracks to focus on the splendour of the fleets, the fanfare of trumpets and panoply of flags. But as you turn each page, you notice that many of the ships are in flames or are sinking into the deep, with planks, barrels and people scattered on the surface of the waves. It is a visual record of maritime might and seaborne disaster all thrown together. Take for instance, the two pages dedicated to Pedro Álvares Cabral's fleet, which left Lisbon in 1500: winds urge the topmost ships on, blowing them across the ocean; but lower down, several ships are sinking, their prows nosediving into the water, their masts and sails wafting final signals of surrender to the sea. On the upturned hull of one vessel, figures stand shouting for help; another, shorn of its sails, is totally engulfed in flames. Other pages illustrate for us crates and barrels tossed into the sea, survivors on a shore, and there is even a cinematic shot of one ship plunging below the water's surface as it makes its descent towards the seabed. Disaster and what people of the period called 'discovery' were inseparable. The bare cluster of facts from this era that most of us have kept in our pockets since school don't capture the untidiness of the past as presented to us in documents like this.

The biography of Christopher Columbus would be another case in point. He died wanting to believe that the Caribbean islands and the coast of South America that he visited were really Asia: he had hoped to reach the riches of China, India and Japan, but hadn't. On his first voyage, the tiller of his flagship the *Santa María* was left in the hands of a ship's boy; the vessel carelessly drifted into a sandbank off the island of Hispaniola (present-day Haiti and the Dominican Republic) and broke up.[11] A stockade was constructed out of the *Santa María*'s timbers and thirty-nine men were left to defend it. When Columbus returned to the Caribbean on his second voyage in 1493, though, all those men had been killed by a *cacique*, or leader, called Caonaobó after the Spaniards had raided the interior for gold and women.[12] His third voyage (1498–1500) ended with him being brought back to Spain in chains, after disputes with other captains who rightly questioned his abilities as a governor. During his fourth voyage in 1502, a fleet sent back to Spain by the governor of Hispaniola, Nicolás de Ovando, was ravaged, despite warnings from Columbus, by a hurricane that sank around twenty vessels.[13] After exploring the coast of the American mainland between present-day Belize and Panama, Columbus himself then ran into a storm while trying to return to Hispaniola. Day after day passed without seeing sun nor stars, the fear of certain death swirling relentlessly in the stormy darkness. The ships that survived were falling to pieces; those aboard so enfeebled that they were capable of little more than constant prayer.[14] They ended up stranded in Jamaica for a year. Curiously, that very term 'hurricane' comes to us, via Spanish, from the word *hurakán* – 'god of the storms' in the language of the Taíno people of the Caribbean. The word's etymology is a little trace of something that comes from outside Europe, and beyond its control, to rock the boat.

Much of what follows is based upon European sources, but it is crucial that we recover forgotten voices and neglected sources in our collective attempts to decolonize the past. I do so by combining historical documents with the recent work of anthropologists and artists, inspired by a range of different indigenous perspectives, who are now creatively reshaping our understanding of the past across different art forms.[15] Nevertheless, there still remains important work to be done with the European material, finding overlooked stories and sounding out their silences and contradictions in order to open up new ways of looking at this period in history. Moreover, there is a strange tension in some historical discourse whereby scholars expose the crushing violence and exploitation of empire yet still cling to a 'great man' view of the past, in which extraordinary individuals crossed frontiers and pushed forward the boundaries of knowledge. Our collective understanding still privileges single moments that apparently 'changed the course of world history', giving the events of the past cleaner edges and clearer consequences than they possessed for those who experienced them.[16]

We need a more realistic view of these individuals, not another tale of exceptionalism. We need to see that these so-called heroes learned from other traditions and relied on other people, whom they often compelled to do their bidding through torture and by stripping away their rights. They were halted in their ambitions by frequent resistance, and they got lost, made tactical miscalculations, and overloaded their ships, causing their own wrecks. At times, Europeans were just an unfriendly blip in the lives of peoples on other continents, arriving to dig up the earth and then shortly after leave again.

The stories gathered here don't pretend to give a complete picture of this period, rather they are episodes that add grist to the progress of empire; a bit of friction to remind us it wasn't all smooth going. You'll see some of that larger picture in the series of timelines in this book, which give a sense of the turbulence felt during the intervals between the stories I tell.

One thing that has become very clear to me as I have put together this book is how alive the histories I am telling still are today. The events of this period, the source materials for them, and the long-enduring afterlives of both, are all being vigorously renegotiated. Indigenous artists in Brazil, for instance, have punctured the visual record of conquest with humorous additions to images and maps produced by Europeans. Across the globe, activists and artists are fighting for indigenous land rights, political sovereignty, and the repatriation of objects taken from their forebears. I see those contemporary actions as part of the historical story. For many, the choice to leave the past in the past is politically, intellectually, morally impossible. In this sense the past still feels unfixed, and it is being reimagined not within the pages of academic books, where scholars reveal the unearthing of new manuscripts and argue over the interpretation of the written record, but rather directly through people's lives, livelihoods and surroundings. Heritage sites, monuments and museums, in particular, have become the focus for debate and protest.

This sense of debate is not just a characteristic of the present, however. The history of protest is as long as the history of empire. What's more, the chronicles and archives that I draw upon often disagree with each other over what really happened and how we should interpret events. I don't dwell on every discrepancy in the sources, but I do guide you through some of the gaps in the evidence and point out what some of the differences of opinion can tell us about the significance of the events being described, and how unspoken agendas have shaped what gets written down and remembered.

None of this – the multiple perspectives; the importance of argument to the production of history; the emphasis on failure – is intended to downplay the impact of Europeans, their weapons and diseases and religion, on the peoples and places that they encountered and often eventually colonized. That would be to forget about the big picture entirely. But it is important to remember that this history was disjointed, discontinuous and disconnected; no less brutal, no less violent, but differently so, not just unrelenting, inevitable domination. During the period itself, questions were often raised about empire, its whats, hows and whys. At times, it looked like disaster might win out over European ships and arms. So it is properly historical to retrieve some of that uncertainty. If we see empires simplistically as unstoppable, even as we condemn them we surrender to precisely those narratives that empires have sought to tell of themselves. Europeans did advance brutally and rapidly across the globe; but if we forget that they met resistance and committed errors, we paint a misguided portrait of Europeans and we rob many of their agency.[17]

In returning to stories of failure, then, we gain a sense that history as we know it wasn't predestined. Designs for imperial dominion, such as they existed, were constantly redrawn in the light of opposition, catastrophe, new knowledge and persistent errors. Stories of failure open up a space for something akin to what visual studies scholar, Ariella Aïsha Azoulay, calls 'potential histories', where 'different options that were once eliminated are reactivated as a way of slowing the imperial movement of progress'.[18] Analysing how documents are written and then assembled to make up what scholars call an archive, acknowledging the limits of that archive, listening to those remaking our sense of the past in the present: all these things call on us to reimagine history, not as a series of predetermined events, but as a space of possibilities – then, now and in the future.

PART ONE

The Explorer Who Asked for Directions

'The discovery of America, and that of a passage to the East Indies by the Cape of Good Hope, are the two greatest and most important events recorded in the history of mankind,' wrote Adam Smith in *The Wealth of Nations* (1776).[1] It's a view of the past that has been hard to shake: Christopher Columbus went west to America and Vasco da Gama went east to India, steering world history in radically new directions and towards greater interconnectedness. In one way, ceasing to be enthralled by this heroic view of the past isn't so much about denying that these men did what they did, but rather looking more closely at their stories to consider what they really achieved, how they achieved it, and what their legacy was beyond the simple fact that they reached a place far from their point of departure. We saw in the introduction how Columbus failed on his own terms, going to the grave claiming America was China. Now we turn to the protagonist of Smith's other great and important event, the Portuguese nobleman Vasco da Gama, who led the first European ship to reach India by sailing round the southern tip of Africa.

Even in the twenty-first century Da Gama is still voted one of ten *grandes portugueses*: Great Portuguese. But he wasn't a likely candidate to become Portugal's national hero. He hailed from the small town of Sines in the lower Alentejo, a place removed from any of the cities – Lisbon, Porto, Faro – that a tourist today might think important. And by the time his king appointed him captain-major of a small fleet that would supposedly redirect the course of world history, he hadn't especially distinguished himself in any field. Scholars have been digging about in the Portuguese state archives for decades in search of information that might explain why the little-known Da Gama was selected by King Manuel to lead the 1497 expedition to India. As yet, though, no crumpled piece of vellum with the answer has been extracted from the vaults of the Torre do Tombo, Lisbon's national archive (which, from the outside, looks more like a nuclear bunker than a research library). Da Gama leapt into history from nowhere. It must be said that captains were primarily selected for being nobles rather than navigators – and were routinely satirized for not knowing their fore-sail from their yardarm – but it does still seem a little odd that the only trace of nautical involvement Da Gama had prior to 1497 was skipper-ing a small expedition in well-known waters some five years earlier. Nothing on the scale of – or the difficulty of – a voyage to India lies in his background.

To explain away this blank space in Da Gama's backstory, some historians have advanced the imaginative theory of Double-O-Da-Gama, suggesting he was a sailor-spy who had led secret reconnaissance missions down the coast of Africa prior to his breakthrough voyage, missions so top secret that they have left no archival trace. This fan-ciful theory tells us less about Da Gama himself than about how uncomfortable historians can find holes like this in the records and what fantasies they have concocted to plug them. A portrait of him from close to the end of his life and a quarter of a century after his first voyage to India, shows a tired-looking man in his fifties clutching a staff and gazing quizzically, perhaps even anxiously, into the distance.

Posthumous portrait of Vasco da Gama, c. 1565

There is little of the thrusting self-fashioning so common in the portraits of other governors and viceroys of the empire. He looks more wizened than triumphant. It is an interesting counterpoint to later and more grandiose portrayals that try to give the impression of a stereotypical adventurer; but, from what we know, Da Gama doesn't appear to have been an upstart or a striver or a man of unquenchable curiosity — those types we typically recognize as history's protagonists. He probably did not know much about the practical business of avoiding shoals and harnessing winds. As we'll see, he was more a short-tempered opportunist. He did accomplish something unprecedented (with plenty of help); but it has been kings, dictators, poets and historians who have made him, retrospectively, into a hero.[2]

When Da Gama set out from the banks of the Tagus river, he sailed in the wake of almost a century of Portuguese exploration down the West African coast. His journey to India was an incremental, if crucial, advance in Portuguese voyaging. Since Portugal's first incursion into North Africa, with the seizure of the stronghold of Ceuta in 1415, the country had been enriched by links with Africa, particularly the wealthy kingdoms in present-day Guinea and Sierra Leone, and had instigated the largest slave market in history. The aim, as the Portuguese sailed ever further south, was to round the southern tip of Africa and enter the Indian Ocean, where they could gain access to the trade in spices and other luxuries from Asia without any middlemen, and, they hoped, meet long-lost Christian kingdoms on the way. After many years of exploration, a crucial step forward was made in 1488, when Bartolomeu Dias rounded the Cape of Good Hope for the first time. But then followed a surprising interlude of navigational quiet lasting the nine years immediately preceding Da Gama's voyage. It seems that King João II, despite ordering timber for the construction of two large ocean-going vessels, got cold feet about the long-standing quest to connect Portugal and India during the final years of his reign, or became embroiled in internal problems in his kingdom, or else was waiting to acquire further scientific information that would be useful for the voyage, such as the astronomical tables produced by the Jewish astronomer Abraão ben Samuel Zacuto.

The next chapter in the book of Portuguese exploration was thus left for João's successor, King Manuel I, to write.

While overseas activities by the end of the fifteenth century had become very important for Portugal, they remained a controversial subject. The court at the time was divided over whether the mercantile ambitions of the king were a good thing or not. Many nobles grumbled that, rather than fixing its sights on Asia, the crown ought to be set instead on a crusade against Islam in North Africa, where the Portuguese had made their first imperial inroads. Fear that their own position might be undermined if the monarchy succeeded in controlling trade with the East, and thereby increasing its revenues, led to further hostility from the nobility. Traditionally, nobles liked to prove their worth on the battlefield and earn their lavish keep from owning land. Trading was for lesser sorts. Indeed, the French king François I allegedly dubbed Portugal's Dom Manuel rather disparagingly the 'grocer king' (*roi épicier*) for turning himself into a hawker of spices. But that might just have been envy talking, given the profits Manuel would make from trade with Asia. The selection of Da Gama was perhaps, then, a product of wrangling at court: nobles wanted one of their own involved if this enterprise was to go ahead. They didn't want to be replaced by an emergent class of merchants and privateers.

The fleet entrusted to Da Gama consisted of two newly commissioned large ships, or *naus*, plus a caravel acquired by the king from a Lisbon-based pilot named Bérrio and a supply ship bought from Aires Correia, a shipowner also from the Portuguese capital.

The timber that King João II had ordered to be cut for two new ships in 1494 had been left unused in the royal storehouses. Within the first year of his reign, King Manuel sent these planks to shipbuilders in the northern city of Porto, where several Atlantic-worthy *naus* had been constructed over the course of the fifteenth century.[3] Production started in the summer of 1496 and was completed during the first months of the following year. It was not a large fleet, which suggests some reticence on the part of the monarch over risking too much capital on this venture. The armadas sent to India in the years after Da Gama's expedition would be several times larger.

The king's instructions for the captain-major, given how little

EO GOVERNADOR·IORGE·CABRALL·MAMDOV·FAZER·MEMO
RIADAS·ARMADAS·QVE·PORTVGALL·PASARAM·AESTAS·
PARTES·ESTA·PRIMEIRA·COM·QVE·VASCO·DA
GAMA·COM·QVE·PARTIO·REINO·ANO·DE·497·

Paullo   *Dagama*

Vasquo   *Dagama*

Honauio Zeneculao coelho q 2 s

Fleet of Vasco da Gama in 1497

the Portuguese knew of the world beyond Europe and West Africa, were somewhat vague. Da Gama was to reach India and hand the ruler there a letter from Dom Manuel written in Portuguese with an Arabic translation. The small matters of where exactly to dock in India, and how to get there, were left to Da Gama and his crew to decide. He set sail at the height of summer, in July 1497. It was not clear when, or if, he would return.

1. Into the Unknown

You might think that Vasco da Gama's departure would be a moment of fanfare, with trumpets blaring and banners festooning the docks at Restelo. But when Luís de Camões – whose place in Portuguese literature can only be compared to Shakespeare's in the anglophone canon – came to write the story of Da Gama's voyage in his epic poem, *The Lusiads*, he somewhat surprisingly had the captain-major depart under a cloud.

Amid teary personal farewells and royal jubilation, an old man appears at the docks of Restelo in the poem. He scowls at the crowd. He shakes his head in grim disapproval. All fall silent as he begins to speak: 'Oh, the grandeur of rulers! Oh, the empty craving for this vanity we call Fame! Oh, the fraudulent desire we call honour which tempts us with its vulgar sheen.' His tirade continues: 'To what new disasters have you decided to drag this kingdom and its people? What perils and deaths are you subjecting them to in the name of some glittering ideal?' For the old man, Glory, Fame, Honour, Strength, Valour were delusions, words used to dress up a wicked enterprise in more appealing moral attire. Call it what you will, he declaims, it doesn't change the cruelty, greed and pride of the undertaking. You can't simply overlook death, disaster, profit-mongering by calling men heroes. This old man, like most old men in literature, was not afraid to tell it as it was.[1]

In some ways, Camões's old man of Restelo is the emblem of this book. He's a disruptive voice from the period of exploration, someone who didn't want to forget what could go wrong and knew that there was always an alternative angle from which to tell a story. His viewpoint, bracingly countercultural though it seems, was still a Eurocentric one: what he wanted instead of trade and exploration in Asia was not peace, it was an anti-Islamic crusade; the lives he was so concerned about were Portuguese, not those killed and exploited by them.

This is not to say that his central point lacks any broader resonance, however. He raised an issue that early modern writers often worried about, namely that the difference between vice and virtue was more a question of language than of morality. The very same action might be called glorious by one man, greediness by another. One person's bravery was another's foolhardiness. Valour might, from a different angle, look like cruelty. Rhetoric, in other words, could twist and contort moral evaluation. Everything was a matter of spin. Greatness, the old man tells us, is conferred by the adjectives and nouns we choose to ascribe to actions. So far, history has tended to lean towards the aggrandizement of Da Gama, but we can find another set of words in the dictionary to describe his actions and what followed. Camões knew that back in the sixteenth century and was admitting it in the voice of his old man, even in a poem that is largely a long nationalistic boast.

That Camões interrupted a key moment of his story with a naysaying harangue also tells us that there were anxieties in the Portuguese court about what a voyage to India was going to achieve and why it was undertaken. Around seventy years after Da Gama's journey, when Camões published his epic poem, there was still a bad taste in Portugal's mouth. Strikingly, no one responds to the old man's vituperations in the poem. No one refutes his claims, as though the conversations at the time had also reached a point where no compromise could be found. This silence sounds now like a tacit admission that, on balance, the prospect of gold did indeed weigh heavier than lives, just as the old man suggested.

Lost and Found in the Atlantic

After Da Gama left the Tagus behind, the first several hundred miles of his voyage should have been smooth sailing, given he was navigating well-travelled sailing routes.

Things weren't so easy, though, because of one of the great unspoken players in history: the weather. A pall of fog engulfed the fleet soon after it had steered out into the Atlantic and the ships, unable to see each other, became separated. They had made plans to rendezvous in

Vasco da Gama's Voyage to India (1497–9)

PORTUGAL
Azores
Lisbon
Canary islands
Alexandria
Cairo
Hormuz
ARABIA
INDIA
Diu
AFRICA
Aden
Goa
Cannanore
Calicut
Cochin
Cape Verde islands
Elmina
Mogadishu
Malindi
St Helena
Kilwa
INDIAN OCEAN
Mozambique
Sofala
ATLANTIC OCEAN
Madagascar
St Helena Bay
Natal
Cape of Good Hope   Mossel Bay

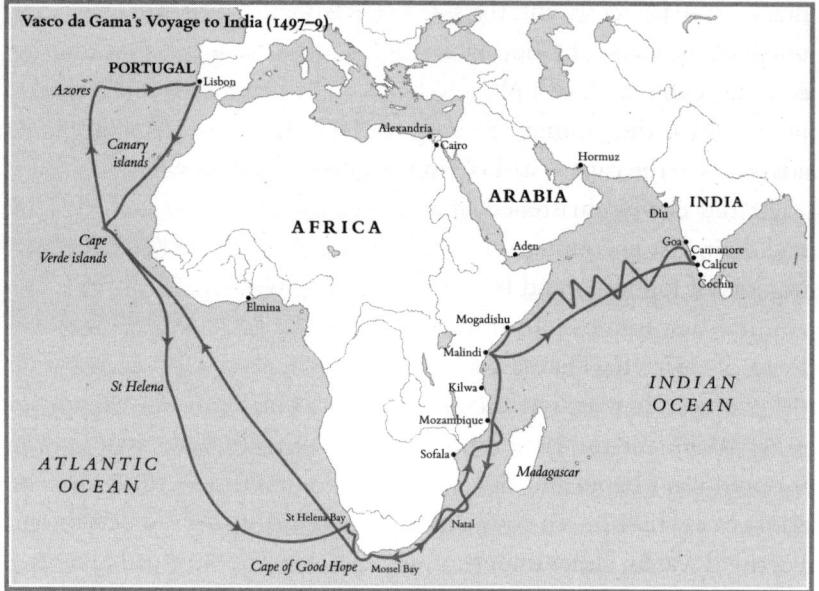

the Cape Verde islands if they lost each other so early in the voyage, but it was not the best of starts. A few days later, we are told by the writer of the only remaining ship's log from the voyage, three vessels found each other. There was still a ship missing, though. It was Da Gama's. Holding their nerve, they stuck to the plan. The fleet without a flagship continued south to the prearranged rendezvous point, but the fickle Atlantic winds suddenly evaporated, stalling them for several days. As the winds picked up again, Da Gama's ship at last appeared in the distance. They fired their cannons and blew their trumpets in delight – and relief. The mission, after all, wasn't over before it had begun.[2]

Reunited, the fleet dropped anchor at Santiago, the largest of the Cape Verde islands, to make repairs and take on provisions. Then, in what seems at first to be a counterintuitive move, they sailed not directly south towards their goal, but west into the Atlantic to catch the favourable winds that would sweep the ships southeast and around the tip of Africa. Da Gama had the right idea by swinging out into the mid-Atlantic – these winds were the breakthrough meteorological discovery his predecessors had made – but he failed to execute the manoeuvre perfectly and the ships reached land some 200 kilometres north of the Cape of Good Hope. A few days later, they again pulled into shore in search of a place to anchor, finding this time a sheltered inlet, which they named St Helena Bay. Their prime geographical adversary – the cape – still lay in wait down the coast.

At the newly christened St Helena Bay, Da Gama and his crew had their first encounter with people they did not know. After reading lots of logbooks and letters – the primary formats for recording cultural first impressions in the period – one begins to get a certain sense of déjà vu. They always note the same sorts of things about the peoples and places being encountered: their clothes, weapons and other goods, and food; the flora, fauna and climate. The catalogues are in some ways banal and obvious; these were tangible things the eye could easily take in. To compare the dogs here or there to pets back in Portugal was an easier undertaking than to grasp the familial or governance structures of a society when they had limited language skills and only a short window of time for observation. And readers back home were always eager for news of anything that seemed different: loincloths, piercings, flying fish. But beyond the blatant exoticizing, what catches their attention – and what gets left out – also implicitly reveals a clear set of imperial preoccupations: potential resources to exploit, opportunities for trade and conversion, likely threats.

On the day after Da Gama's fleet anchored in St Helena's Bay, they took a captive. You'll soon see that hostage-taking became Da Gama's signature modus operandi; one of the few ways he could gain leverage in a new place. After this hostage was fed and held against his will overnight, the Portuguese dressed him in their clothes and set him back on shore. For the Portuguese, one of the key metrics of difference with other peoples was how much a person covered up their body with cloth; the less skin a person showed, the more civilized they were. The forced re-costuming of this man was thus supposed to change him, win his favour, turn him into an ally. Whether the change of attire really worked or not, the next day around fifteen locals paid the ships a visit. Da Gama showed them cinnamon, cloves, seed pearls and gold, hoping that they would lead him to more of the same. They seemed to be uninterested in or unfamiliar with such items.

Curious about these people – and in the fifteenth century, curiosity was often a dangerous vice – one man, Fernão Veloso, wanted
to venture inland to see how they lived. Da Gama at first refused,
concerned for what might happen if he went off on his own. Veloso
insisted. Eventually, as the day was beginning to wane and the crew
returned to their vessels for dinner, Da Gama reluctantly gave him
leave to make his little field trip. While the rest of the Portuguese
supped on their ships, Veloso dined on roasted seal with the locals.
The fatty meat sated his appetite, but not his curiosity. He made signs
to his hosts that he wanted to head further inland to explore their
villages. They waved towards the shoreline. Step no further, their
gestures made clear. He began to walk back in disappointment. Spotting figures lurking in the brush, he started to move a little more
quickly towards the beach. Then he started to shout and run. It was
an ambush. Veloso's cries interrupted the crew's dinner. Da Gama and
his men dropped their plates, clambered into their rowing boats and
sped to land to rescue their imperilled friend. Spears flew through
the air at the Portuguese as they reached the beach. Da Gama had
been right to be cautious. Veloso had been foolish. One of the spears
wounded the captain-major himself. Stupidly, they had no weapons
to retaliate. As the writer of the ship's rutter, or log, concluded: 'we
trusted them, thinking them to be timid and believing that they
would never do what they did; we thus landed without arming our-
selves.' It's a telling admission of hubris.

A Toppled Imposition

Unsure of quite how far north of the Cape of Good Hope he was, Da
Gama tacked close to the shore after leaving St Helena Bay, inch-
ing southwards towards the key geographical obstacle: the Cape of
Good Hope. Before Dias rounded it for the first time in 1488, it had
proved a stumbling block for the Portuguese. Shoals, rocks and uncooperative winds smashed several ships to smithereens as they tried to
round it. On his first attempt to defeat this rocky adversary, Da Gama
failed. The wind was against him. A second attempt brought a second

failure. The winds that had swept Dias around the cape were not catchable from so close to the shore. This was a navigational leap that needed a run-up. It was only on his third try that Da Gama finally cleared the troublesome promontory.

Here, once more, perspective matters in our telling of the story. One can easily turn Da Gama's troubles into the encouraging parent's favourite lesson: try, try, try again, in order to succeed. The Yemeni chronicler Qutb al-Din Muhammad al-Nahrawali al-Makki, writing around 1565 – around when Camões was composing his epic too – saw the prolonged Portuguese face-off with the cape quite differently, however. Nahrawali wrote, with a tinge of schadenfreude, 'This place is so tempestuous that the ships of the Franks [i.e. Europeans] could not cast anchor, and were shattered to pieces, and none of them survived. Thus they persisted for a time, perishing each time at that spot, and none of the Franks managed to arrive in the Indian Ocean, until one of their galleys managed to escape and make its way towards al-Hind [India].'[3] For Nahrawali, the cape was a site of repeated disaster. Rounding it once didn't scrub previous failures from the record. These simply made Portuguese persistence foolhardy, with the occasional lucky escape. Contrasting Nahrawali's account with Portuguese histories, it's clear that Europeans had a long memory when it came to their supposed successes and a short memory for disasters.

Relieved to have passed the cape, Da Gama and his crew anchored at São Brás (today's Mossel Bay). Reluctant to repeat the misfortunes of St Helena Bay, Da Gama allowed the locals to approach only singly or in pairs. The Portuguese traded bells and red caps for ivory. There was still no sign of the fragrant products Da Gama was really after.

Before the Portuguese raised their anchors to depart, Da Gama erected a cross and a pillar, known in Portuguese as a *padrão*, to mark how far they had come. The crew had dismantled the supply ship and distributed its provisions among the other ships while at São Brás, likely using its mizzenmast to create this improvised monument. They were leaving a piece of themselves behind to say: 'The Portuguese were here.'

To the Portuguese, the verb 'discover' possessed a specific, technical meaning, alongside its Eurocentric assumptions about 'uncovering' places that had long been inhabited: it meant 'to chart on a European map for the first time'.[4] And to chart on a map for the first time meant to claim dominion over that place. Empire was, in other words, a high-stakes game of finders keepers for the Portuguese, where the playground was the world, and the only legitimate players were Europeans. In this act of 'discovery', *padrões* served a practical as well as a symbolic purpose. Wherever a captain placed a *padrão*, its latitude was measured and recorded; thereafter it became a link between the three-dimensional world of water and rocks and the abstract lines of the atlas. *Padrões* loom completely out of scale on sailing charts as waymarkers and pillars of dominion, just as they stuck out on actual shorelines. Their enduring symbolic power can be seen on the *Padrão dos Descobrimentos* in Lisbon – a commemorative monument to Portugal's 'glorious' past inaugurated in 1960 by the nation's long-reigning dictator António de Oliveira Salazar – where the muscular figures of Bartolomeu Dias and his fellow explorer of the southern coast of Africa, Diogo Cão, heave a *padrão* up the monument. These pillars were how empire started. They were the sixteenth-century version of a flag on the moon.

At Mossel Bay, though, the locals rejected this tall reminder of Portuguese intrusion into their world. As Da Gama was about to sail off, they tore the *padrão* down. Da Gama's crew must have seen this as an immediate gesture of resistance. A Swahili saying from further up the coast, which spoke of Dom Manuel the Portuguese king, expressed the same spirit: *Enda Manoel, ututukiziziye, / Enda, na sulubu uyititiziye.* 'Go away Manuel, you have made us hate you, go, and carry your cross with you.'[5]

Into the Unknown

Soon Da Gama's fleet passed the furthest point previously reached by a Portuguese ship and entered a world largely unknown to them.

By Christmas Day of 1497, they had sailed seventy leagues (c. 340 km) beyond where Bartolomeu Dias decided to turn back for Lisbon. Seventy leagues of progress. That progress, though, had knocked and bruised the ships. The mainmast of one of the ships split. As the wind pulled at the sails and the waves rocked the hull, this wound in the mast opened and closed, mouthing the ship's distress. The crew carried out makeshift repairs. Then, when the fleet anchored to reprovision, a mooring rope snapped and an anchor sank into the deep. Here, in South Africa, things were beginning to fall apart.

Keen to avoid the obstacle course of shallow waters and shoals along the coast and to make swifter progress, they made for the open sea. But this just meant swapping one set of problems for another. Their barrels of drinking water soon began to run dry. Each sailor's ration was reduced to a *quartilho* (three-quarters of a pint) per day. Another week passed, stuck in this ocean drought. A vista of waves and nothing to drink. At last, the coast re-emerged as a smudge on the horizon and, as they drew close, an inlet with a river appeared, a break in the rocks and sands. The Portuguese eagerly sailed in towards this promise of reprieve and dropped anchor. Here they received a friendly welcome from the locals, who, in turn, received well the gifts Da Gama presented: a jacket, red breeches, a cap and a bracelet.

This would have been a good place to revictual fully, but the wind had different plans. It ushered the Portuguese to be on their way before they had enough time to take on as much water as they needed. Such were the contingencies of their voyage. If the gusts beckoned, their captain had to follow. The Portuguese called the river the *rio de cobre* – the 'Copper River' – after the copper twisted into the hair and around the legs of the people there, and their land the *terra da boa gente* – the 'Land of the Good Folk'.

Much though the act of naming is one of entitlement and often came with a claim to dominion, the naivety of these early territorial labels, the simple correlation between place and experience which they describe, is striking. We are used to overlooking the etymological meanings of place names – the once-utilitarian suffixes marking fords and bridges and settlements no longer seem significant to us. Place names are tags; an arbitrary class of words that might be evocative, but rarely straightforwardly descriptive. By comparison, these new names given by the Portuguese are so bluntly expressive that they seem slightly implausible, almost childish. They preserve in logbooks and on maps the effect of initial arrival at a place: they project the hope, pride, fear, disappointment of the Portuguese onto geography. *Terra da fome, terra da boa gente, terra dos bons senhais, rio de cobre* : hunger, good folk, positive signs, copper – you can extrapolate from them the experiences once had. They indicate resources, enemies, allies and afflictions, warning you off or welcoming you ashore. Renaming can also be an act of erasure, a good way of editing history. The Cape of Good Hope was known for a long time as the Cape of Storms. It was rechristened after Dias's success.

Ports of Deceit

At Da Gama's next port of call, there were promising signs: the inhabitants communicated through gesture that there were other foreigners in these parts, who knew about large ocean-going vessels like the *naus* of the Portuguese. They were now touching the fringe of a new trading network, a web of sailing routes spun between the edges of Africa, Arabia and India. They pushed on, craving the products (and the profits) that flowed between these regions.

After several days at sea, they spotted a bay, which they sought to enter. Nicolau Coelho, captain of the caravel *Bérrio*, misjudged the depth and struck a sandbar. Vessels came from land, directing them away from these dangerously shallow waters to a better anchorage further along the coast. On trying to enter this bay, though, Coelho made another miscalculation and hit land again, damaging his helm. In hindsight, this bumpy arrival would look like an omen.

When they finally made contact with the inhabitants of this region, the Portuguese realized they had stumbled on a rich port with Arabic speakers. One of the crew, who had been held hostage in North Africa and who had thus learned the language, interpreted for Da Gama as he questioned the locals about their way of life and trading. He found out precisely what the captain-major wanted to hear. Merchants from far away brought silver, cloves, pepper, ginger, pearls and rubies to this place. As the ship's log noted, the people here had 'Genoese needles' (i.e. compasses), quadrants and sea charts.

In other words, they were skilled sailors used to long-distance trade voyages. There were even two St Thomas Christians from India. Information that gladdened the Portuguese so much that they cried with joy and thanked God with prayers.

This was the island of Mozambique. A place that, along with the 2,500 kilometres of coastline stretching to the north and south, would eventually become a Portuguese colony until the 1970s. The Muslim ruler of the island turned his nose up at the gifts of hats, coats and coral that Da Gama handed to him. The Portuguese also acted rather suspiciously, raising tensions. The entire time they were at Mozambique, they anchored away from the port, as though they were trying to hide something. They insisted on having two pilots, one of whom always had to stay on board Da Gama's ship, as an insurance policy. The king asked the Portuguese whether they were from Turkey. On receiving the answer that they were Portuguese and, moreover, Christians, relations soured. The pilot whom they had been given revealed that plans were afoot to attack the Portuguese. But unfavourable winds becalmed them there for over a week.

I've always found that word *becalmed* a peculiar maritime euphemism. The Portuguese were hostages to the wind, stuck in a land hostile to their presence. While they were stranded, the ruler of Mozambique sent word that he wanted to make peace with the Portuguese. Separately, a so-called 'pilot from Mecca' came aboard with his son, saying that he wanted to leave Mozambique with them.

By this point, the Portuguese needed to take on water again. Under cover of darkness, they lowered their boats and Nicolau Coelho and a few other men went in search of the watering hole, which was located on the mainland. They took the self-proclaimed pilot from Mecca with them, but he appeared keener to escape from them than show them where they could find something to drink. They searched all night, but returned to their ships in the morning empty-handed.

The next evening, they went back to the mainland once more with the pilot. They found the watering hole defended by men armed with spears. Da Gama fired the ships' cannons to scare them off and it worked. The Portuguese landed and replenished their stocks of this vital resource. The following day, a man approached the Portuguese and told them they could take as much water as they liked. Da Gama suspected the invitation was a trap. He readied the cannons and decided to sail into the trap and show them that the Portuguese could do them damage.

As they approached the watering hole, the locals greeted them with spears, swords, bows and slings. Da Gama in anger bombarded them for hours. He held nothing back. It was a brutal, disproportionate retaliation. The Portuguese later chased boats that were heading along the coast, taking prisoners and grabbing cloth, books and food before they left.

On the next leg of the journey, up the coast of East Africa, progress proved sluggish. The Portuguese relied on the pilot they had acquired at Mozambique, but his information was unreliable and untimely. He seemingly mistook islands for the mainland.

He told them there were Christians on Kilwa only when they had already sailed past it. Da Gama wasted a day constantly adjusting the sails and zigzagging across the waves in a futile attempt to sail into the wind back towards these alleged allies. The gusts pushed them forward. Thwarted, they bore instead for Mombasa.

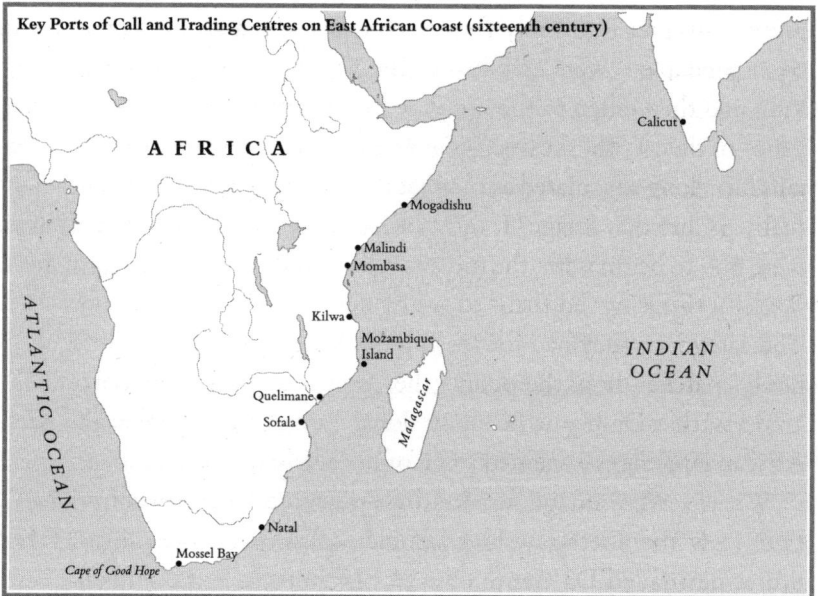

Key Ports of Call and Trading Centres on East African Coast (sixteenth century)

The Portuguese anticipated being greeted by Christians there too. The Muslim pilot had suggested to Da Gama that there dwelt in Mombasa a significant population who shared their faith. Reunion with a long-lost diaspora of their creed allegedly awaited them. Scarcely had they appeared within sight of the city when a boat skidded towards them. The rumours were confirmed: there were Christians in the city, they were told. The crew hoped to celebrate Mass the following day with them. At midnight, however, another boat made for the Portuguese ships, this time crammed with a hundred armed men. Da Gama was immediately suspicious. He permitted only a handful of them on board his ships at any one time, worried that they would overwhelm his crew and take hold of his fleet. Nothing happened. The men looked hostile, but they didn't attack. Perhaps this would be a friendlier place than Mozambique.

The next day was Palm Sunday and the King of Mombasa sent gifts – sheep, oranges, lemons and sugar – and encouraged Da Gama to come ashore. He pledged to supply the Portuguese with the necessary provisions for their onward journey. With his now characteristic caution, though, the captain-major dispatched two dispensable crew members to test the waters. He was not prepared to endanger his captains or other high-ranking members of the fleet in a preliminary recce. This pair – possibly former convicts brought along precisely to be expendable – were escorted to the palace for an audience with the king and then taken to the home of two Christian merchants, who, as proof of their faith, showed them an image of the Holy Ghost. Historians have long speculated as to what this image might have been. Was it really a Christian image? It must be said that the Portuguese crewmen were not, to begin with, the most perspicacious amateur ethnographers. Wishful thinking led them to see evidence of Christians everywhere. The categories they had for sorting the people of the world into boxes rarely matched how the people they met thought of themselves. The 'experts' that Da Gama brought along – speakers of Arabic and West African languages – seemed to be of little help in this regard.

Whatever the image in Mombasa depicted, the news of what the two crew members saw and samples of clove, pepper, ginger and millet persuaded Da Gama to enter the port with his ships the next day. On the following morning, however, Da Gama's ship would not turn. Failing to sail landwards, the fleet dropped anchor once more. Seeing that the Portuguese would not proceed into the harbour, the locals aboard dashed back to their own vessel, which was tagging along at the rear of Da Gama's ship. The two pilots who had come aboard in Mozambique saw an opportunity to escape. They threw themselves overboard and were taken into the locals' boat. Something was definitely wrong. That night, to get to the bottom of things, Da Gama tortured two Muslims who were still aboard. He dropped boiling hot oil onto their skin between his questions to extract the answers he wanted. They revealed that the plan was to attack the Portuguese once they entered the port in order to avenge the bombardment of the village at Mozambique. One man, although his hands were still tied, took his chances with the sea, hurling himself over the side of the ship before a second round of scalding torment. At first watch the following morning, another followed suit.

And so, while the Portuguese experienced each harbour as a discrete point on their journey – *terra firma* momentarily punctuating long stretches at sea – these places were, of course, connected to one another. Rumours and messages sped overland quicker than Da Gama's ships progressed over the waves. The Portuguese were rapidly gaining a reputation in the ports of East Africa. A bad one. News of these dangerous amphibians spread up the coast: beware new predators from the sea who might come on land.

Another night at Mombasa brought more trouble: boats launched from the harbour towards the Portuguese. As they drew near, those aboard slipped into the water, swimming torpedoes who could reach the ships undetected. They began sawing at the cable of the *Bérrio*. Others had already clambered aboard another ship and were hacking at the rigging of the mizzenmast. At first, these marine assailants had been mistaken for tuna bobbing in the waves. When it was realized that these tuna could climb and were armed with knives, the alarm was raised. The attackers scarpered.

Although Da Gama and his fleet faced daily subterfuge while anchored outside Mombasa's harbour, the health of the sailors improved – the 'air' of the city was good. More to the point, they also were able to eat fresh fruit, replenishing their vitamin deficiencies. In one sense, then, they had been fortified. But, at the same time, they had also been depleted when it came to information, after their two hostage pilots had jumped ship. So when the Portuguese, shortly after they left Mombasa, spied two vessels, they immediately gave chase, hoping to capture new pilots and informants. One boat successfully made for land, evading its European pursuers. The Portuguese caught up with the second vessel, whose crew and passengers promptly abandoned ship. The Portuguese fished seventeen prisoners from the water and seized a booty of silver, gold and food from the boat. That Da Gama pounced on the opportunity to take more captives reveals how eager he was for local knowledge. And hence how little he had previously possessed. He was not so bothered about making a 'discovery' through his own efforts, or by the prowess of the crew. He was happy, anxious even, to be guided. He would prefer to be shown the way rather than discover it for himself.

Mutual Advantage

Malindi was the next stop on their stumbling course up the eastern seaboard of Africa. The triangular sails of dhows clustered in the harbour, interleaved with other ships. Some of those anchored there had swept in all the way from Kerala, revealing that not only was passage to India possible, it was habitual. Beyond the docks rose a city of gleaming white coral-stone, flat roofs alternating with the domes of mosques and the thatch of smaller buildings along the skyline. The streets bustled with traders, some naked save for loincloths, others wearing capes and rich turbans, bartering for gold, ivory, wax and textiles.[6]

Once more, rumour beat the Portuguese to the city. Although it wasn't exactly rumour: these sea rovers had in fact pursued ships, looted them and taken prisoners. Aware of this, no boats made their way out to greet the ships when they anchored outside the harbour. Da Gama had to make the first move. He sent the elderly owner of the boat he had captured to the shore, instructing him to inform the local king of his intention to act peacefully and, most importantly, of his desire to acquire a Christian pilot. This venerable man returned the following day with good news. The king would be glad to receive Da Gama and supply him with the navigator he so desired. Da Gama, delighted by this, sent word back that he intended to enter the port the following day, and he dispatched gifts to assure the king of his good intentions. The next day, the king drew near to the ships in a small boat, which led Da Gama to take to one of his rowing boats to converse with him. This waterborne parley went well, although the Portuguese captain-major said his own king had forbidden him from going ashore to visit the ruler's palace – a white lie so that his caution would not cause offence. But to make a further show of goodwill, Da Gama gave the king a tour of his ships and then released all the hostages he had taken en route from Mombasa.

After two days of silence between ships and shore, the king dispatched one of his closest advisers to Da Gama. The captain-major immediately took him hostage and demanded that the king provide a pilot in exchange for the safe return of his *privado*. There was no negotiating. Straight away, the king sent Da Gama a pilot, a native of Gujarat. Da Gama dutifully released his latest captive. This was not deference on the part of the king, a straightforward meeting of the hostage-taker's demands. The speedy dissipation of the tensions here suggests that the king had something to gain from Da Gama. The king was playing a longer-term game. For him, Da Gama was not just a heathen intruder, as he had been at Mombasa and Mozambique. At the time, Malindi was under the tutelage of the King of Kilwa. Da Gama thus brought the King of Malindi the possibility of wriggling out from under this regional yoke, through friendship with a faraway power that might supply him with military assistance and furnish new opportunities for trade.

2. The Portuguese Are Discovered

It is perhaps because of the Gujarati pilot that the final leap of Da Gama's fleet across more than 4,000 kilometres of Indian Ocean receives so little discussion in the surviving ship's log. The crossing to their final destination, to a new continent – and, as historians have often claimed, into a new era in world history – is described in a single sentence. Indeed, Sanjay Subrahmanyam has concluded from the phrasing of the log that Calicut may not have been the objective planned at the outset, but was determined by the connections of the King of Malindi.[1] The pilot knew how to navigate to Calicut, so Calicut was where they went. Well, nearly. The Portuguese made land a league and a half, or around eight kilometres, north of Calicut. Boats from the shore pointed the fleet in the direction of the city itself. They had made it across the Indian Ocean. It was 20 May 1498, more than ten months after their departure from Lisbon.

Da Gama had learned his lesson from the difficulties he faced in Africa and famously did not head immediately on shore himself, but dispatched a former convict, João Nunes, to Calicut. He was, in Portuguese, a *degredado*, a criminal. His punishment was exile, and exposure to the dangers of exploration. For Nunes and others like him, Da Gama's chance of glory was quite the opposite: a kind of penance. To his surprise, Nunes encountered two traders from Tunis who could speak to him in Castilian and Genoese. 'What the devil has brought you here?' they quite understandably asked. Nunes replied that the Portuguese were there to look for 'Christians and spices'.

Nunes's straightforward answer to the North African merchants encapsulates the two principal motivations of the Portuguese in heading to Asia. In a new kind of crusade, they longed to connect with eastern Christians, such as the quasi-mythical Prester John, known throughout the medieval period as a king who was said to rule over a Christian nation disconnected from the rest of Christendom and surrounded by religious foes. In so doing, they would outflank – and hopefully crush – the Islamic powers of the Middle East and Africa. King Manuel dreamed of reconquering Jerusalem and espoused messianic visions in which Portugal would bring a new age of peace on earth, the prelude to Christ's second coming. We've seen Da Gama's eager response to a sequence of rumours about Christians throughout his journey.

Nunes's epigrammatic response also reminds us that the Portuguese left their homeland not in a state of plenitude, but with a sense of lack. The phrase 'maritime expansion', often used in history books, and, even more problematically, the word 'discovery' make the Portuguese (or whichever Europeans they refer to) seem like they had all the agency. Yet imperial seafaring wasn't propelled simply by mere curiosity. The great cities of Africa and Asia enticed the Portuguese with their splendour and the gold and spices they possessed in abundance. European explorers were, at least in part, maritime moths lured by the trading beacons of other continents.[2] In many narratives of the time, Portuguese writers made trade seem like a fortunate side effect of spreading God's word rather than a primary objective. They tried to give the impression that the Portuguese didn't aim to wrest control of the spice trade, but left their shores with their minds preoccupied with God, not gold. Certainly, when Da Gama himself spoke to the ruler of Calicut, he made a show of their search for Christians. As the logbook noted, 'it was for that reason that they had ordered this land to be discovered, and not because they needed silver or gold, for they had those in such abundance that they did not need them from this land'. He wasn't fooling anyone. Upon Da Gama's return to Portugal, the Count of Vimioso is reported to have told him, on hearing of all the goods that the Indians had to trade, that it was not the Portuguese who had discovered India, but India that had discovered the Portuguese.[3]

Diplomatic Dilemmas

In his dealings with the Samudri Raja of Calicut, Da Gama clearly did not have the upper hand. The dishevelled Portuguese did not really convince the raja that they were envoys of a powerful, faraway king. Few in Calicut had even heard of Portugal, so Da Gama's praise of Dom Manuel had little resonance. Indeed, when they first arrived, Nunes had been asked why the rulers of Castile, France or Venice were not the ones to send ships, suggesting that it was something of a surprise that the fleet had come from Portugal. To add to their troubles, the Portuguese had turned up with none of the lavish diplomatic gifts that lubricated exchanges between kingdoms and acted as guarantees of the wealth and power of the ruler being represented. Da Gama had with him only a dozen pieces of cloth, six hats, four strings of coral, a bundle of six basins, a case of sugar, two barrels of oil and another two of honey. The Samudri Raja expected more. The locals witheringly told Da Gama that what he wished to present 'was nothing to give to a king and that the poorest merchant who came from Mecca . . . would give him more than that'. Not exactly the best diplomatic first impression, then. And the longer Da Gama stayed, the more suspicions mounted that he and his men were pirates masquerading as an ambassadorial entourage. On a second audience with the ruler, Da Gama was subjected to a probing set of questions. Why were they really here? Why did he bring such paltry offerings? Where was the letter from Da Gama's king that had been promised at the last meeting?

The merchants in the city grew more and more hostile to these newcomers who threatened their interests. Da Gama became anxious and mistrustful too – and with good reason. After these initial meetings with the raja, he and his men were detained as they made their way back to their ships. The genre of the voyage thus began to tilt from adventure story towards psychological thriller. What rumours, what wicked rumours could cause them to be sequestered in this no man's land, Da Gama wondered. Without a sense of why the locals were acting in such a way – other than, of course, because they were evil heathens – it was difficult to devise a tactic for escape. He had no leverage, no bargaining chips. All he had were protestations and persistence.

The Portuguese were freed after a few fraught days, but by now Da Gama presumed there was little more that he could achieve in Calicut. Denied a final audience with the Samudri Raja, the captain-major again seized hostages and departed with a small cargo of spices.

In other words, Da Gama got *where* he wanted, but did not quite get *what* he wanted: a formal accord with Calicut on future trade with Portugal. As the ship's logbook remarked with resignation: 'We could not manage to leave the land in peace and as friends of the people.'

A Turbulent Return

The Portuguese might have left Calicut, but unfavourable winds meant they had not said goodbye to their problems. Just a day after their departure, a fleet of seventy small boats appeared to pursue them. The Portuguese loaded their cannons and fired. A skirmish ensued that lasted a few hours. Thankfully, the winds began to pick up, carrying the Portuguese ships out to sea and away from this tussle. Days passed. Progress remained slow. They eventually reached Anjediva Island, where they docked to reprovision. Here a young man assured the Portuguese that wild cinnamon was to be found on the island. A trap was suspected, however, when a fleet of ships again emerged on the horizon. The Portuguese gave chase. They found one of the ships abandoned and took the food and arms aboard. A boat approached the following day, its occupants informing them that the fleet had been instructed to attack them. The Portuguese moved on to a different island, but more difficulties awaited. They encountered what they had been taken to be in Calicut: pirates.

Some days later, while they were making repairs to their ships on Anjediva, a well-dressed man who spoke the Venetian dialect approached the ship. He was a convert to Islam originally from Europe. His lord had heard rumours of a fleet that did not speak the local languages of the coast of India. He'd begged his lord to allow him to go and investigate. Or so he said. The locals whom the Portuguese had previously captured suggested that this talkative man was not as he appeared to be, and in fact was the captain of the fleet that had come to attack the Portuguese. The Portuguese therefore flogged the truth out of him. He revealed that he was a spy sent by the Sultan of Bijapur to acquire information about how many men the Portuguese had and what weapons. He revealed that the whole region wished them ill and that traps had been set in all the river inlets along the coast to pounce on them should they try to find a safe harbour.

They remained on the island for twelve days, cleaning their ships and taking on water for their journey back across the Indian Ocean to Portugal. Da Gama and his fleet weighed anchor on 5 October 1498. Out on the Indian Ocean, the spy began to relay more of his life story. It turned out he was a Jewish merchant who had converted to Islam after arriving in India. By the time the fleet returned to Portugal, he had converted to Christianity and been baptized with the name of Gaspar da Gama, in honour of the captain-major. He had switched faith as many times as he had swapped sides, knowing religion to be a useful passport to a life in a new place.

The crossing of the ocean, which had been relatively easy on the way out, proved a race against disease on the fleet's return. Over the course of the three-month voyage, the crew's bleeding gums swelled over their teeth, their hands and feet ballooned monstrously. Scurvy, that peril of time spent at sea, claimed thirty lives, leaving only seven or eight who could navigate aboard each of the ships. The three ships almost became a ghost fleet drifting between continents. The crew prayed in desperation to the saints. When they eventually spotted land, the ship's log said, they were as relieved as if they had reached Portugal itself. Where exactly they were, however, the depleted and disoriented sailors were not sure, as disease had claimed their most skilled seafarers. Without a pilot, or anyone who knew how to determine their position on a map, they could only speculate as to their location. They had to proceed based on their memory of the East African coastline, rather than employing the techniques of scientific navigation.

The fleet returned to Malindi, having fired their cannons (but not dropping anchor) at Mogadishu, on account of it being a Muslim city, and following a brief armed encounter off the island of Pate. They were once again greeted warmly by the ruler of Malindi, who provided Da Gama with a Muslim ambassador and a gift of ivory to take back to Dom Manuel. A few days after they left Malindi, they burned the *São Raphael*, so no one else could use it, as it was becoming impossible to handle all of their ships with so few able men. But the rest of the journey was mostly smooth sailing. Da Gama was not the first back to Lisbon, though. That was Nicolau Coelho in the *Bérrio*, who arrived on 10 July 1499, while Da Gama remained in the Azores to bury his brother, Paulo da Gama, who had fallen ill on the journey home. Anticipation ensured the captain-major was greeted by the people of Lisbon with wild excitement when at last he completed his voyage around the beginning of September 1499.

The Aftermath

King Manuel was deterred neither by the losses suffered by Da Gama's fleet nor by the ambiguous outcome of the negotiations with the Samudri Raja. He declared the mission a success and promptly set about preparations for a new voyage to India. In March 1500, a much larger fleet of thirteen ships and more than a thousand men – and carrying much more lavish gifts – left Lisbon under the command of the nobleman Pedro Álvares Cabral. He returned to Portugal sixteen months later, having hit on Brazil during his outward journey. King Manuel quickly declared himself 'lord of the conquest, navigation and trade of Ethiopia, Persia and India'. Kings were braggarts and prone to one-upmanship, and Manuel wrote to monarchs across Europe proclaiming his country's success and initiating an expensive, extensive public relations campaign. Da Gama was his hero. A hero to match Columbus. The world needed to know.

In celebration of Da Gama's voyage, Dom Manuel commissioned a series of large tapestries. The most spectacular is conventially said to depict Vasco da Gama's arrival in Calicut.

As a vision of that moment, I like this tapestry not for its accuracy, but precisely for how little it matches the reality. Although images, objects and animals – even rhinoceroses and elephants – gradually began to be shipped back to Europe as curiosities for kings and to adorn the homes of the wealthy, at first India had to be imagined from stories and rumours. But there was a fear underlying much travel writing that the world was too weird and wonderful to be believed. Portuguese accounts of their compatriots' overseas activities tried to counteract this by deploying a language of truth-telling.

Tapestry depicting Vasco da Gama's arrival in Calicut in 1498

They always stressed – sometimes suspiciously often – that what they were saying was true even if it sounded like fiction. And yet, at the same time, the monarchy and others invested heavily in forms of magnificent make-believe. They overlayed the truth with all kinds of fantasies.

The ships that the tapestry depicts are overflowing. The Portuguese are unloading a menagerie of exotic creatures from their hulls and onto rowing boats headed for the docks. Ostriches peer out of one boat; camels stand on the deck of a ship while a unicorn is winched over its side. Quite the opposite of the meagre gifts Da Gama actually had to offer the raja in Calicut. The scene gives the impression too that Da Gama was met immediately by an enthusiastic throng and handed his letter directly to the ruler. There is no hesitancy here. There are no suspicions. No misunderstandings. No anxious wait for an audience with the raja. In the ship's log, the Portuguese reported crowds, but the crowds that swarmed around them came to gawp, not to welcome them. The negotiations were tense and unsuccessful.

It would be easy to claim that Da Gama was a remarkable individual for the simple fact that he made it to India from Portugal around the Cape of Good Hope, a route not previously sailed by a single vessel. Nothing of any consequence, though, is ever achieved without an immense effort from all sorts of people. Setbacks along the way are a normal part of breaking new ground. However, look at any monument to Da Gama's voyage, or school history book account of it, and the Gujarati pilot is not there, nor are there any traces of how Da Gama was rebuffed in Calicut. And so when we look more closely at *how* he got to India, that he was directed by someone else, and that fundamentally he did not achieve what he set out to do, then we should start to be a little more cautious about turning this story into a triumph and, in particular, *his* triumph. Nationalist and imperialist historians have, from the beginning, wanted us to overlook the problems that Da Gama faced, his personal limitations, and the resistance and rejection that he faced all along his journey. If we succumb to the adventure story, then we succumb to an imperial vision of the past, one keen to make 'great' men emerge above the tides of history to shore up an image of the world shaped by the agency of Europeans. In reality, Da Gama entered a world where he – and other Europeans – did not automatically have the upper hand.

Indeed, Calicut might have been the gateway to Asia, but its doors would quickly shut as a Portuguese entrepôt. Just three months after Cabral established a *feitoria* (trading station) there in 1500, Muslim merchants attacked and killed its personnel. Cabral launched a counterattack and then abandoned the port, setting up instead a little further south in Cochin (Kochi) and further north in Cannanore (Kannur). The ruler of Cochin, in particular, was happy to ally himself with the Portuguese as the means of gaining greater independence from the more powerful Samudri Raja, to whom he had been paying tribute. As we saw in Malindi, it was often the leverage that the Portuguese offered rulers in their regional rivalries which determined whether they were met with hostility or open arms. Their own ambitions had to be modulated to suit the political game they had sailed into. When a ruler entered into a compact with the Portuguese, it was not always a question of submitting to a superior power, but of exploiting its naval clout for their own ends. With the arrival of the Portuguese, trade in Cochin started to boom. Calicut, meanwhile, remained a thorn in the side of the Portuguese empire for decades.

Over the years following Da Gama's voyage, the Portuguese spread themselves around the Indian Ocean and east to Sri Lanka, Melaka and eventually China and Japan. Their progress was no linear, cumulative process, though. Maps and timelines with their city dots and dates of conquest or arrival can give the wrong impression, that the Portuguese empire reached straightforwardly further and further with each passing year. The reality was jerkier. Infighting among the Portuguese sent fissures through the enterprise. Everyone had their own ideas about how the empire should grow and operate. Successive governors or viceroys of Portuguese Asia set their own agendas for their terms of office, and these could vary quite considerably in tenor and ambition. They headed for India with a list of instructions in hand, but once they were ensconced in Goa, the headquarters of the empire, they were not really answerable to anyone. In their reports they always found an angle (or excuses) to explain their actions. Some privileged private trade and saw little benefit in constructing fort after fort in the ports at which Portuguese merchants successively docked. Official policy, however, was to secure the Portuguese position in the east by erecting a chain of strongholds around the Indian Ocean in a bid to achieve a monopoly over the spice trade.[4]

Afonso de Albuquerque, one of the early governors of Portuguese Asia, was a major proponent of the ring-of-forts strategy. During his tenure, between 1509 and 1515, he established fortresses in Goa, Melaka and Hormuz, all strategically positioned and all well known as trading hubs. His sights were set next on Aden, crucial for seizing control of access to the Red Sea, but he failed to take it and died before he could launch a second attack.

As the Portuguese squeezed this trading world harder, like anything fluid it started to leak through their fingers. Hundreds of kilometres lay between each limb of the empire. They had to give ground in order to win the allegiance of certain powers. The fantasy of total control thus gave way to something like a game of imperial whack-a-mole: each time the Portuguese took over a port, merchants would fight back or flee the oppression and customs duties imposed on them, setting up shop somewhere else along the western coast of India. With Diu dominated, Surat prospered. Calicut cycled through calm and conflict. Cochin's pepper supply would be periodically choked by uncooperative rulers inland. Even Goa, the headquarters

of the empire, was not won easily. Albuquerque captured the town
in February 1510, but a counter-attack by the local sultan forced him
to leave. He regained the port in the winter of that year only with
assistance from Hindu allies. Rulers across Asia frequently threatened
the Portuguese presence and forced it onto the back foot. This was not
a region where the Portuguese could advance without significant and
persistent resistance. Existing networks of trade in the Indian Ocean
adapted around the arrival of Europeans, demonstrating dynamism
and resilience. Such resistance makes the use of that word 'expansion'
in relation to empire again seem too simple. Empires grew, yes, but
they also shrank, had their advances slowed or halted, and repeatedly
had to battle against uprisings and desertions in order to keep those
frontiers intact.

Perhaps you might say that the Portuguese 'won' in the end, in
that they retained an empire across multiple continents for nearly five
centuries. But talk of overall 'winners' or 'losers' means zooming so
far out from the lived experiences of particular people in particular
places that we lose sight of the more conflictual reality and end up
blind to the agency of those who resisted and challenged the Portuguese. It's why I am focusing on individual stories in this book, rather
than telling a sweeping narrative of all that happened: in seeing the
struggles, empire loses some of its might.

The difficulties that the Portuguese faced often led to doubts
over whether the gains outweighed the losses in the balance sheet
of empire. In 1506, the Venetian ambassador to the Spanish court,
Vicenzo Quirini, concluded that the early voyages to India would
not bring any long-term gains for the Portuguese (or long-term competition with the Venetians for the spice trade):

> the death of the King of Portugal, it is believed, will be the occasion
> for the ruin of this voyage [to Asia], and if not the death of this king,
> then that of his successor, and on that account many people think
> that in future times, the said voyage is not destined to be firm. And
> in this thought, they are comforted by the many accidents that have
> overcome the ships and the mariners, in this so very long route that
> the Portuguese pursue, which accidents are such that already there

are few who are willing to volunteer to go on it, both on account of the diseases and on account of the great perils of shipwreck, which have been such that from 114 ships which have been on this voyage between 1497 and 1506, only 55 have returned, and 19 are lost for certain, almost all of them laden with spices, and of another 40 nothing is known as of now.[5]

Quirini was wrong to see the doom of the Portuguese India voyages as so imminent, but the problems he identified were real and the overland trade in spices did slowly pick up throughout the sixteenth century. The Portuguese did not manage the perpetual monopoly they hoped for.

As the empire expanded and the monarchy trumpeted Portuguese achievements, the doubts lingered. And if Da Gama was the hero of empire, he could also be blamed for its negative consequences. With time, then, he transformed from a conqueror into a personification of wrongheadedness. A long-time servant of the crown in Portuguese Goa, Heitor da Silveira, wrote three lines of poetry, probably in the 1560s, that are hard to forget:

> Cruel, cruel Gama, what injuries you do to
> Portugal. So many men are turned to dust for
> the sake of worldly goods.[6]

'Cruel, cruel Gama': such a flat denouncement of the discoverer shows just how conflicted even those – especially those – who participated in the empire felt about it, and about Da Gama as its inaugurator. Those old worries voiced by Camões's old man from Restelo would not go away. Empire was about enrichment and therefore it was dirty and corrupt. It was venture capitalism, high risk for high reward. But it was not just capital that was risked, it was people. The pursuit of worldly goods turned men to dust. The criticisms were never loud enough to change the direction of history radically – or people were too greedy and deaf to hear them – but it is important to remember that, from both inside and out, empire was always contested. Silveira might have intended his *tanto varão*, 'so many men', to refer to Portuguese nobles, but we can read his lines a little against the grain to see in them a larger indictment.

There was a long-lasting PR campaign by the Da Gama family to settle their forefather's place in history and to negotiate their own status in Portugal and its empire. The family were often in competition with others for important positions in the governance of Portuguese Asia and they liked to remind people of Vasco, of their descent from such a great historical figure, when making claims for themselves. Many of the images that we have of Da Gama came from the legacy-building of his family in the decades after his death in 1524. He was someone they did not want forgotten, so they commissioned histories and portraits to sustain his legacy. That they put so much energy into the preservation of his memory suggests there was a risk that he might have been forgotten, which is a curious thought given how central a figure Da Gama now is in most accounts of world history.

In 1599, just over a hundred years after Vasco first arrived on the Malabar coast, a statue of him was erected on the so-called 'Viceroy's Arch', which formed one of the gates to the city of Goa, as part of this sustained promotional campaign by the Da Gama family. Two years later, though, in 1601, the statue was ripped down and the pieces scattered about the city in an act of protest by rivals of the Da Gama clan. To really underscore this act of defiance, the statue's head and one of its hands were placed in the city's stocks so that Da Gama could pay symbolic penance.[7] People have been tearing down statues as long as people have been putting them up. Toppling them has often provided the chance to think about how and why these individuals ended up on their pedestals in the first place.

WORLD EVENTS

1501
Founding of the Safavid empire
by Shah Ismail I – Persia (Iran)

1500
Pedro Álvares
Cabral unexpect-
edly reaches the
coast of Brazil

1502
First African slaves arrive
in the 'New World' –
Hispaniola (Dominican
Republic/Haiti)

1506
Death of Christopher
Columbus – Valladolid, Spain

1502
El Dorado, Spain: Sank
during a hurricane in the
Mona Channel between
Hispaniola and Puerto Rico.

San Antón, Spain: Ran
aground near Port-au-Prince,
Haiti while attempting to
recover gold.

Santa María de Gracia,
Spain: Sank near the coast
of Hispaniola due to
shipworm damage.

1503
Esmeralda and *São Pedro*,
Portugal: sink in a
storm near Al
Hallaniyyah off the
coast of Oman.

1505
Bela, Portugal:
Ran aground on the
coast of Guinea.

SHIPWRECKS

1514
Battle of Chaldiran between the Ottoman empire and the Safavid empire – Chaldiran Persia (Iran)

1509
Henry VIII becomes King of England – London

1513
Vasco Núñez de Balboa reaches the Pacific Ocean – Panama

1517
Martin Luther's Ninety-Five Theses – Wittenberg, Germany

1511
São Pedro, Portugal: Crashed into the previously unknown islets of Saint Peter and Saint Paul in the mid-Atlantic while on a journey to India.

Flor do Mar, Portugal: caught in a storm and wrecked in strait of Melaka

1516
Seven ships and barks lost off the coast of Cornwall

1519
c. Thirty Spanish ships lost off the coast of North Africa due to a storm during attack on Algiers led by Hugo de Moncada

PART TWO

Double Treachery

His name means 'warrior'. The other has become a byword for resistance. One was born in Spain. Another on Hispaniola. Each did the unthinkable: they swapped sides.

When Gonzalo Guerrero left the town of Palos de la Frontera in southern Spain, he was just another sailor on just another ship watching the shoreline recede. Like many Spaniards before and after him, he probably hoped to better his fortunes by leaving Andalusia and crossing the Atlantic. Maybe he'd find gold. Maybe he'd make a name for himself. He couldn't have envisaged that one day a statue of him – hair tied up in a topknot, and wearing nothing but a loincloth and sandals – would be cast in bronze and erected in what we now know as Mexico. With a spear in hand and a child clutching at his shins, he's celebrated today as a renegade who left the 'Old World' to embrace a completely different culture.

Enrique, a Taíno man, didn't leave his home on a ship, but he did decide to quit the Spanish world he had grown up in. He made a life for himself and a whole community on Hispaniola, hidden away from the injustices of life toiling for an imposed master. For fifteen years, Spanish officials complained about the turmoil Enrique and his followers caused on the island. We find in the archives the officials' enduring frustration at being unable to track Enrique down and stamp out his uprising.

'Us' and 'them', 'enemy' and 'ally' – such categories become harder to tell apart when people start crossing between them. It becomes difficult to tell who has the upper hand. And sometimes, in a twist of fate, the life that you never imagined becomes the life you can't imagine leaving behind.

3. Two Worlds in One Person

The island of Hispaniola or Haiti, now divided into the modern states of Haiti and the Dominican Republic, was the second major island Christopher Columbus stumbled upon during his first voyage across the Caribbean in search of a route to Asia.

He soon realized that he had not reached Cipangu (Japan) but wrongheadedly held to the hope that he was at least on the right continent.[1] Hispaniola's size and natural abundance captivated Columbus.[2] He claimed in a letter of 1493 that Hispaniola was a 'marvel', larger than the Iberian peninsula, and gold glittered in the silt of nearly every river that flowed through its lush, tropical vegetation.[3] He noted with surprise that canoes shuttled between the islands of the Caribbean undaunted by the ocean. The Spanish would, in only a few years, come to change the nature and pattern of those interconnections by enslaving people from the so-called 'useless' islands elsewhere in the Antilles and displacing them to Hispaniola, where

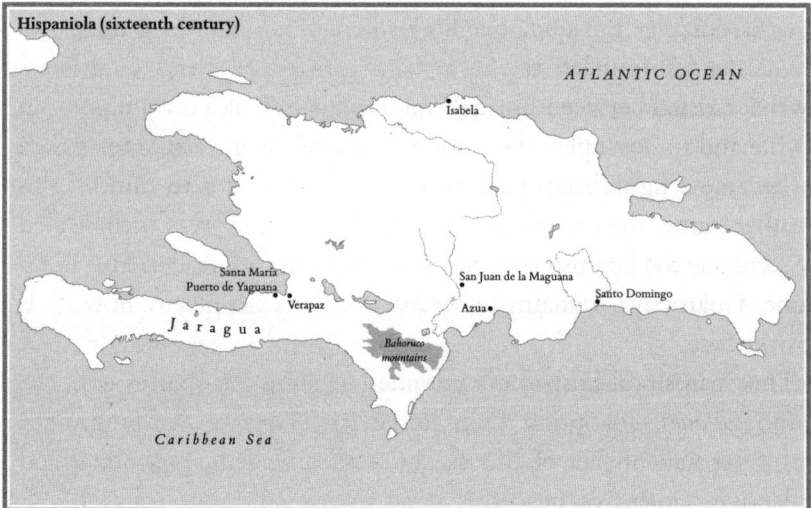

Hispaniola (sixteenth century)

the colonizers were determined to turn a profit from gold mining and sugar production.

Enrique, born after the Spanish arrival on Hispaniola, always straddled two worlds. He came from a line of *caciques*, or leaders, of the indigenous Taíno people, but he was educated by Franciscan friars in a monastery at Verapaz, not unlike boys fortunate enough to go to school in Europe, where he absorbed the tenets of the Catholic religion and acquired skills in one of the prime technologies of colonization: reading and writing. Forging such dual identities was integral to the Spanish strategy for controlling the island. The Franciscans would teach every future Taíno leader for a period of four years, then they would return to their communities to disseminate their learning and their faith. They would be better ambassadors for Christianity than European outsiders, so the Spanish thought, and would be better able to spread its teachings far and wide.[4] By 1513, we know that grammar books and reams of paper were being shipped across the Atlantic to supply one of these Franciscan schools and further its project of cultural assimilation.[5]

One sign that Enrique belonged to two worlds is his name: a Spanish, princely name that he acquired through baptism. In many of the sources that describe his life and his actions that name appears in the belittling diminutive form 'Enriquillo', which the fathers of Verapaz used to address Enrique as a boy. I've chosen to refer to him by the less patronizing 'Enrique', but his nickname is interesting insofar as officials and chroniclers try, in repeating it, to preserve the familiarity that existed between Enrique and the Spanish at a certain point in his life and to downplay the resistance against Spanish rule for which he became a figurehead. Each time the records refer to him by this familiar name, they mark the fact that his uprising was orchestrated by someone the Spanish considered an intimate, an insider. His Taíno name, Guarocuya, remains uncertain and is not typically how he is now known.[6]

The Spanish on Hispaniola intended to build allegiances with the Taíno *caciques*, co-opting their authority.[7] Despite this, resistance was a permanent fact of life on the island. Dissent, individual and collective, violent or peaceful, always crackled in the background.

Columbus learned this quickly when he found that the thirty-nine Spaniards he had left behind at La Navidad on his first voyage to the Caribbean had all been assassinated.[8] There were other ways of fighting the invaders, too: Gonzalo Fernández de Oviedo y Valdés (commonly referred to as Oviedo), a key historian of the Spanish empire in the sixteenth century, tells us that at one point the Taíno, in an act of insubordination, refused to sow crops, which led to starvation, sickness and death among many of the colonists.[9]

The status of the indigenous populations on Hispaniola and across the wider Caribbean was constantly shifting over the first decades of Spanish colonization. While Queen Isabella's 1501 instructions to the governor of Hispaniola, Nicolás de Ovando, made it clear that although indigenous people were required to serve the Spaniards, they were not to be considered slaves but rather free subjects, there remained exceptions to her rules both in theory and in practice. She increased the legal exceptions in 1503, making it lawful to enslave any indigenous people who resisted Spanish governance or conversion to Catholicism. The law kept evolving over the ensuing decade in response to economic, religious and political pressures, opening up various avenues for colonists to abuse or circumvent any legal protections for indigenous groups. Faced with the reality that the Taíno were not going to work willingly in Spanish towns and mines on the island, Ovando instituted a system known as the *encomienda*, which formally subjected indigenous peoples to Spanish colonists: the crown allocated a certain number of indigenous people to a given Spaniard, known as an *encomendero*, who could force them to work in agriculture, mining or other tasks for a minuscule (and regularly nonexistent) wage. The *encomendero* was supposedly responsible for the conversion of his charges and for making sure they were well treated, but abuse was rife. The *encomienda* system quickly decimated the local population through disease, famine and exhaustion from overwork, as well as from outright violence.[10] As one contemporary Spanish observer put it, the colonizers were wild animals who roved around the islands bringing demonic chaos.[11]

In response to this situation, on 21 December 1511, the Dominican friar Antonio de Montesinos delivered a now-famous sermon on Hispaniola, denouncing the cruel treatment of the Taíno under Spanish rule. Though his focus was not on condemning slavery outright, his critique of the abuses within the *encomienda* system sparked debates in Spain which led, in 1512, to the reforms known as the Laws of Burgos.[12] These laws aimed to improve conditions for indigenous groups, but were largely ineffective in practice. More reforms came in 1514, when a significant restructuring of the colonial system, known as the *repartimiento* of Albuquerque, was implemented. Its objectives were to increase the productivity of the gold mines on Hispaniola, give crown officials greater authority, provide indigenous labour to towns that lacked it, and allow for more efficient conversion of the Taíno to Catholicism. This restructuring displaced many Taíno communities from their ancestral lands to mining areas in the centre of the island and to the burgeoning sugar plantations near the colonial capital, Santo Domingo.[13]

When Justice Fails

Enrique and those in his *cacicazgo*, or chiefdom, were among those displaced by these reforms. They were assigned in 1514 to a man called Francisco de Valenzuela and forced to move to San Juan de la Maguana. For five years, Enrique accepted this new home, until the *encomendero* died and his son Andrés was imposed as their overlord. According to the historian, erstwhile *encomendero*, and Dominican priest Bartolomé de las Casas, Valenzuela junior seized Enrique's horse and raped his wife.

Enrique channelled his outrage through the structures of the law. He appealed for redress to the lieutenant governor of San Juan de la Maguana, Pedro de Vadillo, demanding that action be taken against these clear abuses. Vadillo was unsympathetic and uninterested in providing justice. He told Enrique to drop his complaint, and discredited him as a troublemaker. Undeterred, Enrique travelled more than 150 kilometres across the island to Santo Domingo in order to have his case heard by the *audiencia*, the highest court on Hispaniola, which also had a broader administrative remit.

Bohíos in Hispaniola

The buildings of Santo Domingo were not like those of much of the rest of the island. The traditional *bohíos* of the Taíno were constructed from wooden pillars driven into the ground with roofs thatched with palm leaves.

Here, though, the buildings were of stone, and laid out on a regular gridwork of streets which would become the prototype for towns all across the Americas. For a moment, walking down the Calle de las Damas, Enrique might have thought he had been transported to somewhere in Spain, surrounded as he was by the architectural language of Andalusia and Extremadura, with its hybrid vocabulary of Moorish, Gothic and Renaissance styles. The first-floor window on the corner of the Casa de Tostada has two pointed arches that sprout leaves and fronds in stone; the lintel above the door of the old governor Nicolás de Ovando's house is so finely wrought it appears to be made of malleable silver rather than stone. Foliage and buds seem to grow out from the undulations of its sinuous curve.[14] Columbus had seen storms flatten *bohíos*, but these stone buildings wouldn't budge much in a hurricane.[15] Such solidity, to Enrique, was perhaps less reassuring and more a tangible reminder that the Spanish, come what may, intended to stay. Each of those stones had been quarried, carried and mortared into place by forced labour.

At the head of the Calle de las Damas, close to the River Ozama, sat Enrique's destination: the *audiencia*. The building plays its cards quite close to its chest. The exterior gives little away; a string of small arched windows on the upper floor peer over the banks of the river, surveying arriving and departing ships. But step through the arched doorways of the ground floor and there are grand rooms and colonnaded courtyards within.

The judges of the *audiencia* found in Enrique's favour, ordering that his horse be returned and that his wife be protected from the predatory advances of Valenzuela. But these instructions for redress went straight back to Vadillo himself to enforce, so you can imagine that they were not greeted with any enthusiasm, let alone action.

Las Casas isn't considered by historians the most reliable witness to sixteenth-century events, so some doubts remain as to whether these specific crimes were indeed committed by Andrés de Valenzuela. But what is incontrovertible is that, in 1519, Enrique was driven to leave San Juan de la Maguana with a small group from his community and flee to his ancestral homeland up in the Bahoruco mountains in the region of Jaragua. The catalyst may have been these specific abuses or an accumulation of more general grievances: persistent maltreatment by Spanish *encomenderos* and the depletion of the indigenous population through overwork in the mines and sugar plantations, as well as through the ravages of diseases imported from Europe and Africa which decimated the Taíno year on year. Estimates for the population on Hispaniola before the arrival of Columbus put it at upwards of 400,000 people. After a smallpox epidemic in 1518, there were only 3,000 native Hispaniolans left.[16]

Enrique's flight was the start of fourteen years of persistent challenge to the Spanish. Curiously, Las Casas, Enrique's most sympathetic Spanish chronicler, hesitated in calling Enrique's defiance a rebellion or an uprising. He was keen to differentiate between the possible words – rebel, enemy, fugitive, insurgent – one might use to describe Enrique, as each label brought with it a particular judgement about the legitimacy of his conduct. Las Casas wanted to show that Enrique was in the right:

> He [Enrique] decided not to serve his enemy [Valenzuela] any more, nor send him any of his people, and thus to defend himself in his own land. The Spanish spoke – and still speak today – of Enrique and the Indians rising up and being rebels; but, truthfully, it was nothing more than fleeing from their cruel enemies, who killed and consumed them.[17]

Las Casas's words hint at the broader issues behind Enrique's decision to flee to the mountains. By running away, Enrique rejected the *encomendero* system, refusing to send his people to work for the Spanish. They became literal outlaws, living outside the oppressive regime that had so harmed them. For Enrique, fleeing was a way to reclaim his home and his autonomy from the Spanish.

Las Casas eschewed the word 'rebel' in order to legitimize Enrique's actions: he wanted to emphasize that his refusal to engage with Spanish colonial society was justified, a last resort in the face of an enemy that was bent on annihilation through murder or exploitation. A rebellion or an uprising implied, in the Spanish mindset, an unjustified act of defiance that would need to be quashed. Las Casas sought a different set of words to persuade his compatriots to see Enrique's actions in a different light.

For Enrique, resistance to the Spanish seems to have run in the family. Enrique's great-aunt, Anacaona, was a prominent *cacica*, or leader, in the region of Jaragua. This area, located in the southwest of the island, was far from the main Spanish settlements. Because of this, many people from across Hispaniola fled to Jaragua to escape the colonizers. In 1503, Nicolás de Ovando, the governor at the time, headed to Jaragua with sixty horses and 300 men to crush this enclave of resistance. Yet he did not ride in and immediately wreak havoc. Las Casas recounts that Anacaona welcomed Ovando with festivities and dancing. Subsequently, Ovando invited her and several chieftains into a *bohío* for a discussion. On Ovando's cue – a finger to the gold chain strung around his neck – the Spanish inside the hut rounded up all the chieftains and restrained them with ropes. He escorted Anacaona outside then torched the hut with the bound captives screaming inside.[18] Anacaona herself was dragged to Santo Domingo and hanged publicly in the main square as a warning to anyone who did not comply with Spanish wishes.[19] In a Latin translation of Las Casas's account, from later in the sixteenth century, an illustration depicts the horrific fire on the left and Anacaona's harrowing fate on the right.

Reports from early in the life of the colony point to frequent desertions by slaves of different kinds. In 1503, Ovando had complained about enslaved Africans fleeing the gold mines and then colluding with groups of Taíno living far away from the Spanish settlements. These slaves had been brought to Hispaniola from West Africa to make up for the ever-diminishing population of the Caribbean islands after waves of disease and Spanish mistreatment. By 1509, there were more Africans on Hispaniola than Spaniards and indigenous people combined.[20] Taíno and Africans collaborated with each other in

The execution of Anacaona and the *caciques* of Jaragua in 1503

various ways. One habit that quickly translated was smoking tobacco to stifle hunger and fatigue while working at the gold mines. Spanish observers, however, did not take warmly to the early colonial cigarette break.[21] The establishment of an official post of *recogedor*, or slave catcher, was requested in 1518, again signalling the scale of the problem of indentured labourers resisting and fleeing the yoke of the Spanish. Following Enrique, other *caciques* rebelled too, spurred on by his example, some of them joining his community of renegades in the mountains.[22] In other words, Enrique's rebellion was not the first, nor would it be the last.

Escape to the Mountains

Upon learning of Enrique's desertion, Andrés de Valenzuela took eleven men and chased after the *cacique*, his family and followers. The pursuers, armed with lances and spears, clashed with the runaways and tried to force them to return. Two of Valenzuela's band were killed and Enrique's defiant rebels hurtled off into the Bahoruco mountains as the enraged *encomendero* lobbed insults behind them. The terrain, deeply familiar to the Taíno, deeply hostile for the Spaniards, became their natural fortress; the forest sprawling between valleys and peaks was green camouflage for their settlements, the topography a labyrinth to wear down those who chose to enter. Sometime later, Taíno warriors, presumably linked to Enrique, ambushed a group of Spaniards transporting gold near Verapaz. The incident triggered another Spanish attempt at retaliation. A patrol of eighty men was authorized to go and hunt down Enrique and his rogue community. The Spaniards underestimated their adversaries, however, who killed the patrol's commander and eight of his men, forcing a hasty retreat.

Those who fled Spanish rule were known as *cimarrones*, which gives us the English word 'maroon'. Although that word today tends to summon up ideas of Robinson Crusoe and castaways on desert islands, originally it had more radical connotations. In Spanish, *cimarrones* were animals that escaped and became wild, but the term was soon extended to humans, first to indigenous people who deserted and then, from at least the 1530s, also to African slaves who ran away. It's a word which evokes the daring choice to flee the colonial world and make a life free from the shackles of enslavement.[23] Maroon communities were practical experiments in reversing the brutal treatment of Europeans which stripped people of their rights and land, and tried to decimate cultures and languages that were not their own. They arose all across the 'New World' in the sixteenth century. Two famous examples were those of Bayano, an enslaved African who revolted with several hundred others in Panama in 1552 and founded a settlement near the Chepo river, and of Miguel de Buría in Venezuela, who forged a coalition of displaced Africans and Jirajara indigenous people working in the Spanish mines in order to defy their colonial overlords and set up their own autonomous community, or *cumbe*.

Patrol after patrol ventured into the thick forests of Hispaniola on the hunt for Enrique's enclave of fugitives. Every one returned depleted by hunger and thirst, unable to make the mountains of Bahoruco yield up any of the deserters. It was a vast warren of forest, crags and waterfalls. The Spaniards had to lug water and food on their backs as they scrambled over the roots and rocks, trying to keep a secure footing. They struggled against this rugged terrain, far from their own settlements, often spending weeks or months searching the forest with no sign of Enrique or his village. They tried large expeditions – some numbering up to 300 men – and small, nimble hunting parties to smoke the fugitives from their hideout. None of them caught up with their elusive quarry, yet they were constantly reminded that it was out there somewhere because of the raids Enrique's followers made to steal their supplies.

Gradually, the Spanish strategy evolved: detachments of soldiers were deployed defensively to try to stop the raids, and that, at last, began to reduce the impact that the rebels were having on Hispaniola at large. The war was a challenge, not only because the Spaniards' foes knew the region well and were well adapted to the environment, but also because they were conversant with Spanish customs, habits, military organization and weaponry, which they themselves seem to have managed to steal.[24] It is the familiar story of guerrilla warfare through the ages. The arrogance of the more technologically advanced and the better-resourced did not adapt well to a scenario of skirmishes and concealment so different from the short-lived campaigns of conventional full-scale warfare. In this long game of survival, the Taíno persistently outmanoeuvred and out-thought the Spanish.

Unfindable, Enrique and his fellow fugitives held the island in a permanent state of fear; the threat of ambush lurked by every roadside. In 1524, five years after Enrique fled from San Juan de la Maguana, officials in Hispaniola petitioned the crown in Spain for support, revealing the impact that the groups of maroons were having. They told how Indians and Africans had banded together to rob travellers, *pueblos* and *estancias* (towns and estates), and that they were utterly incapable of limiting the damage and harm done by the outlaws.[25] The *ingenios*, or sugar mills, were a focus of the hatred of African, Taíno and other indigenous groups, and were often attacked. Worry that the idea of rebellion would percolate through even peaceful communities, fomenting disobedience in every quarter, leached into the writings of officials. Some were nervous that even the African slaves who were employed to track Enrique and his people down would be shown an alternative path to take.[26] The fear was well placed: in 1521, the first uprising of the African diaspora in the Spanish Americas erupted.

It started on Christmas Day, at a sugar mill owned by Columbus's son Diego, who had become viceroy and governor of Hispaniola after his father's death. The rebels took advantage of the Christmas lull to make their move. They advanced from Columbus's plantation at Isabela towards Azua, the centre of the sugar industry, ransacking the ranch of Melchior de Castro, who was also involved in gold mining. They killed several Spaniards on their way, another during the raid, and took over a dozen captives, torching everything that they left behind. Columbus sent a group of soldiers on horseback to quash the rebellion. For a week, the squad rounded up dissidents or killed them. Those who were captured were hanged as an example to any remaining would-be revolutionaries. New ordinances were brought in swiftly after the rebellion in a bid to limit the possibility of future uprisings. Slaves were not allowed to move between *ingenios*, and communication between them was limited as much as possible; lines of communication were channels for discord. Slave owners were required to keep detailed information about their slaves and their movements, which, by implication, suggests how little control and information they did in fact have.[27]

The costs of Enrique's rebels to the Spanish, over time, were multiple: the expense of feeding soldiers and equipping expeditions, and the loss of labour and time.[28] So many of the documents sent from Hispaniola back to Spain during the later years of Enrique's rebellion contained references to the ongoing difficulties that the colonial administration had in limiting the damage and preventing Enrique's numbers from growing.

In their world, the rebels cultivated yucca, and ate spiders, crayfish, snakes and roots, all deemed unpalatable by the Spanish, but a diet that was able to sustain them for more than a decade. Enrique's fugitives were careful about the traces they left of their presence in the landscape: they never took too many branches from one place, so that the broken boughs or cleared ground didn't set out a trail for the Spanish, and fire, with its tell-tale smoke, was carefully controlled. They even cut out the tongues of the cockerels that they raised so that they would not crow and alert any soldiers to the location of their settlement.[29] They knew which spots were isolated, what would grow and where, the places that drinking water could be found; a local knowledge that allowed them to defy the Spanish for so long. They were perhaps also sustained by another invader of the island, eight of whom had arrived in 1493 with Christopher Columbus: pigs. Historians of the sixteenth century all commented on the 'swinish multitudes', the pigs that had proliferated, with litter after litter finding ample food for themselves on the tropical island. The porcine invaders were incredibly successful and became the chosen breed of colonizers across the Americas if they needed to infest a region with a reliable source of protein.[30]

Across the Chasm

In 1528, nine years after Enrique fled to the mountains, a captain named Hernando de San Miguel finally found him. San Miguel had shifted tactics, focusing on destroying the fugitives' crops and making life difficult for them so they would be drawn out from their hideaway. But still he roamed through the thick forests of the mountains without finding Enrique. He was an old Hispaniola hand who had arrived with Columbus as a young man; over his decades on the island, he had grown accustomed to the people and the terrain. Which I think means that he was prepared to do whatever was needed to get what he, and the Spanish more broadly, wanted. He was such a tough guy, Las Casas tells us, that he sometimes even trekked barefoot over the serrated rocks of the Bahoruco mountains while searching for Enrique.[31]

One day by chance, however, the two men came close enough to have a conversation. Their meeting, as Las Casas describes it, was worthy of cinema: they stood on either side of a gorge, a chasm of 500 fathoms (or something like 900 metres) slicing perilously down between them. Across that ravine – physical, political, cultural – they began to talk. The gap between them gave them mutual security; they could talk frankly. San Miguel lamented how difficult the disruption from raid, theft, robbery and desertion had made the lives of the Spanish; he knew this perpetual strife must be sapping the energies of the rebels too. Enrique, after more than a decade as a fugitive, confessed that he had wanted to seek some sort of agreement for a while, but, in his eyes, the Spanish needed to ask for peace and make the first move, not wait for his surrender. San Miguel, as proof of his trustworthiness, held up the document given to him by the *audiencia* in Santo Domingo, which granted him the authority to broker peace. Enrique was too far away to read the handwriting on that piece of paper, but San Miguel assured him that he and his community would be allowed to live freely on the island in a place of his choosing without being disturbed by the Spanish. All he needed to do was end the hostilities and hand back the gold that his men had stolen from the Spanish near Verapaz. Enrique was clearly relieved.

They agreed to meet, accompanied by eight men each, near the coast to settle the terms.[32]

But trust is a friable material. Enrique made his way to the coast with his eight men to ratify the verbal pact made in the mountains. They went about making a small shelter out of logs and branches and set up a table laden with food and the gold that they were returning to the Spaniards. Enrique expected a quiet conclusion to years of animosity, but when he spied San Miguel approaching, he was beating a drum and escorted by more men than the agreed entourage of eight. At the sound of San Miguel's procession, and the sight of a ship anchored worryingly close to the beach, Enrique scrambled back into the forest for cover. He suspected that he was walking into a trap. If the Spanish couldn't keep their word on the matter of how many people were supposed to meet, what grounds were there to trust that he and his community would receive what they had been promised? Sheltered by the forest, he dispatched eight followers to meet San Miguel. He instructed them to tell his Spanish counterpart that he was too unwell to be there in person, and to offer them the gold and spread of food that they had prepared. The tough guy had, in short, screwed up. His overeagerness to celebrate the conclusion of hostilities ended up prolonging the tension between Enrique's renegades and the Spanish for five more years.

Other attempts were made in the interim to bring a close to the fighting. These were disastrous. A Franciscan whom Enrique knew from his childhood in Verapaz was dispatched at least three times to meet him. On one, or possibly two occasions, he accompanied a *cacique* identified in documents by his Hispanicized name, Don Rodrigo, who was supposedly related to him. On that likely second mission, Don Rodrigo was killed and the friar was stripped down to his smalls before being released.[33]

The weary officials in Hispaniola made another appeal to the Spanish crown for help. Their plea was answered in 1533 with the arrival of a large expedition, led by Francisco de Barrionuevo. The men he brought were not professional soldiers, but farmers and artisans who were probably entirely lacking in experience of the Caribbean and thus ineffectual in the face of the challenge. He selected in their stead thirty-five local Spaniards and an equal number of indigenous people, who knew the terrain, and enlisted two of Enrique's relatives, women who were seemingly happy to be involved in the delicate negotiations.

Barrionuevo sailed along the coast from Santo Domingo to the vicinity of Bahoruco. Ten weeks of searching ensued, but not a trace of Enrique's settlement emerged out of the difficult landscape. Barrionuevo sought out an informant, as it was clear he was not going to find Enrique's hidden community without some inside knowledge to orient him through the terrain. He requested guides from a nearby official and was helpfully sent a Taíno who had fled from Enrique's fugitive community. It was this runaway from the runaways who led Barrionuevo and his group deep into the centre of the island to a large lake, which is still today known as Lake Enrique. There, finally, they encountered some of the community and sent one of the Taíno relatives of Enrique as an envoy to broker a meeting the following day. Barrionuevo handed over an official pardon to Enrique, the first in a series of reassurances to coax along the peace agreement, more cautiously this time.

The next day, Enrique bid farewell to Captain Barrionuevo, sending delegates to escort the captain back to his ship. In a gesture of goodwill, they returned with gifts from Barrionuevo for Enrique: wine, oil, biscuits and other goods. They were taking care to smooth the way at each step. The judges of the *audiencia*, keenly aware of how challenging it was to bring a fugitive community back within the orbit of the *pueblos* of the island, moved cautiously, offering Enrique every assurance in order to avoid any perception of deceit.

Enrique also sent a representative with Barrionuevo to meet the *audiencia* officials. They, in turn, ordered the public proclamation of the peace accord in the towns near to Bahoruco and in Santo Domingo itself. Gonzalo, Enrique's envoy, went from town to town – La Yaguana, San Juan de la Maguana, Azua – to watch the Spaniards declare peace, so that he could report back to his community that the Spaniards were keeping their word. A letter written by the *audiencia* recording these proceedings suggests that Gonzalo actively participated in them, taking off his hat each time peace was proclaimed in every place.[34]

To ensure that the next phase in the delicate negotiations advanced without any undue hiccups, the *audiencia* consulted widely on whom they should send back to Enrique as their representative. They settled on Pedro Romero, a trusted figure who was known to Enrique from the past and who had been with Barrionuevo on his last diplomatic mission to Bahoruco. Accompanied by an interpreter and two high-ranking Taíno, Romero travelled first by ship to Azua then trekked westwards and inland into the mountains, laden with gifts for Enrique – clothes, devotional images, a bell, wine and practical tools such as axes and hoes. The accoutrements of religion in this list are a reminder to us that Enrique remained a Christian – or at least observed Christian rituals – throughout his time in the Bahoruco mountains. One report suggests that Romero found crosses hanging in each of the wooden *bohíos* in Enrique's community. The borders between rebel and oppressor were blurrier than the long conflict between them can make it seem.

Romero's visit succeeded. He was warmly received by Enrique and stayed eight days in his hidden village, home to about 400 people by this point. Enrique expressed his gratitude to the Spanish crown for the pardon and pledged his friendship. He gave his own diplomatic reassurance by handing over six Africans who had fled from captivity. And he promised to surrender to the Spanish authorities any future fugitives – African or indigenous – who came to join him. The agreement drew a line under the past, but also drew a line around the future: the inclusion of this clause acknowledged the power of these communities as a magnet for those who refused to comply with Spanish dominion. Enrique betrayed those he put back into Spanish hands. An axis of solidarity against the Spanish had been broken.

The final ratification of the peace accord came when Enrique visited Santo Domingo in the summer of 1534, accompanied by twenty of his men. The rebellion had lasted some fifteen years. Enrique and his men spent nearly three weeks being entertained by the judges of the *audiencia* and other prominent citizens. Enrique settled near Azua with his wife and people and offered to assist in controlling other rebels. The *audiencia*'s strategy had paid off. Enrique and his followers were integrated into Spanish colonial society, and Enrique had pledged to help maintain peace. The officials tactfully rejected the king's suggestion to exile Enrique, citing his value in maintaining order on the island as an ex-fugitive.[35] Sadly, he did not enjoy peace for long, as he passed away in September 1535.

Enrique's reconciliation with the Spanish marked the end of concerted indigenous rebellion on Hispaniola – something that was only achieved with the first agreement between the empire and an insurgent group within it. The terms of that agreement, though they may seem compromises, tell us of the reality of rebellion and the diplomatic and legal manoeuvres required to prevent rebels banding together and causing formidable problems for the Spanish. Enrique's story defies simplistic timelines of arrival and then conquest. It isn't just a linear story about cultural assimilation or colonization, where one thing leads predictably to another: greater understanding, deeper European entrenchment, more forced conversion. Hispaniola's narrative arc displays a series of unexpected turns – the rebellion of an insider, defiance as well as assimilation, mistrust, peace on compromised terms – all set against the perpetual challenges of disease, demographic transformation and the relentless exploitation of both people and the environment.

4. The Lost and the Found

In February 1519, the same year that Enrique fled San Juan de la Maguana to form a new community in the mountains of Hispaniola, the Spanish conquistador Hernán Cortés set sail from Cuba with a fleet of ships bound for the Yucatán peninsula, in what is now Mexico. His instructions were to retrieve shipwrecked Spaniards said to be held captive there by Maya chiefs, as well as to trade with them for gold.[1]

During the first night of the voyage, winds scattered the ships and the signal lantern supposed to keep them together drifted out of view of many of the fleet. The dispersed ships had instructions to rendezvous at the harbour of Santa Cruz on the island of Cozumel.

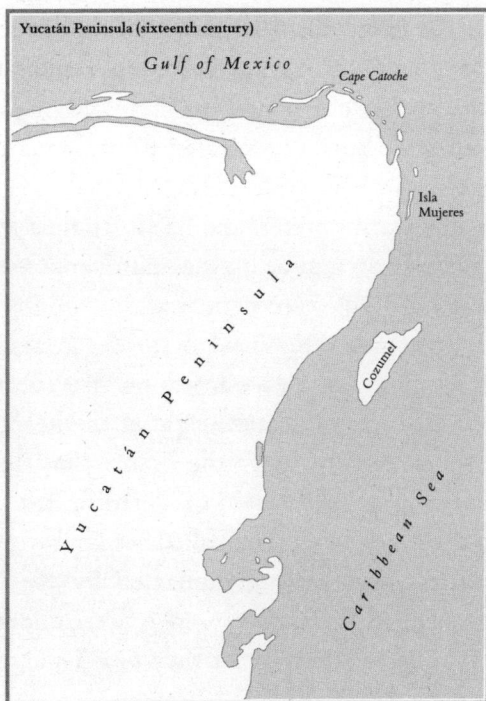

Yucatán Peninsula (sixteenth century)

The flagship and another vessel, captained by Francisco de Morla, stayed in sight of each other but were struggling to reach their intended destination. The weather, or perhaps just good old incompetence, caused Morla's ship to lose its rudder. They set alight a flare as a distress signal, so Cortés's ship hove to and waited for daybreak to help them. By the time the sun had risen the following morning, the waves had dropped and the missing rudder was spotted drifting on the surface of the ocean. With a rope tied round his waist so that he could be winched back in again, Morla dived into the sea and swam across to retrieve the vital piece of broken apparatus. He managed to haul it back to the ship, where it was slotted back into place so they could once again steer themselves more easily.[2] Cortés and Morla made their way towards the Isla Mujeres, where they encountered all but one of the fleet, and then together they sailed on to Cozumel.

Two years earlier, an expedition to Yucatán led by Francisco Hernández de Córdoba had reported hearing the locals say 'Castilan, Castilan', as if to suggest that they already knew about the Spanish. On Cozumel, Cortés set about enquiring into these intriguing utterances with the help of one of the Spaniards who had accompanied Hernández de Córdoba, and of a Maya fisherman captured in 1517 and subsequently christened Melchor (although the Spanish, much as they did with Enrique, referred to him by a diminutive of his name, Melchorejo). Having learned some Spanish, Melchor was able to serve as a basic interpreter, and he ascertained from the locals that Spaniards were known to be on the mainland. Cortés wanted to track down these long-lost countrymen as they might be able to act as more reliable interpreters to speak with the locals. An anecdote that dates back to these early encounters on the Yucatán peninsula puts the problem of communication right at the heart of the Spanish experience there. According to the Franciscan friar Antonio de Ciudad Real, writing in 1588, when the Spanish first arrived in the area they asked the locals what they called the land where they lived. Their interlocutors, unsurprisingly puzzled by the sounds being uttered at them, replied, '*Uic athan*' – 'We don't understand.' None the wiser, the Spanish recorded what they heard and established the name of the region as 'Yucatán'.[3]

Cortés struggled to persuade any of the people on Cozumel to act as his messengers, because they feared that the chieftain on the mainland who held the Spaniards captive would kill anyone trying to send word to them about setting them free. Cortés pleaded with some men and bribed them with gifts. Dressed as they were, in just a loincloth, there were few places on their person where they could conceal a note. Cortés came up with the idea of stashing the folded paper in the hair of one of the men and provided them with glass beads with which to ransom the captives. One of the Spanish ships transported the messengers across the strait to the mainland.[4]

Cortés waited a week for a reply, but there was no news. The messengers failed to return, suggesting that their fears about the chieftain on the mainland were well placed. Once the Spaniards had completed the repairs to their storm-damaged ships, they hoisted sail again, setting course back to the Isla Mujeres. After anchoring there for a day, they headed for Catoche, on the northern tip of the peninsula. En route, the supply ship carrying most of the expedition's provisions sprang a leak. It began to take on water more quickly than its two pumps could cope with; if it didn't make land soon, the ship would sink. So Cortés made the decision to return to Cozumel, where there was a good harbour and their treatment by the locals had been friendly.[5]

Bad Luck Becomes Good Fortune

Back where they started, the Spanish set about repairing the supply ship, plugging the hole and making the hull more securely watertight. Before they left once again, a canoe slid up over the horizon and towards the island. A handful of local-looking men got out and began to head in the direction of the Spaniards. Cortés instructed one of his men, Andrés de Tapia, to investigate. At the sight of Tapia and his sword, all but one of the men retreated. But one continued to come forward, undeterred, and started to speak. He asked in clumsy Castilian whether they were Christians and who was their king. When the answer came back that they were Castilians, the questioner burst into tears. This man was Jerónimo de Aguilar.

In Spanish that had shrivelled without an interlocutor for eight years, he told his story. He was a Franciscan priest from Écija in southern Spain and had been part of an expedition in 1511 led by Juan de Valdivia which was headed to Spain from Santa María de la Antigua del Darién. Located in the Gulf of Darién, an inlet of the Caribbean Sea to the northwest of present-day Colombia, right in the crook where the Isthmus of Panama connects to the South American continent, Santa María de la Antigua del Darién was the second Spanish settlement in the region. (The first, San Sebastián, had been abandoned because of attacks by the indigenous Urabaes, the ravages of disease and malnutrition, and the dangers of the local wildlife – a crocodile reportedly ate one of the Spanish horses.[6]) Valdivia's ship was seeking provisions and reinforcements for the colony, but it was also carrying around 70 kilograms of gold for the King of Spain. This bounty, designed to encourage the king to redouble support for the colony at Darién under Vasco Núñez de Balboa, made the vessel Aguilar was travelling on one of the most richly laden in the early period of colonization. The ship, however, hit a sandbar close to Jamaica and most of the crew perished in the wreck. A few managed to escape in a small boat; but without food or water, only half survived as they drifted on the current to the mainland. Of the eight or nine who made it to shore, most were killed when they arrived. Only Aguilar and one other man survived.[7]

Aguilar attributed his endurance of enslavement by the Maya to his faith. He told how he had tried to keep the Sabbath, even without ever truly knowing what day of the week it was, and maintained his vows of chastity despite frequent attempts on the part of his captors to seduce him. His time as a captive, however, had served as an immersion course in Yucatec Maya, albeit an unwelcome one. His proficiency in the language enabled him to facilitate negotiations as a go-between, and made him one of Cortés's key assets in his early conquests in Mexico. He formed a crucial pair with a woman named Malintzin, herself a speaker of Maya and Nahuatl, famed as the translator who brokered the fall of the Aztec empire.

The other Spanish survivor mentioned by Aguilar was a more mysterious figure, and all the more intriguing for it. His name was

Gonzalo, and he was often given the surname 'Guerrero', which means 'warrior' – it was most likely a fabricated epithet reflecting the role that Gonzalo was said to have played in the resistance that the Spanish faced in Yucatán over the ensuing years.[8]

After Aguilar received the urgent message carried by Cortés's couriers from Cozumel island, he promptly set out to find Gonzalo, who had been sold to a chief called Nachan Ka'an of Chetumal. Aguilar expected Gonzalo to leap at the chance to return to the Spanish, but Gonzalo's time among the Maya had profoundly transformed him. He had married and had children. Gone was the sailor in search of riches; in his place stood a man with the tattoos and piercings of a Maya warrior. His skin bore the marks of his bravery, etched into his flesh through painful incisions filled with pigments. The Spanish priest Diego de Landa, writing later in the century, noted that such tattoos were a sign of immense courage because of the agony endured. While we can only speculate about the exact designs of Gonzalo's facial tattoos, scholars such as Alfred Tozzer have pointed to carvings from the Maya city Uxmal, on the Yucatán peninsula, which depict intricate facial adornments. These designs, often described as 'breath', involve swirling patterns extending from the corners of the mouth.[9] The ears and lips of elite Maya were often pierced and filled with plugs of jade or bone. It has been suggested that the holes made in the flesh to accommodate this jewellery created channels for vital energy to flow into and out of the body, emphasizing the vitality of these individuals. The materials used for the plugs were associated with these life forces too, and thus were not just signs of wealth but also manifestations of power and charisma.[10]

Gonzalo's body therefore testified to his total immersion into the Maya world. And according to reports by Cortés and later historians, when he replied to Aguilar's invitation, it was these bodily alterations that he cited as a barrier to reinserting himself into Spanish society. His new life had been grafted onto his skin. Consequently, he would always look different from other Spaniards, his experiences in an unfamiliar culture would never go unnoticed. While the comments the chroniclers made about Gonzalo underline, on some level, the plasticity of identity – languages can be learned; we can adapt to or be seduced by a wholly different culture – the claim that his tattoos and piercings prevented him from returning to Spain reminds us that identity in this period was not endlessly flexible. Some circumstances – and, more importantly, others' attitudes to those circumstances – restricted some individuals' ability to change.

It wasn't just Gonzalo's assimilation into Maya culture that prevented him from returning to and readopting his old Spanish identity. He had a family and a life in Yucatán. Indeed, several of the chronicles report that Gonzalo's wife told Aguilar to shut up and go away. It's hard to tell what exactly was embellished as Gonzalo's story was filtered through the accounts of Cortés's time on Cozumel and of the struggles that the Spanish later underwent, but we can glean possible glimpses of Gonzalo's perspective even from the way that such historians disparaged him. Oviedo, for instance, who was perhaps the most critical of all, called him 'vile' and 'lowly', terms that are loaded with moral reproach but also highlight his social status: he was a sailor, not particularly wealthy, and not high in the pecking order. For Oviedo, a more privileged individual, one could expect little more of such a person than to give in to a totally alien culture. Yet, within that criticism, we perhaps see exactly what the appeal of Gonzalo's new life was: in Chetumal he seems to have won respect, to have built a family and a life for himself. He was not lowly and vile in the eyes of his adoptive community. Why would he give that up?

Another slur against Gonzalo centred on his apparent lasciviousness for taking a Maya wife.[11] Such comments have to be seen in the light of a generalized worry around *mestizaje*, cultural and racial mixing, as it was construed in the past. His behaviour suggested a porousness of boundaries and a receptiveness that flew in the face of the religious zeal that accompanied European expansion, its predication on a belief in the spiritual, moral and cultural superiority of the colonizers. Aguilar, who avowedly kept himself chaste and enthusiastically rejoined the Spanish after receiving Cortés's letter, was Gonzalo's foil in this respect: the perennially pious man who does not give in to carnal desires. At the same time that texts about travel obsessively dwelt on bodies and sexual mores – nakedness, sodomy, the practices and apparatus of chastity and pleasure – Europeans also worried that lust would lead their own astray. After rule number one – be true to God – the next regulation given to Cortés before he left Cuba demanded that he guard especially against fornication.[12] Desire was a peril that could entice men to breach the invisible line between them and us. Desire in the eyes of church and commander alike was a kind of slackness. It was another way to discredit Gonzalo's choice: he just did what he did out of lust.

In the moment that he rejected Aguilar's request to flee Yucatán with him, Gonzalo finally became fully and irrevocably Maya. Before then, his life among the Maya was probably more something assembled from the flotsam of circumstance, pieced together incrementally with what was to hand, without any underlying intention other than to survive in the situation in which he found himself. The possibility of returning to his Spanish life must have appeared so anomalously small to him that it wasn't worth shaping his identity around it. Instead, his existence probably revolved around the *milpa*, the patch of ground where a Maya household cultivated maize, beans and squash. It was the province of men – fathers and sons, and, for a time, the son-in-law fulfilling his period of bride service to his wife's family. They would have worked hard to keep the forest at bay, as it tried to reclaim the clearing and entangle their crops. After a few years, though, they would have to let this natural process take its course, in order to replenish the soil, and they would find another location for their *milpa*.[13]

Perhaps one morning, on his way to the day's labour, Gonzalo followed a swarm of bees off the path and back to the hollow tree that contained their hive. The bees of the region were stingless and sacred. They did not produce honeycomb, but instead a kind of wax blister that, when pierced with a stick, oozed sweet liquid.[14] The honey was fermented with water and the bark of a particular tree to create *balche*, a mead-like drink that was said to purge the drinker and was offered to the gods and used in a range of sacred ceremonies.[15]

Bees were revered for their orderliness, how they worked together in a community like humans.[16] It was disorder that the Maya associated with the arrival of the Spanish. The *Book of Chilam Balam of Chumayel* is a fascinating compendium of Maya texts written over the

course of the colonial period in Yucatec Maya using the Latin alphabet. Looking back at the time before the Spanish arrival, it tells us:

> Then they adhered to the dictates of their reason. There was no sin;
> in the holy faith their lives were passed. There was then no sickness;
> they had then no aching bones; they had then no high fever; they
> had then no smallpox; they had then no burning chest; they had then
> no abdominal pains; they had then no consumption; they had then
> no headache. At that time the course of humanity was orderly. The
> foreigners made it otherwise when they arrived here. They brought
> shameful things when they came.[17]

In contrast to the highly centralized world of the Aztec empire, settlements in Yucatán were not politically unified and this meant that
the Spanish could not sweep in and conquer the region in a single
blow. They were persistently thwarted, struggling to adapt to the
Maya guerrilla tactics, just as Enrique equally foiled the Spanish
on Hispaniola for more than a decade by hiding in the mountains
and raiding unpredictably. Gonzalo reared his head in the Spanish
chronicles of these desperate skirmishes in Yucatán as a spectre of
resistance, aiding and abetting the fight against his former countrymen. His insertion into these stories – although he only ever appears
in brief, passing comments – speaks of a desire to explain Spanish
failures beyond their own shortcomings and their enemy's skills:
something more dangerous had to be at work. A renegade had to be
supplying knowledge that would help the Maya outwit the Spanish. It's a persistent myopia of history-making during the sixteenth
century: always imagining events to be determined by one of the
historian's own.

Rough Breaks

The stories of Enrique and Gonzalo are not straightforward fables,
but point to the rough edges of choices made in difficult circumstances. Enrique's rebellion challenged Spanish rule, but after fifteen
years he was ready to negotiate peace. Watching and listening to

yourself so you don't give yourself away, always looking over your shoulder – the clandestine life of the freedom fighter brings confinement as well as liberation. Still, it was obviously better than the grim indentured existence of hard labour under Spanish rule. The story of Enrique's community in the Bahoruco mountains gives us an alternative geography of the island of Hispaniola, where there are patches of the unknown and the free. Maps so often are just political outlines, revealing fantasies of national boundedness but little of the flux that surges within those territorial confines. Indeed, the fact that Enrique held on to the religion he learned in a monastery reminds us that running away isn't necessarily a clean break: a splinter of the before may stick in one's memory.

The energy spent by the Spanish chroniclers in discrediting Gonzalo for his apparent lowliness, lasciviousness and lack of Christian faith shows just how much his choice to stay in Yucatán among the Maya bothered (and fascinated) his former compatriots. Despite the scantness of the official records, he appeared consistently in a range of sixteenth-century chronicles of the early days of imperial history. He reminded the Spanish – though perhaps they never fully digested the lesson – that conversion cuts both ways: if they forced people into their religious fold, it was only logical that there might be traffic in the other direction.

Both Enrique and Gonzalo appear in colonial documents and chronicles as figures that couldn't be grasped or controlled. They were disruptors: each in different ways pointed to the thrilling possibilities, yet also the practical difficulties, of following a path outside the colonial regime, especially one in defiance of long-standing habits of body and mind. You can't entirely get away from the violence that characterized the beginnings of Gonzalo's and Enrique's tales, but their stories do nevertheless suggest that, after the wreckage, something new could begin.

PART THREE

Around the World in 150 Deaths

A snake hadn't bitten him, but it was serpent venom that seeped through his flesh, extinguishing his nervous system like a gust blowing through a candlelit room. He fell to his knees. Then collapsed completely. The final darkness descended over him on a sunny beach while his crew splashed through the surf in retreat. Beyond the reach of their cannons; their musket rounds all fired. They were outnumbered, outmanoeuvred. Defeated.

'Although Ferdinand Magellan must have been a brave and spirited man in his thoughts, in his appearance he did not have much authority, because he was small and didn't show himself destined for much nor possessed of much prudence.'[1] This is a surprisingly cutting description of the favourite voyager of many an armchair historian or would-be explorer: a man long famed for finding a navigable sea route from the Atlantic into the Pacific, and thereby becoming the first to circumnavigate the globe. The words, written in the second half of the sixteenth century, belong to the Spanish historian Bartolomé de las Casas. His conclusion, if we translate across time, was that Magellan suffered from that quintessentially blokeish ailment of the ego: short-man syndrome. Rude as this is about Magellan's stature, and stereotypical in its extrapolation of what that meant for his character, Las Casas did nonetheless get to the nub of Magellan's story. He possessed unshakeable self-belief but struggled to have his authority recognized by others and often threw caution – quite gladly and quite literally – to the wind. Around 150 of those who set off from Spain to find a route to the Pacific with Magellan died out of a total crew of about 240. The captain-general himself would be one of them.

We have no portraits of Magellan from his lifetime to offer a different view of him, and Las Casas's snide remark goes down as the most extended description of Magellan that we have. A portrait of him was painted in Italy after his voyage, though, which we know to have been in the collection of the humanist Paolo Giovio in 1535.[2] That painting is now lost, but copies of it were made which can still be seen in Vienna and in Florence.

Posthumous portrait of Ferdinand Magellan, mid-sixteenth century

In that posthumous portrait, Magellan looms against a dark back-drop, the chiaroscuro attracting our eyes to his sober-looking face, his thick beard tinged with grey. He looks out over our right shoulder as though he has seen someone coming into the room behind us. The man painted from memory or from description has gravitas, a quiet authority. You cannot tell from his appearance his ambition, anger and ruthlessness, how he drove his fleet so hard that such a high proportion of its crew did not survive.

5. Beleaguered Beginnings

By now it should be clear that Magellan's voyage west to Asia through his now eponymous strait ended badly. It started badly too – with treason. Magellan was Portuguese, but a Spanish king paid for his fleet.

After serving as a young man in the Portuguese royal household, Magellan left Portugal in his twenties to spend a decade in various parts of the country's growing empire.[1] He departed in the fleet of the first viceroy of the Estado da Índia, Francisco de Almeida, in 1505. It was the largest armada yet assembled by the Portuguese, a demonstration of their commitment to consolidating their presence around the edge of the Indian Ocean and vying to control its trade through whatever means. Magellan battled in port cities and fortresses from Kilwa, Socotra and Malindi on the African coast, to Diu in northern India, and Calicut, Cochin and Goa further south. All these cities were crucial trading posts for the busy Indian Ocean commercial networks or essential waypoints for Portuguese ships shuttling annually between Lisbon and the African and Asian regions of its empire. By 1510, Magellan was prepared to cash in on his exploits by investing in a cargo of pepper which would make him a huge profit when he and it reached Portugal. He also intended to seek recompense from the king for his 'services' in the name of the empire, as was usual for the age. His hopes sank, however, off the Maldives when a storm wrecked the Portuguese fleet and consigned his lucrative freight to the deep. Magellan was rescued by Portuguese ships travelling in the opposite direction, which carried him back to Cochin.

By that time there was a new governor, the notoriously brutal Afonso de Albuquerque, who had his sights set on expanding the Portuguese empire eastwards. A key target was the port of Melaka on the Malay peninsula, the richest emporium in Southeast Asia at the time. A famous world map from 1502, created by a Portuguese cartographer, but purloined by a spy and taken to Italy where it remains today, described Melaka as the city through which all the merchandise passed on its way west – cloves, sandalwood, precious stones of great value, pearls, porcelain or other goods from China.

The Strait of Melaka as depicted in the Cantino Planisphere, c. 1502

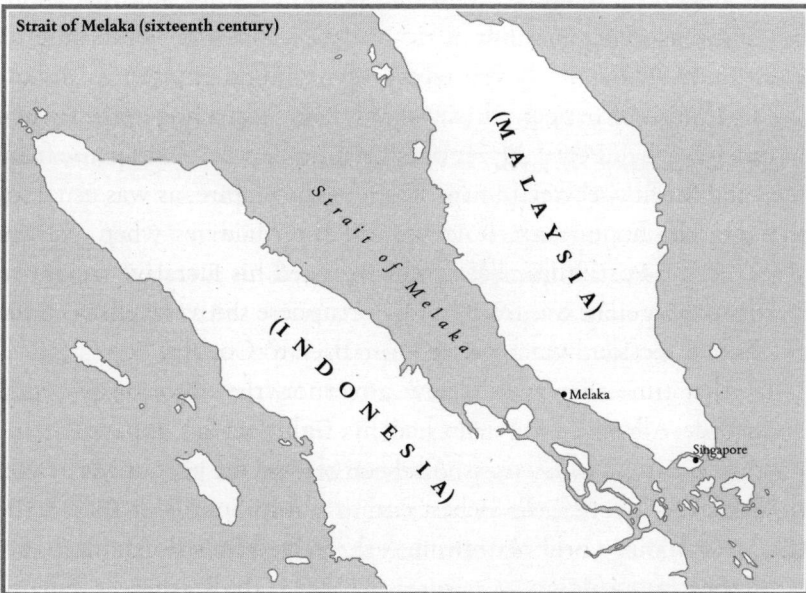

The Portuguese had reached the city in 1509, but its ruler, Sultan Mahmud, had been forewarned by Gujarati and Indian merchants that they were not to be trusted. He sent a clear signal that he rejected their diplomatic overtures: Diogo Lopes de Sequeira, the expedition's captain, was almost stabbed during a chess game. According to one Portuguese historian writing in the sixteenth century, it was Magellan who saved the captain from this assassination attempt. Many of Sequeira's men were killed as they tried to escape the city and twenty were thrown in prison. One of the prisoners, Rui de Araújo, later wrote to Albuquerque informing him about the city and its defences.

The letter spurred Albuquerque to try to take Melaka in 1511. He set sail with eighteen ships, 800 Portuguese, 200 Malabar mercenaries and Magellan. The city was torched in their brutal assault, and a fort promptly constructed amid its smouldering ruins. It became a gateway to Southeast Asia for the Portuguese, but their arrival in Melaka displaced many of the resident merchants from the broader region, so that trade shifted elsewhere. Despite their efforts, the Portuguese never truly controlled maritime trade in the Indian Ocean. Centres, entrepôts, peripheries – these moved around in response to European incursions.

After Melaka, Magellan ventured even further east, as far as the famed spice-growing islands of the Moluccas (the Maluku islands), in what is now Indonesia, before returning to Lisbon in 1513. Less lucrative and longer than he perhaps wanted, Magellan's time in the Estado da Índia was a practical apprenticeship in trade and violence. He also became friends with a man named Francisco Serrão, supposedly after saving his life during the first Portuguese expedition to Melaka. Serrão went on to establish himself in the Moluccas in 1512 and remained there probably until his death. His letters addressed to Magellan back in Portugal extolled the uncountable riches of these five spice islands. Almost from the day they were written, Serrão's letters have been claimed as a key influence on Magellan's future trajectory – or maybe it would be better to say they have been blamed for it.

Back in Lisbon, Magellan continued to involve himself in trade with Asia. His dealings brought him into the orbit of a Spanish merchant called Cristóbal de Haro, who was then based in the Portuguese capital.

Magellan sought out the reimbursement of a loan with the father of a former trading partner whose untimely demise had prevented repayment. Later, Haro would return home to Spain at around the same time that Magellan decided to seek his fortune across the border, and he proved a crucial conduit for the latter's networking there.

In the meantime, overseas action called once again, and in 1513 Magellan joined an expedition to take Azamor in North Africa. He had to buy his horse on credit in order to participate, such were his finances. But disaster struck when the mortgaged steed received a lance to its side and died, leaving Magellan to beg the crown for compensation to cover the cost. The Portuguese victory at Azamor, however, brought with it captives and cattle, and Magellan seized the opportunity for profit by selling some of the livestock back to the locals. This bovine embezzlement hung over him when he returned to Lisbon. He was eventually cleared of wrongdoing and sent back to Morocco, but the taint of suspicion lingered, undiluted by his formal acquittal.

All these episodes spell out a clear concern: money was on Magellan's mind. Unsurprisingly, then, he approached King Manuel for an increase in his yearly stipend as a knight of the royal household. In 1515, he asked for 200 reis more per month on top of his regular monthly allowance of 1,000 reis. The increase was not a huge amount of money. As if he were negotiating a raise with his boss, he argued that his compensation did not match his value and that others, who had served and suffered less, received more generous remuneration. A monarch, though, is a very particular type of boss and one not known for consistency. Magellan was granted only half of what he'd been seeking.[2]

Magellan did not like that reply. A few years later, when Magellan was in Spain and planning his voyage to Asia under the auspices of the Spanish crown, a Portuguese agent was dispatched with the objective of persuading Magellan to return to the fold. In a letter dated 18 July 1519, the agent wrote to Dom Manuel that his earlier snub still had Magellan's ego smarting. Small, symbolic actions can lead to big problems. Pettiness and pride can be a historically explosive combination.

Mapping the Way to Spices

Tempting as it is to imagine, as early historians did, that Magellan immediately stormed off to Spain in a huff after the king's rejection, this was not the case. He stayed in Portugal for a few more months, although he clearly began making plans that would not depend upon the generosity or favour of the King of Portugal. The path to neighbouring Spain was well trodden by the disgruntled or just plain ambitious. Many a Portuguese before and after Magellan sought to make their names and their fortunes across the border. Indeed, it was a network of Portuguese in key positions in the Casa de Contratación (a crown agency responsible for matters relating to overseas trade) who were partly responsible for Magellan managing to get a hearing for his plan and convincing the king to grant his financial and political support for his mission to Asia. This king was Charles I of Spain, better known by his future title, Charles V, Holy Roman Emperor, which he assumed in 1519.

The target of the proposed voyage was those Moluccas which Magellan had visited in 1512, and about which he had received so much enticing information since from his friend Francisco Serrão. The five islands that composed the archipelago at the time – Ternate, Tidore, Makian, Motir and Bacan – were tiny specks of land, but they possessed an enormous reputation. Nutmeg and mace, cloves and sandalwood grew there in abundance, and multiplied in price several-fold between their place of origin and Melaka, one of their principal ports for onward sale. To harvest them where they grew and hawk them in Europe would be very lucrative.

Beyond the apparent fragrant bounty of these islands, the imperial geopolitics of the time made Magellan's venture a particularly attractive prospect from the Spanish perspective. One of the most hyperbolic acts of imperial arrogance committed by the Spanish and Portuguese was to divide the world beyond Europe into two at the Treaty of Tordesillas in 1494. The western hemisphere went to Spain, the eastern to Portugal. The monarchs drew the dividing line in the Atlantic, 370 leagues west of the Cape Verde islands. The slight hitch in their attempts to split the world between themselves was that figuring out exactly where this line lay was rather more difficult in practice than in theory. Longitude was notoriously challenging to measure at the time, particularly at sea where measurements could not easily be made and captains had to make a best guess at their position on the basis of their speed, direction and how long they thought they had been travelling. It didn't help, either, that the two kings couldn't agree which of the Cape Verde islands to take as the starting point. In many ways, it was a line drawn in the dark: neither Spain nor Portugal knew what fell either side of the line. For all the claims to its fixity and its strict grounding in science, it was a demarcation that would move and bend through negotiation.

The problem of the line in the Atlantic also raised a parallel problem on the other side of the world: the antimeridian, the place where these two hemispheres joined. The edges of the world had not yet been stitched together at this point: Magellan's voyage itself would do some of that hemming together by showing it was possible to sail from South America to Asia across the Pacific. Cosmographers, mapmakers and pilots had not yet completely settled the exact location of the Moluccas. Enough doubt remained as to whether they lay far enough east to fall into the half of the world claimed by the Spanish. If Asia could be reached by sailing west from Europe, as Columbus had supposed at the end of the fifteenth century, then the Spanish could have direct access to the products of the Moluccas and the broader Southeast Asian world which hovered on the eastern horizon of the Portuguese.

Over the course of the first decades of the sixteenth century, the Spanish and Portuguese had begun to explore the Isthmus of Panama – as we saw with Gonzalo Guerrero and the ill-fated colonies in Darién, where he resided before being shipwrecked near Jamaica – and they had sailed as far south as the River Plate (Río de la Plata). On some maps, a conjectured strait appeared towards the tip of the South American continent, which gave access to the Pacific, known then as the Mar del Sur (South Sea). Magellan intended to prove the existence of this imagined entrance to Asia and to reach the islands of Southeast Asia.

Magellan made a multimedia pitch to Charles V at the beginning of March 1518. He and his co-proposer, the cosmographer Rui Faleiro, brought one of Serrão's letters, a map – most likely by the renowned Portuguese cartographer Pedro Reinel – that indicated the strait, and two enslaved men, one of whom now went by the name of Enrique de Melaka, as interpreters to help with negotiations in Southeast Asia. In a note that he left with the king on setting out on his voyage, Magellan detailed his knowledge of the Moluccas' whereabouts, and remarked that he left this information 'in case a time should come when it would be needed' – that is, in case the King of Portugal should complain that his royal neighbour was encroaching into a space they had agreed belonged to him.[3] Magellan, then, already had the knowledge, the know-how and the key crew members to make a success of the voyage. He made conjecture appear concrete.

On 22 March 1518, Charles approved the mission. The instructions from the crown were clear: sail west, find the strait, head for the Moluccas. Recently, though, historians have discerned that Magellan probably intended to disobey these instructions in one or more ways. Whispers circulated from the beginning that Magellan, in his eagerness to reach his destination and its apparent riches, would take the easy route, which in his age meant the known route. Unable to find a strait, he'd turn around and sail brazenly east into Portuguese-controlled waters with a Spanish fleet, making his way to Asia around the tip of another continent: Africa. No diplomat would advise that course of action.

More than this, Magellan appears to have wanted to find further islands than the five that made up the Moluccas, because, in the documentation about the voyage, he was promised that if he were to find more than six islands then he would be able to choose one for himself – something from which he could derive, he no doubt hoped, significant profits. Adventurers sought *encomiendas* because they offered steady profits from others' labour. Given the route that Magellan later took, and the fact that he knew very well where the Moluccas sat on the map, Magellan seems to have deliberately steered a course that would take him beyond his stated objectives. Certainly the Portuguese apothecary Tomé Pires, who wrote an account of Asia while residing in Melaka and India during 1512–15, knew about the islands that now make up the Philippines, where Magellan died. Pires mentions the *Luçones* (derived from 'Luzon', the name of the island that today houses the archipelago's capital), suggesting that they lay ten days' sail from Borneo. Magellan wanted to bump into islands he could claim for himself – and the Philippines may have provided such a destination.[4]

Over the course of preparations for the voyage, concerns were raised about Magellan's suitability as its leader. Indeed, the king removed Rui Faleiro, who was due to captain one of the ships, from the prospective expedition altogether; the sources tell us he was not in his right mind . . . When Magellan hoisted banners bearing his personal crest on his flagship while it was being prepared for the voyage, Spaniards suspected him of being disloyal to the king. These suspicions and tensions persisted throughout the voyage, as we will see.

The voyage, however, was not an entirely Iberian affair. You might be surprised to look at the ships' manifests and see just how international they were, but ships at the time were cosmopolitan. Crew in Magellan's fleet came from Bristol in England, Galway in Ireland, France, the Low Countries and Germany, the Mediterranean islands of Rhodes and Corfu, and even from Brazil. There were slaves from North Africa, as well as the two in Magellan's retinue whom he'd bought in Melaka but who probably came from Sumatra. An Italian, Antonio Pigafetta, who had met Magellan in Barcelona in 1519 while serving with the papal ambassador, joined the journey in search of excitement. Pigafetta kept a record of the voyage, and his account has proved by far the most popular and influential over the centuries. In retrospect, he appears as Magellan's onboard PR: he wrote relentlessly in favour of the captain-general and steered clear of the messier and more brutal dimensions of the voyage. The presence of men like Pigafetta and the other non-Iberians on the voyage smudges the national boundaries that typically keep imperial histories in separate lanes.

Weathering the Atlantic

After more than a year of preparations, on 20 September 1519, the fleet set sail from Sanlúcar, downriver from Seville.

From testimonies afterwards by those both for and against Magellan, we know that he kept their intended route close to his chest.

The crew had a vague idea of the final objective – the far side of the world and its spices – but little more than that. Magellan, in his flagship, the *Trinidad*, thus deliberately disobeyed the instructions of the king to share his charts and route with the other captains and pilots. He instead wanted the *San Antonio, Concepción, Santiago* and *Victoria* to play follow-the-leader. Lanterns on the stern of his ship would light their way and they would communicate with a reduced lexicon of lamp signals. Two lights meant they were about to change course; three lights indicated they were to slow or that they needed to take in the bonnet sail because of unfavourable weather. It wouldn't be too much of a stretch to think that Magellan, the short-statured man described as lacking authority, liked this limited form of communication between the ships. The captains could not answer back to this lamp semaphore.

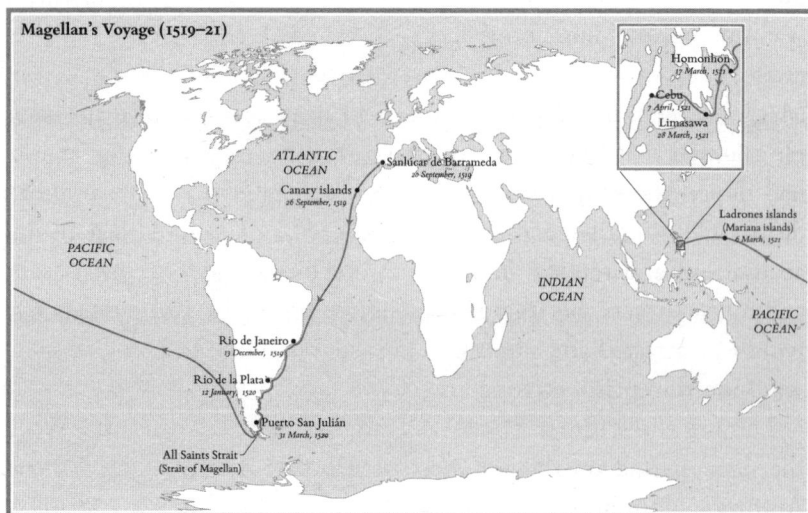

Magellan's Voyage (1519–21)

The fleet's first stop was Tenerife. From there, any sensible captain would steer southwest into the Atlantic, riding the southern Atlantic winds that had been essential to European long-range sailing for decades. Instead, Magellan took the surprising decision to head due south, a route proven challenging by many a sailor before him. It was as though Magellan chose to suffer an avoidable nightmare. And nightmare it was. As the fleet crossed the equator near the Guinea coast, angry gales and uncooperative currents ambushed the ships. The rain harangued them incessantly for sixty days – a more than biblical deluge. After this furious tirade, they received the meteorological equivalent of the silent treatment. The winds left them to sit on the ocean and drift without a breeze they could harness. All they could do was wait out the return of the wind. Storm. Storm. Silence. A rhythm that would not take them forward.

On several of the stormy evenings, the mastheads shone with eerie St Elmo's fire, a phenomenon which makes pointed objects glow with a blueish halo of luminous plasma in an atmospheric electrical field. Antonio Pigafetta described one occasion when the light was so dazzling that the crew's eyes struggled to adjust after it ended, making them call out for mercy, certain that this temporary blindness signalled their collective end.

Juan de Cartagena, the captain of the *San Antonio* and the fleet's number two (or equal number one, depending on whom you asked), was not pleased with how the fleet was progressing and with the course they were taking. Towards the end of October he approached Magellan's ship in a skiff, clutching a sheaf of complaints in his hand. He claimed that Magellan did not know what he was doing, that he had duped the king and that he was leading them all to a pointless death. The captain-general took little heed of Cartagena's damning accusations and replied angrily that not only should he just shut up and follow orders, but that if he continued to show such insolence he would be arrested and punished. One source suggests that Cartagena was indeed imprisoned for a few days.[5]

Despite the stillness of the weather, all was not peaceful. While the fleet drifted on the windless ocean, the master of the *Victoria*, António Salomón, was caught having sex with a ship's boy, Antonio

Genovese. Such behaviour at that time demanded an onboard trial. Most historians skip over the subject of the hearing, as though its only interest stemmed from the fact it assembled all the captains together, precipitating another face-to-face confrontation between Magellan and Cartagena. Cartagena apparently referred to Magellan in a manner that was not sufficiently deferential. It may seem trivial, but tetchiness about forms of address was widespread in the early modern period: you had to calibrate between lords and majesties, 'thou' and 'you', an entire panoply of options for flattering or snubbing; there were laws about it, even if words and their uses have always been hard to police. The linguistic misfire ignited Magellan and brought the power struggle between the two men to a head. Magellan arrested Cartagena and replaced him temporarily with Álvaro de Mesquita, a Portuguese, as captain of his ship. It was an episode that marked an important point in the ongoing ructions that rocked the fleet.

The reason for Salomón's trial, however, and the manner in which it was conducted speak to the atmosphere of early modern seafaring and to a broader obsession in the period's travel accounts with documenting (and moralizing over) sexual mores. Even while writers denounced any kind of sexual deviance, they seem to have a constant fascination with it. The unfortunate captain's conviction may have been a formality, but the sentence was not immediately enacted. It was October and he had to wait for his punishment until they reached the far shore of the Atlantic, where he was strangled to death on 20 December. His execution beside the bay of Rio de Janeiro means that the first member of the fleet's crew to die did not perish from the hardships of the ocean, from disease or in battle. He died by the hands of his shipmates. There was tragically no need to sentence the young man: he threw himself overboard on 27 April 1520 after being hounded and taunted by the rest of the crew. His drowned body resurfaced on 21 May. The records pass no judgement on the outcome of this unhappy story, the fate of its wretched victim or the actions of those who drove him to his pitiful end. Sailors and soldiers knew many ways to dehumanize, many forms of cruelty, active bullying and passive callousness. And it seems that no one cared to confront the death that had occurred.

Looking for an Opening

The voyage across the Atlantic to the coast of Brazil took much longer than it would have done if the fleet had taken the more usual route west. It unnecessarily depleted the stores that fed and nourished the crew, and supplies would repeatedly present problems for them as their journey progressed. They reached the bay of Rio de Janeiro in late December 1519 and stayed there for around two weeks to replenish their stocks. The accounts of this land sit between fantasy and reality. Pigafetta implanted rumours and words that he took from other contexts into his descriptions of the people and the natural world around them: parrots, toucans, tapirs, as well as birds that ate the faeces of other birds and ones that apparently had no anus. A Portuguese pilot, João Lopes de Carvalho, somewhat improbably was reunited with a child he'd had with a Tupinambá woman some years earlier. We will revisit Brazil in Part Five, so I will keep our sojourn here as short as it was for Magellan and his fleet.

Two days after Christmas, Magellan gave the order to recommence their voyage. They journeyed as far as the River Plate, the southernmost point achieved by Spanish and Portuguese explorers. The estuary harboured hopes that it was the mouth of a strait leading to the South Sea, but as Magellan once again proved, it was fresh water, and therefore a river not a passage to another ocean. This did, however, mean they could refill their water barrels, and they stocked up with fish.

At the beginning of February, they resumed their progress south. They groped their way along the coast, testing every inlet for signs of a potential avenue west. All the while, storms smashed and soaked them. Magellan was now about as lost as the captains he kept in the dark about his intentions. Worries over continuing the voyage bubbled up. Could they survive the winter that would soon be upon them? Would making port be their end or a waypoint providing salvation?

Each opening in the coastline was invested with possibility. No, it was just a river. No, just a bay. On 31 March 1520, they reached the natural harbour of San Julián in today's Argentina. Its wide bay was encircled by a vast, semi-arid terrain. Winds whipped over the grasses, adding a sharp edge to the temperature, which probably seldom rose above freezing in the months they spent there. Amid this stark land-scape of washed-out colours – ochres and greens – white and red foxes darted, and a strange new animal was found nibbling at the turf and low-lying shrubs. This novel creature had, in Pigafetta's words, 'a head and ears as large as those of a mule, a neck and body like those of a camel, the legs of a deer, and the tail of a horse, like which it neighs'.[6] It was a guanaco, a species closely related to the llama.

Magellan's fleet had been scrutinizing the coast for some 1,800 kilometres since the River Plate, looking for a way through to the South Sea. It had been a long stretch of disappointment. San Julián looked like a safe harbour for the ships, but for some on board, it proved a dead end.

Winter of Discontent

Soon after arriving, Magellan assembled his crew to tell them that a mutinous plot was afoot among the captains of the rest of the fleet: schemers were planning to kill him on Easter Day and overthrow the mission. He wasted no time in throttling the conspiracy. That evening, he invited the highest-ranking officers to dine aboard the *Trinidad* after Mass. Only his ally Álvaro de Mesquita attended the supper. That tells you everything. The others sensed the dinner was a trap. The tense equilibrium between Magellan and the other captains ended. They were readying to battle for control.

After Mass, Álvaro de Mesquita retired to his cabin on the *San Antonio*. All was quiet. Then the door was flung open and Gaspar de Quesada, captain of the *Concepción*, stormed in, flanked by Juan de Cartagena and thirty men. Metal soon pressed against Mesquita's chest. He was forced below deck and shackled. He went from captain to prisoner on his own ship in a matter of minutes. A nautical coup had begun.

A priest, Pedro de Valderrama, stepped into the fray to persuade

Quesada to desist, but he wasn't going to heed anyone who quoted psalms at him. The scriptures had no place in his playbook. Juan de Elorriaga, master of the *San Antonio*, accosted the chief mutineer, demanding again that he free the captain and give up his rebellion. Quesada refused. Elorriaga tried to muster a counter-mutiny, but this caused Quesada to explode in anger and stab him repeatedly. Elorriaga didn't immediately perish, but he never recovered; he died a few months later, after a long and painful decline. Unconscious, he was dragged to the *Concepción* by the rebels, and then they confiscated the weapons of the *San Antonio*'s crew so no one else would risk standing in their way like Elorriaga. Juan Sebastián Elcano, master of the *Concepción* – who would later lead the final part of the fleet's circumnavigation after Magellan's demise – was brought in to supervise the guns. The shift in the balance of power brought disorder that would subsequently endanger them all. The mutineers celebrated their victory by raiding the stores and letting the men feast on what they could find, without thinking of how that would lead to fast later in their voyage.

With rebels in charge of three of the five ships in the fleet, they could not now be ignored. Cartagena commanded the *Concepción*; a colluder, Luis de Mendoza, captained the *Victoria*; and now Quesada had seized the *San Antonio*. Their demands to Magellan centred on communication and leadership: stick to the king's orders; stop plotting to get rid of detractors, and listen to them and their plans for the rest of the voyage. Magellan suggested meeting on his ship, the *Trinidad*, to discuss their differences. They refused, obviously. They weren't going to walk so easily into an ambush; equally, Magellan refused to step aboard any of the vessels under the rebels' control. He needed a go-between to break the impasse. So he sent a message to Luis de Mendoza on the *Victoria*. But the message wasn't in words: the blank slip of paper carried by Gonzalo Gómez de Espinosa was a decoy. The true message was a stab in the neck with a dagger and a second blow to the head. With Mendoza eliminated, some fifteen men swept in to seize control of the ship. The tables were turning back.

The next day, the *San Antonio* made a bid to escape and to desert Magellan for good, but they couldn't easily slip by the flagship, which

was anchored at the entrance to the inlet. There was no way to manoeuvre past it and into open water, so the captain had to drop anchor.
That night, some of the crew on the *San Antonio* nudged their ship
silently nearer to the flagship as the chief conspirators against Magellan slept. Magellan's men asked those on deck whose side they were
on. Had they come to attack or to surrender? The crew on the *San
Antonio* swore their loyalty to Magellan. The mutiny ended there
and then. Magellan's men seized the mutineers, which left Cartagena, who was on the *Concepción*, with no choice but to admit defeat.
His plot had failed. It turned out that enough of the ordinary sailors
believed in Magellan, even if their officers did not.

Mendoza's body was taken ashore, but not for burial: he was
quartered and the parts impaled as a gruesome warning. A few days
afterwards, on 7 April, Quesada lost his head and his body received
the same desecration, hacked to bits so that the threat of such brutal
punishment inflicted by Magellan would prevent anyone else from
daring to act against him. Juan de Cartagena and a priest called
Pedro Sánchez de Reina, meanwhile, were sentenced to marooning;
it would not have looked good to execute a man of the cloth and the
most senior figure representing the Spanish crown, Cartagena. These
punishments were supposed to persuade the rest of the crew not to
cross Magellan, but the problem is that violence acts more as a deter-
rent than as a means of truly winning people over. Mutilated bodies
mounted on display couldn't really quell anxieties about leadership
and direction, even if they could discourage anyone from acting on
those doubts. According to one early record of the voyage, the execu-
tions and the strandings meant that 'hatred settled more deeply in the
hearts of the Spaniards'.[7]

The chatter among the crew began to focus on the cold weather.
They were concerned about spending a frozen winter in San Julián.
Although there were penguins and seals to hunt that could pad out
their rations, the prospect of staying for months at such a latitude
seemed bleak and the men made their feelings known to Magellan.
They argued that they had advanced far enough beyond the bounds
of the world known to Europeans that their exploits were already
a triumph. To push on would be reckless: they should know their

limits. The boldness of their venture might slide into foolhardiness if they didn't seek a milder location soon.

You can imagine the reply. Magellan would not abandon his plan under any circumstances. He shot down their attempts to already call themselves heroes, insisting that they ought not to deviate from the original objective of finding a strait to the South Sea. They could, he said, make do if they would just show some self-control, taking what was needed and not what they wanted, supplementing their rations with fish, and sourcing wood that they could find in their environs, rather than using up their stores as the rebels had done after taking control of some of the ships.

Thoughts for their own survival, however, did not prevent them from endangering others. Once, twice, three times Magellan's men set out on kidnapping raids among the local Tehuelche people, who fought back, killing Diego de Barrasa during one of these skirmishes. This death set a lighted match to the powder keg of Magellan's anger. He rampaged towards a nearby settlement in revenge, but finding no one to explode at, torched the abandoned houses. Eventually he succeeded in seizing three Tehuelche and clamping them in irons, their capture a slow death sentence rather than an immediate execution.

At the end of April, the *Santiago* was sent ahead down the coast-line to resume the search for the strait, which Magellan hoped could not be too much further south. The ship found an estuary, which its captain christened the Río de Santa Cruz on 3 May. It was not the opening they sought through to the Pacific, but it had potable water and seals to eat. Storms, however, descended before the *Santiago* could turn back to rejoin the fleet. The weather struck with such violence that it smashed the ship apart on the rocks of the estuary mouth. Remarkably, all but one of the thirty-seven aboard survived. Unable to salvage enough from the wreck to construct a boat or raft big enough for all of them, the survivors resigned themselves to staying put until help could reach them. They knocked together a tiny raft from the drifting planks, which was able to carry two men north across the river so that they could make their way back to the fleet by land. Drinking snow and foraging for molluscs along the shore, the pair laboured their way north for eleven days back to where the rest of the fleet was anchored.

Now that Magellan had news of the stranded men, he dispatched a rescue party to retrieve them, and they all arrived back around 9 June. Although most of its crew survived the destruction of the *Santiago*, the loss of the provisions it carried for them dangerously diminished the fleet's overall resources when strict rationing was already necessary. The new bay, however, with its fresh water and animals for eating, was deemed a more hospitable place to sit out the rest of the winter and so they moved their base there on 24 August. They took on wood, tried to salvage bits of the wrecked *Santiago*, and fished to see them through the remaining dark and cold weeks.

Months passed. October finally crawled in. Now summer was on the horizon and it was time to resume their journey.

Cracks Appear

The strait that the fleet eventually reached on 21 October 1520 forms a perilous crack in the tapering end of the South American continent: 570 kilometres across, it is a chaotic gauntlet of rocks and channels and shoals. Still, today, only those certifiably familiar with the strait's dangers and obstacles are permitted to pilot ships along it. Magellan made tentative, messy progress through this craggy and confusing channel. Moving forward, doubling back, dodging hazards, testing routes. The *Concepción* and *San Antonio* formed a vanguard, scouting out a safe passage for the *Trinidad* and *Victoria* through rocky obstacles and shallows. All in all, it took thirty-six days to cross the strait.

Once Magellan was aware – or at least fairly sure – of a western exit to the narrow maze, he uncharacteristically asked for advice. The fleet was approaching the fulcrum of their journey, the moment of crossing into the South Sea and at last turning northwards again. But not everyone was convinced, as they neared the oceanic threshold to Asia, that they should sail across it. Estevão Gomes, the Portuguese pilot of the *San Antonio*, issued the first plea to turn back. A 'great gulf' lay in wait, an ocean not yet traversed by Europeans – they did not know that Polynesians had swept across its waters a long time before. The journey so far had depleted their stores. They were setting themselves up for starvation and disease if they continued.

The captain-general's reply: 'Even if we have to learn to eat the hides that wrap the masts, we must go forth and discover what has been promised to the Emperor.'[8] When Magellan asked for the crew's opinions, what he sought was a chorus of praise and positive affirmation of his own decisions. He did not expect or allow dissent. Any consultation was, at heart, a sham, a test of loyalty and belief in him.

Surprisingly, considering Magellan shut down any discussion of the depleted stores or of abandoning their onward journey, the experienced pilot Andrés de San Martín – whose latitude readings during the voyage were startlingly accurate for the time – wrote a note to Magellan the next day, urging him to turn back: 'the crew is weak and weary, and the supplies are insufficient for a voyage to the Moluccas and thence to return to Spain.'[9] 'Weak and weary: their bodies and resolve were withering. For San Martín, the question was not one of triumph or failure – they had already sailed further in this direction than any European ship had done before. It was existential: to live or die. He assessed the knowns and the unknowns, calculated their likely toll and argued for prudence over recklessness. The passage between oceans existed – they now knew this. The spices, the islands, could wait.

Even as the fleet reconnoitred success, then, troubles intensified among its crew. During a scouting expedition, the *San Antonio* went missing. The *Concepción* waited behind for a number of days, but there was no sign of the other vessel. The *Victoria* retraced the fleet's journey, like Ariadne following her string through the labyrinth. Still nothing. The *Concepción* and *Victoria* regrouped with the *Trinidad* to discuss the mystery: what had happened to the *San Antonio*?

Mutiny. Again. At Magellan's behest, the *San Antonio* had headed off to reconnoitre a channel to the south of the main strait. They planned to rendezvous with the *Concepción*, but it never happened. After looking around for four or five days without sighting any of their fellow ships, the crew of the *San Antonio* decided to head back east. The captain, Álvaro de Mesquita, objected to their abandoning the rest of the fleet. There was a fight. Mesquita stabbed Gomes the pilot, but he was overpowered and clapped in irons. Gomes survived the brawl. He'd already made it clear that he thought the whole fleet should return to Spain, and that was exactly what the *San Antonio* then did.

One advantage of returning before the rest of the fleet – if indeed the fleet would ever make it back – was that the crew of the *San Antonio* could set about framing the narrative of the journey in their favour. When questioned upon their return home, they made Magellan seem dishonest and incompetent. The tensions in the fleet, they said, derived from Magellan's unwillingness to comply with the king's orders: he wouldn't listen and he kept his plans a secret.

6. Adverse Endings

One ship wrecked, one ship having deserted, the remnants of the beleaguered fleet entered the South Sea – or, as Magellan would rename it, the Pacific. The crossing of this ocean was transformative, for it was the moment of realization that the world was mostly blue, not green and brown. The Ptolemaic vision of the world handed down from antiquity – and remarkably resilient even in the face of gradually emerging evidence to discredit its principles – represented the world as a crater, a bowl of earth holding the ocean in its well. After Magellan's voyage, it became clear in Europe that the reality was the reverse: continents and islands were solid encrustations poking out from the vast encompassing ocean.

It took the fleet four months at sea to next set foot on land. That was a long time for hunger and scurvy to emaciate and rot the crew's bodies. The wind blew them along, steadily, unremittingly, but for far longer than they had imagined they could stay at sea. On leaving the strait, they first followed the current north, then gradually pulled away from the shoreline, letting the wind hurtle them northwestwards. The prevailing wind was a kind of autopilot; the crew barely had to touch the tiller or the sails to maintain their course. In this restless, endless motion, all they could do was wait until they reached the other side, watching the seemingly unchanging view of ocean and sky. We are all now familiar, at least by proxy, with the psychological poison that enters the mind in lengthy sequestered waiting. To not know where the journey would end, when it would end, that must have been tough. They sailed and sailed and sailed.

For sustenance, Pigafetta said,

> we ate biscuit, which was no longer biscuit, but fistfuls of powder swarming with worms, for they had eaten the better part (it stank strongly of rat urine); and we drank yellow water that had been putrid

for many days, and we also ate some ox hides that covered the top of the main yard to prevent the yard from chafing the shrouds, and which had become exceedingly hard because of the sun, rain, and wind. We left them in the sea for four or five days, and then placed them for a few moments on top of the embers, and thus ate them; and often we ate sawdust from boards. Rats were sold for one half-ducat apiece, if only one could get them.[1]

Archipelagos of Possibility

Relief was the feeling when two islands were spotted protruding out of the waves on 6 March 1521. Guam and Rota, the southernmost pair of the Ladrones (now Mariana islands) were the twins that promised an end to their misery. As the fleet grew nearer, flocks of triangular sails swooped towards them from the islands. The small vessels were proas, probably like those illustrated in a Spanish manuscript from later in the century created in the Philippines by local artists.

They were not a peaceful welcoming party. They surrounded Magellan's fleet, their crews climbed aboard, and set about pilfering anything they could get their hands on. They cut the tow rope of the flagship's boat and stole away with it. A fight then broke out on board, and the islanders retaliated by throwing spears. Hopes of replenishing the fleet's water and stores were dashed, but in their first interaction with the indigenous Chamorro people, Magellan's crew lost yet more.

Manila galleon received by Chamorro proas in the Ladrones islands, c. 1590

The captain-general ordered a raid in retribution. Forty men landed on the island, killing seven male Chamorro and, in a now familiar tactic, burning fifty houses to cinders. They recovered the flagship's boat and snatched sorely needed food.

As Magellan's ships scarpered, hastily putting distance between themselves and the islands they'd left smouldering – now dubbed 'the Thieves' islands' – local boats sped after them, weaving deftly in between their hulls. People aboard held out fish, as if to offer them to the Europeans, but then they would throw stones instead of passing across the food. It was a kind of mockery, and a celebration of their departure.

The fleet headed (or fled) to the southwest, passing the island of Samar before landing the next day on Homonhon, which was an island uninhabited at the time.

There, safe from any hostility, they set up camp to tend to the sick and weak and to find water. Eating mostly nuts that they found on the island and depleting further what was left of their supplies, they spotted a small boat going past. Magellan, wary of the response they would get, told no one to attract its attention. But when its crew came ashore, Magellan's fears this time were proven misplaced. They exchanged gifts, a sign of diplomacy or at least the absence of immediate hostility. The Europeans received coconuts, fish, and fruit that Pigafetta thought were like figs. In a wordless conversation of gestures and props, the visitors conveyed to the Europeans that they would return with further provisions in a few days' time. Magellan showed them his ship, and more importantly the merchandise he was seeking: cloves, cinnamon, pepper, ginger, nutmeg, mace, gold – and they suggested that they were indeed familiar with these things. A few days later, as promised, they returned with more coconuts, as well as sweet oranges, palm wine and a chicken: this was a relief after months of a reduced and unappetizing diet.

Once the men had begun to recover, Magellan started to travel around the archipelago. As they sailed on, they began to touch on the fringe of the world they had long sought. This was made evident when the people they next encountered understood the Malay-speaking slaves aboard Magellan's ship.

Magellan's Route through the Philippines (1521)

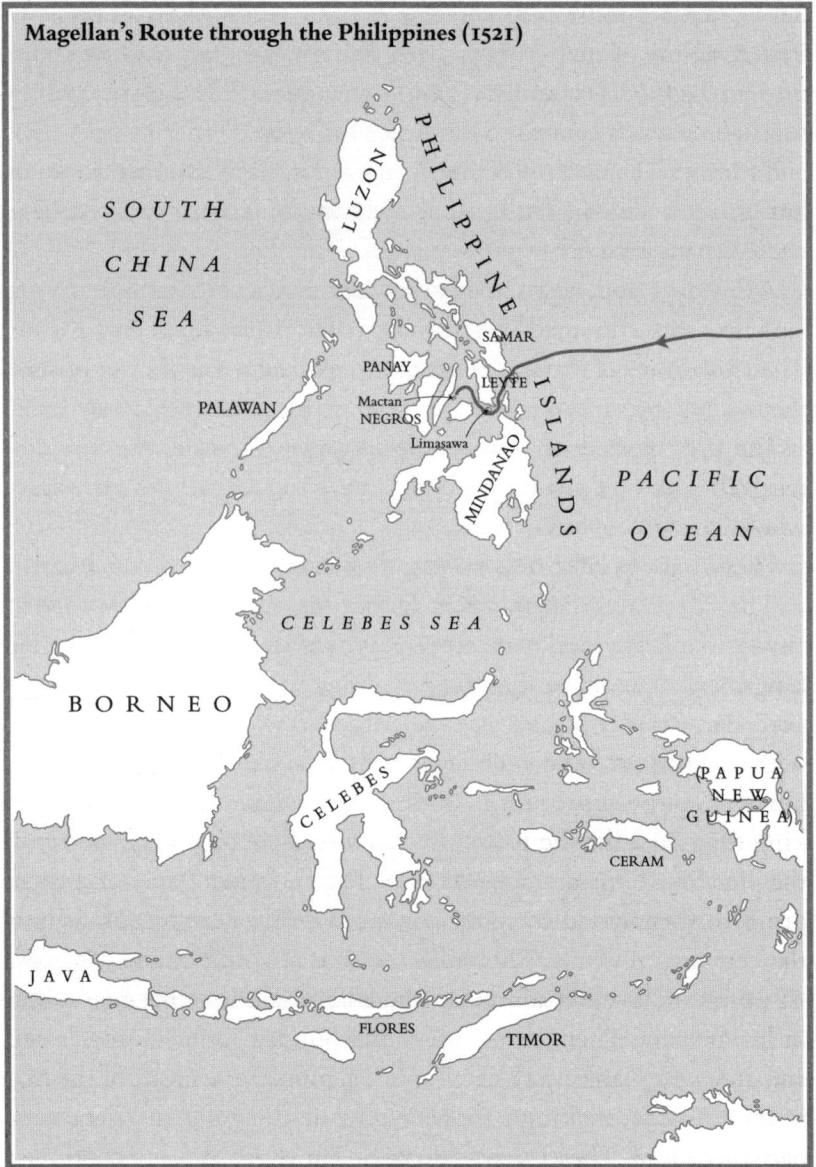

The Philippine archipelago as we now know it is a vast agglomeration of islands stretching across 1,850 kilometres from the South China Sea to the Celebes Sea. Rugged mountains, some crowned with active volcanoes, dominated parts of the island landscape, while dense, verdant rainforests sprawled across the lowlands and valleys. The coastline of many islands had ribbons of pale sand that spilled into impossibly clear water teeming with visible coral and schools of fish. The sea was central to the way of life there, not just for fishing and for travel aboard the nimble proas shuttling between the islands, but also as a link in the broader network of trade routes that connected them with other parts of Asia.

A few days later, now some 150 kilometres from Homonhon, Magellan's crew spotted a small boat passing by and tried to attract its attention. The captain-general tried to entice its crew near by tossing towards them a red cap and other presents attached to bits of wood, which would help them float on the water. The gifts appeared to be gladly received and, as a result, the boat's crew went to fetch their leader, whom Pigafetta referred to as a 'king', from the nearby island of Limasawa. Two hours later, he arrived in two large boats called *balangays*.

The next day, Magellan sent one of his interpreters ashore as an envoy to ask for food and to reiterate that they came in peace. The king then came out to the *Trinidad* with six or so men, who brought porcelain jars filled with rice and large fish. Magellan reciprocated with a gift of a red and yellow garment and a red hat for the king and knives and mirrors for his men. Over a meal on Magellan's ship, the king suggested that he would like to formalize their relationship by the practice of *casi-casi*, a blood pact. Each cut their arms, and added drops of their blood to some wine, before they both took a sip of the ceremonial drink. This was a bond that could not be violated.[2] As postprandial entertainment, Magellan had one of his men suit up in his armour. Then, three others surrounded him, swords drawn, and attacked, clanking their weapons against the armour of the man in their middle, making a show of how invulnerable his metal carapace made him. The king was amazed. The show-and-tell continued. First, Magellan displayed some more cuirasses, swords and bucklers, then they walked together to the stern of the ship and up to the poop deck, where he exhibited his sea charts and compass.

On Easter Day, Magellan celebrated Mass with great ceremony and asked to erect a cross on Limasawa. While this had religious motives, it was also, as Magellan himself pointed out, a practical emblem. It would indicate that he had been there, and that future Spanish visitors should treat the locals well; they would know that this was a place where it was safe to land. After permission was granted and Magellan had duly raised his cross, he asked the king about the best places to trade. It was suggested that Cebu was the largest island with the most trade, and so

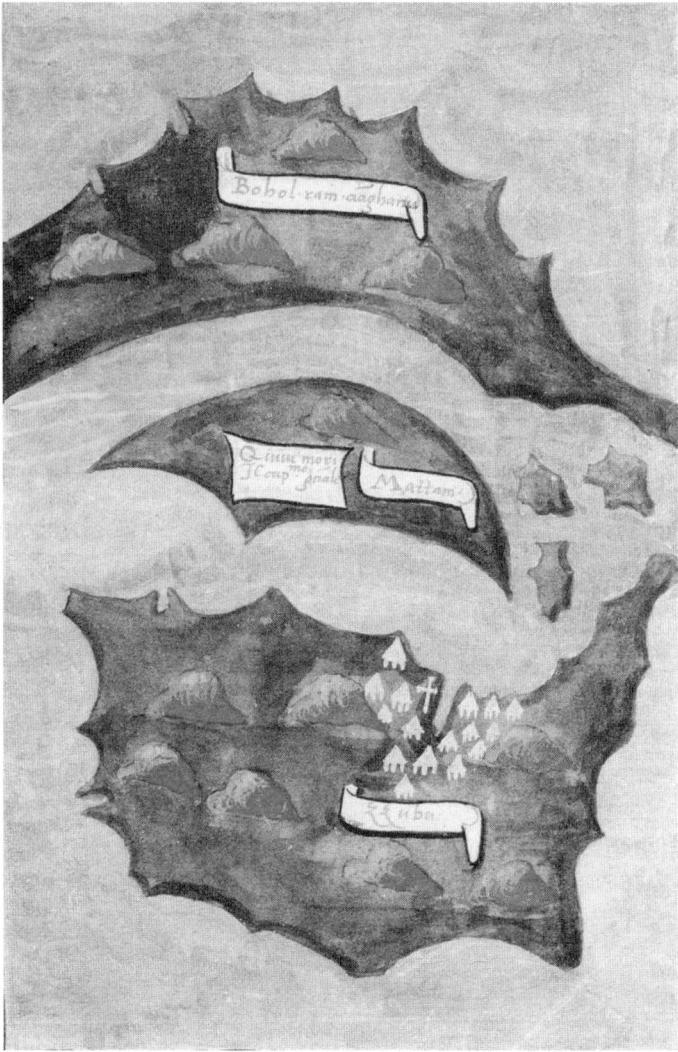

Islands of Bohol, Cebu and Mactan as depicted in the only surviving Italian manuscript of Pigafetta's account of Magellan's voyage, c. 1523–5

it was decided that Magellan would go there next. The ruler of Limasawa accompanied them as they hopped from island to island on their
way.

Their arrival on Cebu was not smooth at first, because Magellan
refused to pay a customary toll for boats and instead threatened violence.

A Muslim merchant from Siam (Thailand) suggested to Humabon,
Raja of Cebu, that he should be careful: Europeans were known –
even by those who had never met them in person – to act horrifically
if crossed. With the intervention of the ruler of Limasawa things did
not turn sour. Once more a blood pact was enacted, between Humabon and Magellan, to seal their diplomatic ties, and that evening they
gathered together again to discuss what their alliance would entail.
The Raja of Cebu was willing to accept baptism in order to secure
Magellan's and Charles V's support. Magellan promised that allegiance to Christ and to the crown of Spain would lead the Raja of
Cebu to become even more powerful. It was a ruse to consolidate
power for Spain's benefit. As the raja was the first to accept Christianity, Magellan would help to make him the most powerful ruler
of the region. When the raja reported the following day that some
local chiefs refused to obey him and considered themselves his equal,
Magellan intervened. He called all those chiefs to him and told them
that unless they obeyed the Raja of Cebu he would have them killed
and all their possessions given to the raja. The threats worked.

That same day, Sunday 14 April 1521, a cross was erected and
Magellan, dressed in white, preached that if the islanders truly wished
to become Christians, as they said they did, they would have to burn
what he called their 'idols' and worship daily at the cross with joined
hands. According to Pigafetta, some 500 people were baptized that
day after the raja.

Three Ways to Die

Towards the end of April, reports reached Magellan which suggested
that Lapulapu, one of the *datu*, or chieftains, of the nearby island

of Mactan, was refusing to provide the quantity of provisions for Magellan's crew that had been demanded as tribute.

As you should know by now, a refusal to do his bidding was not something that Magellan liked. He immediately made preparations to force Lapulapu into submission. Voices among Magellan's own men and some of the local rulers were quick to suggest that it wasn't a good idea to wade into battle. But by night two ships, with a flotilla of Humabon's smaller vessels, slid across the narrow channel between Cebu and Mactan, which today is spanned by a bridge. What happened next is the matter of intense speculation. Today, historians like to offer a single version of the story, but the process of elimination that is required to get to that point removes the intrigue of the various different versions of events presented to us by the sixteenth-century chroniclers. So here, for a moment, I will let you choose your own adventure and select Magellan's exact demise for yourself:

Scenario 1 (Fernão Lopes de Castanheda)

The King [of Cebu] asked Magellan to assist him in battle against the king of the neighbouring island of Mactan who had refused to obey him and thus brought about war between them. Because the king was now a vassal of the emperor, Magellan granted him the support that he requested and fought against the King of Mactan on two occasions, both times killing many of the latter's men. But that king still refused to obey the King of Cebu and fought against him a further time, and on this occasion he was routed and killed. The cause of this was that the King of Mactan had ordered many trenches containing pointed stakes to be dug in the area where the battle was to take place. As the battle commenced, he made out that he was fleeing with his men. Magellan was pleased with this and did not follow them. However, as he gathered his men, the enemy pounced and forced them back onto the stakes where they killed Magellan, Duarte Barbosa and João Serrão, along with more than twenty other men.

The survivors retreated to the boats and once back aboard the ships headed back to the island of Cebu.[3]

INSVLA MATHAN.

Death of Magellan on Mactan, as portrayed in 1626

Scenario 2 (Gaspar Correia)

The King [of Cebu] became a Christian along with all his people, so that Magellan would assist him against his enemies. And Magellan offered to do this, and with some armed men and the local people from that land, he went to attack his enemies and killed a great many of them and burned the place where they were; and the enemies received help from some other men, and a large number came to fight against Magellan, who defeated them and pursued them very far. One cunning thing that they did was to hide some men in the bush who were to ambush them. And when they saw the Castilians getting exhausted, they leapt out and killed a lot of them, and in another attack they sprang out of the bush to take the longboats which were on the shore, unmanned. At this point, the King of Cebu appeared and fought with them and defended the longboats and captured the men.

The fleeing king, seeing that he had been thus defeated, plotted an act of betrayal with the Christian king [i.e. of Cebu] and made an agreement for the latter's daughter to marry him, swearing oaths to the effect that, upon his death, as he was already old, everything would be left to the King of Cebu, and they would always live as friends. This was because the Castilians would leave and, if he did not act, he would be at war with him forever. And this came with the condition that he would find a way to kill the Spaniards. The Christian king, being a vile man, agreed to this act of betrayal and arranged a great feast and a banquet for thirty men, the highest-ranking and best-dressed among them; and while they were rejoicing at the banquet, their armed enemies burst in upon them, and they killed Magellan and all the Castilians and no one escaped, and they stripped Serrão naked and dragged him to the beach, where they sentenced him; and having dragged him there, they killed him.[4]

Scenario 3 (Antonio Pigafetta)

The musketeers and crossbowmen shot from a distance for about a half-hour, but uselessly . . . The captain cried to them, 'Cease firing, cease firing!' but his order was not at all heeded. When the natives saw that we were shooting our muskets to no purpose, crying out, they determined to stand firm, and they redoubled their shouts when our muskets ran out of ammunition. The natives would never stand still, but leapt here and there, covering themselves with their shields. They shot very many arrows, bamboo spears (some of them tipped with iron); at the captain-general they launched pointed stakes

hardened with fire, stones, and mud. We could scarcely defend our-
selves. Seeing that, the captain-general sent some men to burn their
houses in order to terrify them. When they saw their houses burning, they were roused to greater fury. Two of our men were killed
near the houses, and we managed to burn twenty or thirty houses.
So many of them charged down upon us that they shot the captain
through the right leg with a poisoned arrow; on that account, he
ordered us to retreat slowly, but the men took to flight, except six
or eight of us who remained with the captain. The natives shot only
at our legs because they were naked. So many were the spears and
stones that they hurled at us, that we could offer no resistance. The
mortars in the boats could not aid us since they were too far away, so
we continued to retreat for more than a good crossbow flight from
the shore, still fighting in water up to our knees. The natives continued to pursue us, and picking up the same spear four or six times,
hurled it at us again and again.

Recognizing the captain, so many turned upon him that they
knocked his helmet off his head twice, but he always stood firm like
a good knight along with some others. We fought thus for more than
one hour, refusing to retreat farther; an Indian hurled a bamboo spear
into the captain's face. The latter immediately killed him with his
lance, which he left in the Indian's body. Then, trying to lay hand
on sword, he could draw it out only halfway, because he had been
wounded in the arm with a bamboo spear. When the natives saw that,
they all hurled themselves upon him. One of them wounded him
on the left leg with a large *terciado*, which resembles a scimitar, only
being larger; that caused the captain to fall face downward. Immediately they rushed upon him with iron and bamboo spears and with
their cutlasses, until they killed our mirror, our light, our comfort,
and our true guide.[5]

When we look at these three scenarios, what is interesting is their
different tenor. Tactical error, treachery, pits with spikes, wounds to
the face or the leg – each has a different flavour and presents Magellan in a different light. Pigafetta was the only eyewitness; the two
other Portuguese historians cited here composed their accounts later.

It would not be lost on the sixteenth-century reader how much some of these stories resembled other stories of great heroes. Writing at the time was indebted to the past, governed by what was known as 'imitation'. Originality, so far as the concept existed, was less about creating something that was totally new than about creatively emulating literary forebears in their style and substance. Young men of a certain social status were schooled in the classics and their reference points for greatness were often the heroes of epics and histories written in Latin or Greek (the latter usually in Latin translation).

Once you're aware of this, it's curious just how much the now accepted story of Magellan's demise, plausible and realistic as it is, resembles the story of Achilles, killed by an arrow to the leg. This resemblance would definitely have resounded in the heads of early modern readers, whose pleasure in reading was deeply connected to the recognition of these subtle allusions. A death banquet – which is Correia's scenario for Magellan's demise, although other sources have it as a piece of later treachery – was also a famed way to go in stories passed down from the ancient world. And such a death came with the suggestion that treachery and false pretences were the only way to bring down the most powerful commanders.

How to Think about Defeat

Beyond these ancient parallels, it is clear that Magellan underestimated the situation he was in and that his soldiers did not know how to fight effectively on the beaches of Mactan. Pigafetta has Magellan battle for more than an hour after being wounded by a poisoned arrow. But he does, nonetheless, point out the crucial weakness of Magellan's men: the inefficacy of their firearms. Both shipboard cannons and handheld muskets had limited range, were inaccurate and took a long time to reload – and the muskets may not have worked at all if they couldn't be kept dry during the fighting in the surf and on the beaches. The Mactan fighters easily avoided the gunfire by moving about and keeping out of range until the Europeans had used up all their shot.

From the evidence, then, it is clear that each side was fighting a different kind of battle, and that means their philosophies of warfare differed as much as their weapons and tactics. War, though it might seem a simple question of brute strength and survival, is a cultural phenomenon. It too is subject to the slippery laws of translation.

In the world of the Pacific archipelago, rivalry between *datu*, or local rulers, was frequent as they sought to demonstrate their relative *dungan* strength (spiritual potency). These quarrels between *datu* proved to a community that their leader was worthy: it was not just a means of proving prowess to outsiders. Yet, in these skirmishes, the aim was not territorial conquest or obliteration of an enemy. The risks of outright battle were typically avoided and more emphasis was placed on intimidation and underhand tactics than hand-to-hand combat. This was because direct combat depleted human resources. Unlike European battles, where controlling the battlefield was key, and slaughter was critical to success, the aim for *datu* was to conserve and consolidate people power, not expend it wastefully.[6]

Reading between the lines of European accounts of the battle on Mactan, you can see this philosophy at work: Lapulapu's fighters kept their distance until the majority of Magellan's men had fled the scene. The sheer number of forces marshalled by Lapulapu, in the indigenous scheme of warfare, would probably have been intended to intimidate and thus avoid outright violence. The use of long-range projectiles similarly was not intended to be lethal: if an enemy could be scared into submission, captured and assimilated rather than killed, that would bring additional resources. Obliteration served no one.

This clashed with Magellan's outlook, where personal and national pride resided in small forces defeating larger foes. In his early career, Magellan had repeatedly seen the Portuguese win battles against the odds, as we saw in Melaka. Portuguese identity was founded on this idea of being small but mighty, summed up in a line of Camões's epic poem which addresses the Portuguese as 'as strong as you are few'.[7] Extra honour was found in the improbable odds, in the impossible victory. Magellan and Lapulapu were not playing the same game. From Lapulapu's perspective, Magellan's attitude must have seemed foolish.

Early modern European historians often automatically cast retreat as cowardice, an implicit concession of victory. But seen through other eyes, retreat was tactical regrouping, resistance, a decision to endure, to preserve life and other resources. Over the long colonial history of the Philippines, as elsewhere in the world, retreat constituted a key manoeuvre of defiance. To take the example of the island of Luzon, where the Filipino capital Manila is now situated, the Spanish fantasized about total control of the island, yet they mostly occupied the lowlands by the coast. The uplands were unruly, populated by renegade communities who never succumbed to Spanish rule.[8] This is again not to say that Spanish rule was not brutal, and did not have a brutal and lasting effect on all the inhabitants of Luzon, but it does add nuance to the picture to emphasize that European conquest was never total.[9] For Europeans, indeed, territory mattered most, but for those on the other side it was often a loss that could be absorbed: somewhere else could be found, people and possessions could be moved, new settlements or trading posts established. This territorial attitude sometimes worked against the Spanish and Portuguese in Southeast Asia, where they thought the establishment of a fort would guarantee their control of a region. They did not expect communities simply to find somewhere else to live, where they would not have to answer to the Europeans. In the Moluccas, for instance, a consortium of kingdoms fought against the Portuguese precisely by abandoning their islands. It was a kind of reverse siege: a withdrawal of all labour and resources that would allow the Portuguese to survive.

Understanding the terms of engagement matters. And that has involved a continual process of historical revision and of questioning the principal sources that historians have relied on in their writing. That means looking beyond what might, in the Euro-American academy, count as evidence. One of the most compelling, challenging and humorous reframings of the so-called 'Battle of Mactan' in recent years has come not from universities, but from an art gallery: Filipino artist Kidlat Tahimik's installation *Magellan, Marilyn, Mickey and Fr. Dámaso. 500 Years of Conquistador RockStars.*

Tahimik's counter-reading of the Battle of Mactan emphasizes not so much the victory itself as the means by which it was achieved. He refers to it as a *kapwa* victory, one where solidarity in the face of the

Kidlat Tahimik's 2021 installation, *Magellan, Marilyn, Mickey and Fr. Dámaso. 500 Years of Conquistador RockStars*

aggressor achieved this act of resistance. He connects this moment to a long history of Filipino cultural resistance against the colonialism of both Spain and the USA. Statues representing the winds blow back the material, cultural, social and economic forms of influence and oppression. Inhabian, the wind goddess of the Igorot peoples of Luzon, lifts Marilyn Monroe's skirt in a comic and subversive rewriting of an iconic image of American cultural supremacy in a world of globalized media. By emphasizing the *kapwa* dimension of the battle, Tahimik highlights the value of indigenous worldviews as vantage points from which to write alternative historical narratives and as ways of conceptualizing resistance. To have a different vocabulary is to have a different understanding. It is an act of pushing back against the authority of written history: Tahimik's visual and oral works exceed what historians tend to think of as 'valid' sources. They challenge the 'hierarchies of credibility', as historian Ann Laura Stoler has put it in a different context.[10] I also find Tahimik's approach important because it steps away from the obsessively forensic desire to pin down what *really* happened in the past and instead ponders how we frame particular events – was the Battle of Mactan Magellan's defeat or Lapulapu's victory?

Right from the beginning, Magellan's story was about who controlled the narrative. The sources all conflict. Our evidence comes from second-hand accounts by early modern historians and commentators, as well as from participants in the events themselves, both documents written in their own hands and transcripts of their interviews with bureaucrats. Indeed, wherever the surviving adventurers went they were interrogated about what happened, whether they were the mutineers on the *San Antonio*, who were questioned when they returned to Spain without the rest of the fleet, or those who were captured by the Portuguese at waypoints in Asia and the Cape Verde islands on their slow way back to Europe. No one has yet been able to iron out the story completely. The issue, of course, was competing motives and personal interest at the time. Each individual needed to portray the journey and its protagonists in a different light. Later historians have aggrandized Magellan – and continue to do so – out of national pride and blokeish admiration (it is no surprise to me that most of the work on Magellan has been done by men). I can't help but think, however, when I look at Tahimik's installation, that both the sixteenth-century interrogators and some historians since have simply asked the wrong people for answers.

WORLD EVENTS

1527
Sack of Rome by
Charles V's troops
– Rome, Italy

1526
Battle of Panipat,
establishing the
Mughal empire in
India – Panipat,
India

1529
First Siege of Vienna
by the Ottoman empire
– Vienna, Austria

1526
San Lesmes, Spain:
Disappeared after
passing through
the Strait of
Magellan.

*Santa Maria del
Parral*, Spain: Ran
aground on
Sangihe Island,
Indonesia.

1523
Trinidad,
Spain:
Wrecked in
a storm at
Ternate,
Indonesia.

1521
2 MAY
Concepción,
Spain: Deliber-
ately abandoned
and burned in the
Philippines.

1520
Santiago, Spain

1525
SV *Corpo Santo*,
Portugal: Ran aground at
Cape Roçalgate, Oman.

1527
Santo António, Portugal:
Foundered in Gunwalloe Bay, Cornw
en route from Lisbon to Antwerp.

SHIPWRECKS

1532
Francisco Pizarro captures
Atahualpa, leading to the
fall of the Inca empire –
Cajamarca, Peru

1534
Henry VIII breaks from the
Catholic Church, establishing
the Church of England –
London, England

1539
Guru Nanak,
founder of Sikhism,
dies – Punjab, India

Hernando de Soto explores
the southeastern United
States – Southeastern USA

1533
Ivan the Terrible begins his
reign as Grand Prince of
Moscow – Moscow, Russia

1536
John Calvin publishes
*Institutes of the
Christian Religion*
– Basel, Switzerland

1540
Capitana,
Spain:
Wrecked in
the Strait of
Magellan.

1537
Concepción, Spain: Wrecked
at Ponta Loyola, Argentina.

PART FOUR

False Diamonds and True Survival

Marguerite decided to go. It was a decision that had been subject first to inner doubts, then to the surprise of others, but now mostly to the humdrum annoyance of waiting. The captains of the fleet were struggling to corral the necessary crew to man the ships and to populate that promise of a New France across the water. They were supposed to have left France last spring, but summer came, then autumn, then winter, and here they were in spring again and still in France. This year, though, Marguerite would depart. But she struggled in her daydreams of the future to picture the place where she would be going. A region called Canada, a river called St Lawrence, a village called Stadacona: in her mind's eye, it must have been a collage of cold midwinter days, sea and sand and sky all blended into barren greys, animated by the rumours she had heard of ferocious peoples, their bodies painted, wearing pelts – like the figures she might have seen parading with the Tupinambá and the inhabitants of Cochin along the frieze adorning the treasury of the church of Saint-Jacques in Dieppe.

Frieze in the church of Saint-Jacques in Dieppe, c. 1525–35

Maybe she had heard talk of the ten people captured by Jacques Cartier and brought back to France five years ago, all but one of whom had died as a result of their intercontinental abduction, either during the journey or after they arrived in France. But I'm sure she didn't want to dwell too much on that.

Although Marguerite could gaze out on the Atlantic from La Rochelle, the distant reaches of the ocean existed for her only by proxy. Fishing fleets from La Rochelle, Dieppe and Honfleur ventured far into the North Atlantic, returning from the cold waters off Newfoundland with their hulls filled with cod, gutted, filleted, packed in salt. But the taste of *morue verte* did not help with the problem of picturing a whole life out there, in Canada. The fishermen always returned to their lives here. No one had tried to settle there permanently before. Jacques Cartier, on his first voyage to Canada, had described the landscape as rugged and rocky, scattered with moss and stunted shrubs which crouched close to the ground, timid in the face of the harsh weather.[1] He had stepped into the land given to Cain in the Bible, an unfertile earth, punishing to cultivate. On his second voyage, he ventured inland, up the St Lawrence river to where the landscape was lusher and the local Iroquois spoke of gold beyond the Lachine Rapids that barred his way. A bit more promising than he initially thought, La Rochelle was one of the wealthiest and busiest towns in France, surrounded by thick fortifications and overlooked by watchtowers. The city wore its strength on its sleeves. Marguerite was leaving behind white stone and its reassuring weight for a life that would mostly be lived surrounded by wood: the tarred planks of a ship, the encampment on the St Lawrence river that would be her new home.

Reader, Beware

Marguerite de Roberval's story is a complicated one. We can read multiple versions of it in various books of the sixteenth century; but, in this case, a surfeit of printed evidence brings more problems than solutions. Every author who reported her voyage clearly amplified the bare facts, adding to what they claimed to have heard their own special spin. They cared less about rigorous truth-hunting than making the tale advance their own arguments about empire or faith. The documentary record – the kind of scribbled, handwritten papers that historians rummage through as their trade – is very slim, despite the number of archival adventurers who have set out to track Marguerite down in municipal rolls and family papers. The only option left is to work by induction, to sketch a Venn diagram of the available sources and see where the overlap of their facts in the intersecting rings gives us reasonable grounds to trust them. A little supplementary imagining can also be found in the next two chapters, signalled as I go along by the textual flags 'must have' and 'likely', but I do not want those to end up distracting you too much, so I have avoided including them in absolutely every sentence.

Despite the scarcity of hard facts, Marguerite's is a story that has been thought worth telling and retelling many times over the centuries. In part, that fascination with the story is itself of historical interest. The reception of the tale shows us what people in the past thought was worth recording and how they perceived the actions of colonists in their own time. What they made of Marguerite is an index of their own preoccupations and aspirations. And those preoccupations and aspirations in turn became some of the major issues for later colonial expansion: religion, enrichment, cultural imposition and appropriation, escape. Looking at how her story has been told gives us a window into how people saw or wanted to see voyages between continents.

7. Convicts, Captains and Lovers

When news reached the Portuguese and Spanish ambassadors to the French court that King François I was making plans for another exploratory expedition to the 'New World', they bristled. France and Spain had been enemies on and off for years; tensions simmered down, then boiled over again in their volatile diplomatic relationship. Peace had supposedly arrived in 1538, but Charles V, the Holy Roman Emperor and King of Spain, had failed to make the concessions that François had hoped for in Italy, where they had been quarrelling over the edges of their respective domains for years. The Spanish monarch had riled the French king by bequeathing Milan to his son, the future King Philip II. It was a slap in the face after François I had let Spanish forces march across his lands when a rebellion had erupted in Flanders.

Now, in 1540, François I was not going to listen to the entreaties and arguments of his fellow monarchs. He manoeuvred around them by claiming that he was not transgressing against their dominions. The Iberian rights, he argued, extended only to *inhabited lands*, not to the unpeopled soil where he intended to plant and cultivate his new colony.[1] Pope Alexander VI, who had solemnized the claims of the Iberian kingdoms to the 'New World', had no right to do so from the French king's perspective. The head of the church had spiritual jurisdiction, but he had no temporal authority to distribute land between kings. Eventually, in 1533, Pope Clement VII decreed that the earlier papal declaration applied only to known lands, and this freed up the French from a legal perspective.[2]

The Spanish and Portuguese crowns, however, did not see it that way. In a letter to the Cardinal of Toledo in November 1540, Charles V noted that all their diplomatic attempts to dissuade François I from pursuing empire on the other side of the Atlantic had failed, so they needed to collect information on the French preparations, and, when their ships set to sea, 'engage and destroy them . . . and let all the men taken from their ships be thrown into the sea, not saving any one person, for this is necessary as a warning against the undertaking of similar expeditions'.[3]

Accordingly, as the preparations progressed in Saint-Malo, on the French coast, there were eyes watching Cartier and his men. The logistics of the voyage were complex, with supplies and men drawn from various locations across France. Cartier would leave France from Saint-Malo with a first contingent of the fleet; the second part of the fleet, in which Marguerite would depart, visited Saint-Malo, Honfleur, Brest and La Rochelle before setting out across the Atlantic.

Observing, listening, while Cartier's ships were being prepared, was one of the Cardinal of Toledo's spies, who pieced together intelligence on the nature and scale of the operation Cartier was planning and dispatched his findings back to Spain in April 1541. Questions were asked of the looser-lipped members of the crew. Sailors were not

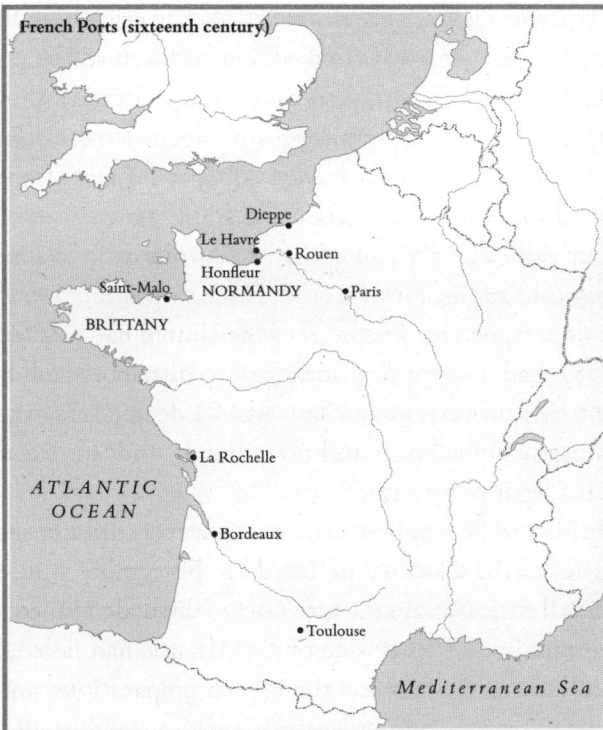

French Ports (sixteenth century)

Dieppe
Le Havre
Honfleur • Rouen
Saint-Malo NORMANDY
• Paris
BRITTANY

ATLANTIC
OCEAN

• La Rochelle

• Bordeaux

• Toulouse

Mediterranean Sea

good at keeping secrets. A man named Jean Rolin offered up many of the details, with a side of critical gossip, to the foreign agent. How many ships and men; what provisions; how long they planned to stay in Canada; their intentions upon arrival; when, if at all, they would return – the spy greedily jotted it all down. Cartier would need to build smaller craft when he reached the St Lawrence river in order to navigate it. Three of the ships and their men would stay to build a colony; the rest would return to France. Alongside the human passengers, cows, sheep, goats and pigs would travel to feed and support the fledgling settlement. Tools and equipment – everything needed for a prosperous town – and the skilled individuals to operate them, all would make their way across the ocean. There is something of the Book of Genesis in the livestock that the spy catalogued: the captain represented a new Noah, assembling ewes and wethers, cows and oxen, men and women on ships, to start new lives again after four weeks on water. The difference was that Cartier, unlike Noah, was not selected for his task on the grounds of virtue – or at least not for the kinds of qualities that we would necessarily recognize as such.[4]

The clandestine report also tells us that Cartier, who had already been twice to Canada, was certain of finding gold. In his parleys with the St Lawrence Iroquois, they had told him of the land of Saguenay, upriver from the village of Stadacona, describing it as an abundant trove of all the kinds of riches Cartier sought to reap. He was already counting the chests of precious metals and rare gems, his future fortune. His confidence was dented, though, when it was hit by the scepticism of João Largato, a Portuguese pilot, who quipped at a dinner with the French king that he thought Donnacona – the Iroquoian chief of Stadacona, whom Cartier had kidnapped and carried back to France – was fanciful in painting a land of plenty in the cold latitudes of Canada; it was all a fib to earn himself a passage home (and who could blame him?). Largato likened the chief to the devil tempting Christ with promises of everything: *haec omnia tibi dabo* – 'All these things I give to thee' – he joked. The king laughed off the remark. But perhaps it was yellow laughter, as the French say, *rire jaune*: he would later be laughing on the other side of his face.[5]

Jean-François de la Rocque, Sieur de Roberval, Marguerite's relative – and, following the death of her parents, her guardian – was brought in to head up the expedition in the final few months before departure. Cartier, experienced in navigating the North Atlantic, familiar now with Newfoundland and the banks of the St Lawrence, was displaced in the pecking order of the third French venture to the north and west. After he had received his royal commission as the expedition's 'captain and pilot-general' in October 1540, the impetus of the voyage shifted away from exploration towards colonization, and that needed a different skill set. So, in January 1541, the king slotted in Roberval above Cartier by naming him viceroy, or as I like to think of it, deputy king. The ruler and lawmaker of the new colony was a military man; his career had seen him command battalions and withstand sieges, and he had privileges over mines and mills.[6] As an engineer, endurer, extractor, he had all the experience necessary to build a settlement, defend it against hostile forces, and find a way to claw profit and sustenance from its land.

The only contemporary portrait we have of Roberval is a drawing. His countenance is sober, his velvet gown is the attire of military men and functionaries. In the Renaissance, hair mattered: people of the period read dress and appearance for clues to status and allegiance. We can do the same: Roberval's tawny beard speaks, as beards were thought to do, of 'gravity, wisdom, discretion, and virility'.[7] The artist,

Portrait of Jean-François de la Rocque, Sieur de Roberval, 1535

François Clouet, asks us to take his sitter seriously, even in the faded outlines we have on this piece of paper. A note jotted overleaf by the painter reveals, though, that Roberval's hair is beginning to grey; he is a man edging into middle age. His hat hides a receding hairline, his skin is slightly yellowing. He is serious, then, but a little worn by his experiences. The sketch dates from 1535, before Atlantic storms, the Canadian winter and poor diet had further wearied him.[8]

A Crew of Misfits

The preparations for the voyage were slow. The two leaders of the expedition decided to split it into two fleets: Cartier would assemble one at Saint-Malo, Roberval the other at Honfleur. By the spring of 1541, Cartier had the necessary provisions and personnel to depart. Roberval decided to let him leave, thinking that he would soon follow suit. Cartier weighed anchor on 23 May and crossed the Atlantic in a month. He stopped off in Newfoundland to reprovision and wait for Roberval. But Roberval did not come. Cartier, concerned about a Spanish attack in this exposed location, headed off after a month in order to spend the winter in the St Lawrence estuary near Stadacona (close to present-day Québec City). It would be nearly a year after Cartier's departure from France before Roberval could pull together all the people needed for the expedition and all the provisions and military hardware to ensure the survival of a colony in a place populated with hostile locals.

As the month of April began in 1542, the sailors of Roberval's fleet at last started to heave the final provisions aboard the ships docked at La Rochelle. And there, amid the barrels and sacks, he was: the real reason Marguerite had decided to embark. Her clandestine lover – a man who is not named in the accounts of Marguerite's story, and so will remain nameless here. They knew not to look at each other when Roberval was nearby. Courtiers were well instructed in the interpretation of glances and gestures; shared smiles could unravel a secret affair. So far so secret; so far so good. Their relationship had stayed under its veil and Marguerite had not yet had to answer any questions from Roberval. She suspected he would not approve of the match, but at least in New France the couple might serve a purpose. The colony would need children for it to survive longer than a generation. She did not think about how much harder it would be to conceal their affections when they were sequestered together on a ship.

The passengers were the very definition of a motley crew, every social rank forced incongruously together. Few had volunteered for the voyage – it was long, harsh, dangerous, poorly paid – so the king had given Roberval permission to hunt for recruits among those who had few other options in life: prisoners. François instructed the bailiffs of Paris, Rouen, Caen, Orléans, Blois, Tours, Maine, Anjou and Guinne to make available convicts to serve on the ships. Cartier and Roberval had their pick of every kind of criminal, save those who had committed heresy or *lèse-majesté*: those who betrayed their superiors or God himself would be sure to corrupt the new colony. The criminals selected would be released from their sentences into a different kind of hardship. Like slavery, it was another way of forcing migration, assembling empire from those who were dispossessed.

We know the names of seventy-five convicts enlisted by Roberval and Cartier and can count among them men and women, murderers, rapists and thieves: Jehanne de La Veerye, thirty years old, sentenced for trafficking children; Simon Dagoubert, lawyer's son and klepto-maniac; Pierre de Ronsart, from Bourges, a counterfeiter – all aboard, all aboard.[9] Many were not from the lowest levels of the social heap, because this was not a welfare voyage: the criminals had to pay their own way. They were forced to fork out for their journey and for the three years of provisions assigned to their name. In order to pay, they needed cash, or belongings that could be sold; their exit from prison came with multiple prices to pay. The counterfeiter might come in useful too, if they found gold.

Roberval and Cartier's recruitment drive behind the bars of France's prisons was not simply a matter of striding into a penitentiary and grabbing some felons. The extrication of criminals, then, as now, was a far more bureaucratic endeavour. The clogged French courts and overwhelmed judges eagerly sought to offload the least wealthy inmates from the country's bursting jails, keeping the wealthier criminals inside as they would take a cut of any property seized by the legal system.[10] Consequently, Roberval had to enlist friends and contacts across France to move along the jammed legal processes and push the right papers in front of the right people. He deployed over forty agents in his headhunt and its associated administration.

Two of the prisoners were joined by their wives. One of the women, Mondyne Boysrye, resisted attempts to dissuade her from accompanying her husband, François Guay. As they departed from Toulouse in the south of France, to head north to La Rochelle, she was offered money to stay behind, as women were often considered disruptive on board ships. She declined: the ties of her marriage to François proved to be stronger than any monetary lure. And so Marguerite, romantic as her situation seems, was not wholly unusual in her priorities; other affairs of the heart were carried aboard the ships at La Rochelle too.

Men commanding ships receive the greatest attention in books on early modern exploration, but the presence of women is nonetheless important right from the beginning, as you will see further when a Spanish ship is wrecked on the coast of Brazil in Part Five and when the Portuguese carrack the *São João* sinks off the coast of South Africa in Part Six. Early Portuguese raids on the Guinea coast took women as slaves from the start, and women who were slaves or former slaves later became important intermediaries on ships all along the African coast. Often ships would leave the ports of Europe only for their captains to discover stowaway women in their hulls, quite to their surprise, sneaked aboard by their husbands or their lovers. In between their religious duties, priests hunted for hidden women, whom they blamed for distracting sailors on watch and for causing fires by carelessly knocking over candles.[11] It was clearly thought to be a big problem, as Vasco da Gama had to crack down on these covert passengers just as he was leaving Lisbon on his third voyage out to India in 1524: any women found on board the ships would be whipped; if they were married, their husbands would be clapped in irons and returned to Portugal; and if the women were slaves, they would lose their right to be freed.

Passion's Narrow Berth

Roberval's fleet of assorted miscreants, nobles and seamen sailed from La Rochelle harbour on 16 April 1542.

But the weather hindered them from immediately striking out into the open Atlantic. The wind buffeted them back to shore, forcing them to anchor for some time off the Breton coast until the worst had passed.

With the wind in their favour once more, it took around four weeks to cross the ocean. The ship's log of the voyage, however, gives us no details and, perhaps surprisingly, survives only in a later English printing; it was written, we presume, in French by the pilot João Afonso, a Portuguese known better by his Frenchified moniker, Jean Alfonse de Saintonge. Its route to us speaks volumes of the interconnectedness of the navigational world. Pilots and sailors moved in

Depiction of Jacques Cartier's ship, c. 1697

an international job market; knowledge moved around and between different people and places.

We might, in the absence of a report from Roberval's fleet, defer to one by a Frenchman destined further south, but who described the terrors of the North Atlantic with gusto:

> we were seized by a surge of the sea that continued for twelve days, during which – even aside from being very ill from the usual sea-sickness – there was not one of us who was not terrified at the ship's swaying. Those especially who had never smelled sea air, nor danced such a dance, and who saw the sea so high and roiled up, thought at each instant that the waves were about to take us to the bottom. It is an amazing thing to see a wooden vessel, however large and strong, resist the fury and force of that terrible element. For even though the ships are built of heavy wood tightly bound and pegged, and heavily tarred – indeed, the one I was in was probably about one hundred ten feet long and twenty-seven feet wide – what is that compared with the width and depth of that gulf, that abyss of water that is the Western Sea?[12]

For Marguerite and her lover, the claustrophobic confines of their ship restricted the opportunities for assignations. Around twenty-five metres at its longest, and six metres at its broadest, the ship did not allow their passion much space. The alleys and streets of La Rochelle and Honfleur, or the chateau at Roberval, its corridors and closed doors, offered a whole theatre of possible unnoticed exits and nonchalant entrances, an endless variety of plausible pretexts – a dropped glove, a turn outside – that would allow for a rendezvous. Aboard ship, Marguerite was unavoidably watched, exposed to more than just the wind and rain that buffeted her on deck.

But prudence had stayed in France. Marguerite allowed herself to stand close to her lover, to eke out the conversations they contrived with each other, lingering, perhaps, for just a few minutes longer than the excuses they had invented would really support. Those awkward pretences probably drew the attention they were supposed to deflect, as the contrived performance of happenstance so often does.

Sometimes they must have descended below deck, where the air was clogged with the musty blend of tar, stale provisions, bodies increasingly sour. Down another level to the cargo holds, the barrels and sacks that shifted heavily when the waves rocked the ship. Down there, you didn't want to think about how only three fingers' width of planking separated the dry from the wet, deep and dangerous. In the gloom, the sounds were muffled, but livestock, caged or restrained, breathed and snorted, the ship creaked rhythmically, straining with each move to and fro.

In the recesses of the ship, in a corner or a gap between provisions, maybe it was there it happened. Or perhaps it was above deck, in the upper cabins, gigglingly slipping away, barring the door, recruiting a lookout. All we know from what comes much later is they did it, and that people, as they do, noticed.

Meals on board grew less appetizing as the weeks progressed and the love affair advanced. The water sitting in the barrels for their refreshment would have gradually turned rancid. Weevils and rats had the first bites of the ship's biscuit, one of their staples. It was double baked into dense slabs of sustenance, but it needed to be softened to make it edible, and with time it crumbled. Cartier and Roberval had stocked up in Normandy, so there was cider to drink too. Peas and beans, meat and fish made up the rest of what they ate. A diet similar to what they consumed in France but increasingly less fresh as they made their way across the ocean. In dire straits, almost everything became a potential source of nutrition. Passengers on long-distance

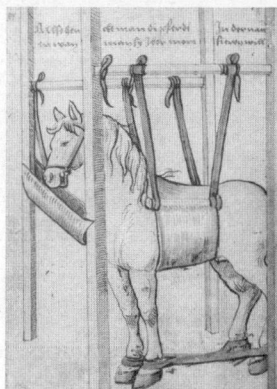

Horse being transported in a ship, c. 1530

voyages cooked exotic birds and forced leather shoe-soles, sawdust and nautical charts down their gullets when they got hungry
enough.[13] The chronicler Jean de Léry described having to separate
morsels of bread from worms and rat droppings, then making an
unappetizingly black gruel out of these crumbs by adding water.[14]

During the less hectic moments, when they weren't being tossed
about until they were sick, or having to scramble to adjust the rigging, to unfurl or take in the sails, they sang and told stories, played
cards and prayed. The apple of Marguerite's eye – if we believe one of
the accounts of Marguerite's life – liked to draw the attention of the
whole crew by strumming along on a guitar to long-winded verses
about his feelings. (I'm not just being scornful: the songs in François
de Belleforest's account are really long and not especially interesting.)

The captain was not the first to hear the whispers or spot the signs.
But rumours scurried everywhere like rats, and Roberval was not
pleased to encounter them. Chastity was a prize and a virtue in those
days and reputation was everything. A liaison between a woman of
his family and a passenger sullied both. At first, Roberval simply
watched. As the evidence stacked up, he began to seethe within. His
own relative, the subject of gossip, carrying on with a man on his
ship. A family like theirs was supposed to be better than the rest of
the colonists and crew, an example to them of how to behave. Her
actions had broken that tacit pact of superiority; they had tarnished and
begun to corrode his sense of command. The decision about whom
she married was his, not her, prerogative. And so, in secret, he thought
about how to set things right; skimming through the options available to him, he decided on a course of justice – by which, of course,
I mean revenge. He would demonstrate that his justice showed no
bias in favour of family or rank and would strike uncompromisingly
against those who erred. He would have order at any cost.

8. The Lady's Isle

On 8 June, the French ships completed their crossing and pulled into the coast of Newfoundland at Saint-Jean (St John's), a North Atlantic touchstone for fishermen, where they encountered no fewer than seventeen fishing boats docked. After weeks at sea, the crew and indeed the animal cargo were relieved to stretch their legs and sip fresh water. Stocks needed to be replenished for the final leg of their journey around Newfoundland and up the St Lawrence river where, after a long year of delays, they would reach Cartier and the first batch of colonists.

Or that was what they planned. So imagine Roberval's surprise when, in breach of his orders, Cartier and his ships appeared at Saint-Jean, clearly heading back to France and abandoning the settlement they were supposed to have set up.

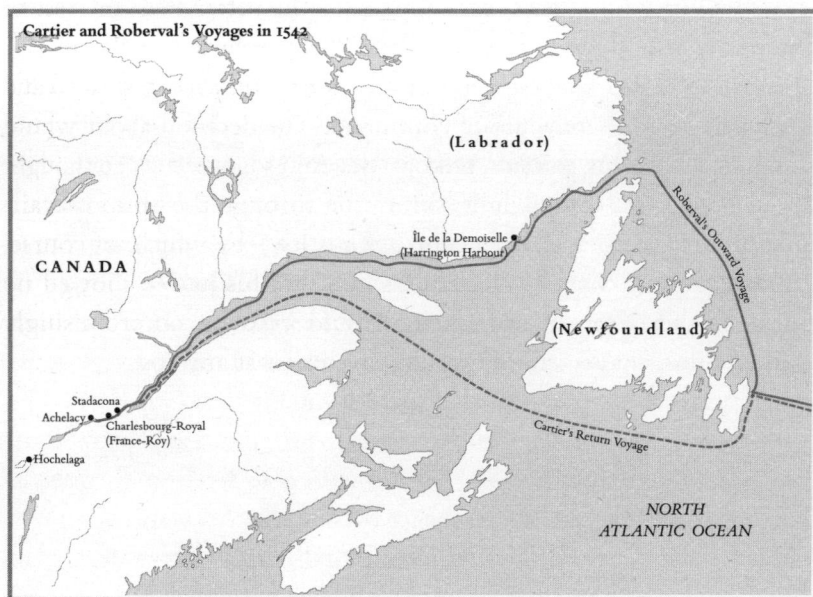

Cartier and Roberval's Voyages in 1542

Cartier related to Roberval what had happened to him over the months since they had last met. After reaching Stadacona in August 1541, he had established a fort where the Cap Rouge tributary meets the northern shore of the St Lawrence river and called it Charlesbourg-Royal. Three kilometres of wooden palisades – logs felled nearby and replanted as fortifications – defended the two parts of the settlement: a lower fort at the level of the river near the ships, and an upper stronghold at the top of a cliff, up which they had fashioned a stairway. Construction had started immediately and progressed well in the first weeks after their arrival; so well, in fact, that it gave Cartier the chance to explore further up the St Lawrence in the direction of Saguenay, where, he had been told, he would find riches. Cartier made it almost all the way to Hochelaga (near present-day Montreal), but was thwarted by the rocks and intense current of the Lachine Rapids and had to get out of his boats and walk. He found a path, testament to the footfall of people before him, leading to a settlement. He was welcomed in a friendly fashion, before being led by a group of men to another village. There he learned, by way of a map of sticks laid on the ground, that yet another set of rapids lay on the river ahead towards Saguenay. Buoyed by the information, he retraced his route back towards Cap Rouge.

Something wasn't right. Two boys left behind on their journey up the St Lawrence at the village of Achelacy (near present-day Portneuf), to learn the local language, relayed that its ruler had departed for Stadacona, immediately raising Cartier's suspicions that the settlements along the river were plotting something against him. What they plotted had been investigated, however, by his own men. With no captain to keep them in order, a cruel band of French youths, supposedly testing the sharpness of their weapons, had attacked Stadaconans for sport, slicing off their limbs in an act of unprovoked cruelty.[1] This brutal act sparked a deadly retaliation, resulting in the loss of thirty-five woodsmen crucial to the colonists' construction and fortification efforts. The Stadaconans, once daily visitors bearing fish and other provisions, now ceased their support, leaving the settlers to fend for themselves through a gruelling winter. As the ice thawed, there was still no sign of Roberval and survival prospects were dwindling, so Cartier decided to abandon Charlesbourg-Royal and set off back to France.

Cartier told Roberval with substantially more glee that he'd seen shimmering seams in rocks near the fort which promised riches, and that he'd also chanced upon sparkling diamonds and gold. His hull was packed with ten casks of gold ore, seven of silver, and seven quintals (around 317 kilograms) of 'pearls and precious stones' to take back to France. A small furnace was set up at Saint-Jean to test the rocks for their lucrative content and they were found to be good. After Cartier returned home, these rocks would give rise to an enduring idiom: *faux comme un diamant du Canada* – fake like a diamond from Canada. The marvellous gems were quartz.

The log from Roberval's ship notes that Cartier was eager for glory and not disposed to suffer the difficulties of establishing a colony. He wanted to beat Roberval back to Europe, to give his story and show off his sparkling prize. Roberval insisted that Cartier dispatch only a few of his ships across the Atlantic to fetch more provisions for the colony while he and the rest of his men sailed back to Charlesbourg-Royal with Roberval. Under cover of darkness, Cartier disobeyed. He had had enough of Canada. He was heading home.

Despite this desertion, Roberval departed from Saint-Jean, voyaging north around Newfoundland towards the shore of Labrador. It was still summer then, warm and promising, and sighting a pleasant and seemingly uninhabited island off the coast of the mainland, the ships anchored again to reprovision. The captain told Marguerite to come along, to take a moment to enjoy stepping on solid land before the fleet made its way towards its final destination.

The Lady's Isle

Marguerite was helped into the ship's boat and along with her lover and a group of men they swiftly rowed to shore. A few of the men began unloading some stores brought from the ship. She thought they were only going to be here a few hours; those weapons and boxes seemed like an excessive cargo for a fleeting visit. She expected, come nightfall, to sleep again on the ship. She must have started to wander around the island, enjoying the air around her, the ground beneath her, while her uncle and his men were busying themselves with their tasks. Some of the men started clambering back into the boat. They must be going to fetch others or more supplies. Maybe they'd forgotten the fishing nets. The final two men began pushing the boat off the sand into the water, wading ankle- then knee-deep before climbing in themselves. Marguerite paced towards them, a flutter of panic rising up from her stomach until her whole body was vibrating with it. Where are you going? she shouted above the sound of the breaking waves. Where are you going? Are you leaving me? It was too preposterous to grapple with in her mind. What was going on? The look on her uncle's face dissipated any lingering confusion.

His wrath, for weeks bottled up during their voyage, was uncorked. He told her that her punishment would be this: an island home to share with her lover. She had betrayed him, her uncle, her captain. She had behaved like a common whore – in one French account, the expression is *fille publique*, a 'public girl'. Women and wives, under the *ancien régime*, were imagined by men to be private property that needed to be guarded. It was not unknown for sexual activity on board ships to be severely punished, especially when it was perceived to cross the carefully patrolled boundaries of social status: on a vessel captained by Afonso de Albuquerque, a man was hanged when he was found having sex with an African slave in the captain's quarters.[2]

Marguerite's betrayal was not an obvious legal infraction of the kind for which plenty of other passengers had been tried and sentenced back in France, but an affront to his command. As viceroy, Roberval was judge and jury rolled into one. Though he framed this punishment as a stay of execution, in choosing and enacting it in all its obvious cruelty he assumed all those responsibilities spelled out by the king in his commission. He needed to keep order if he wanted to make his colony a success. Even the pilot of the voyage, mostly so sparing with his words, noted Roberval's swift and unwavering meting out of punishment during the voyage. A man named Michael Gailion was hanged for theft; others, both men and women, were clapped in irons or whipped. It was, said João Afonso, by these means that 'they lived in quiet'. A sinister euphemism.[3]

Marguerite's panic turned to tears. Her lover had run into the cold water, raging at the sudden ruling against their relationship. Marguerite must have known, there on the edge of that island, that there was no room for appeal, no place or person that could hear a petition for mercy. Her uncle, who had planned and executed this brutal surprise, was not going to change his mind. Regret might bring him back later, but chances were slim. He had a military determination that had seen him through battle and siege. His only kindness, in marooning them there, was the provisions and tools that his crew had dumped on the shore for them. But they all knew the food would not last long. Their lone consolation was not having to hide their affair any longer.

I imagine that he turned to her, not yet prepared to let go of his anger, and pushed away her attempts at consolation, spitting a shanty of curses at Roberval, kicking pebbles into the water in frustration. It's hard to conceive of quite what that would feel like, being stranded so definitively. Even the writers of the period who claimed to be friendly with Roberval acknowledged the cruelty of his actions in their accounts of Marguerite's fate.

The island where Marguerite was abandoned sat near the mouth of the St Lawrence river, and is now conventionally identified as Harrington Harbour. There have been many attempts to locate it and describe it from the sixteenth century onwards. Despite the archival difficulties in verifying much of the story here, an island called the 'Île de la Demoiselle' crops up in a map of the region made not long after the voyage by the pilot of the expedition.

Although Afonso did not mention the episode in his report – he probably knew that any word against Roberval would not be wise – his map offers us important evidence that the later stories were true. The island is green with fir trees and grasses. Today you can visit a place known as 'Marguerite's Cave', where she is supposed to have lived.

André Thevet, a French Franciscan priest and cosmographer, in his *Cosmographie universelle*, mentioned the island and the story that unfolded there, and included an engraving of the island with a ship pulling away . . . or is it about to come to the rescue . . ? Right in the centre is a tree that looks peculiarly out of place: a palm, a botanical transplant from a warmer clime. Historians put it down to a pictorial

L'Isle où Y-
ne Damoisel-
le Françoise
fut exilée.

'The island where a French lady was exiled', as portrayed in
Thévet's *Cosmographie Univeselle*, 1575

shorthand for the exotic and the distant. Perhaps, though, there is
another meaning, given that this was a story which became, once
the shipboard love affair part of it was over, about endurance, about
what it took to stay alive against the elements and far removed from
any form of society. In this respect, the palm has something to tell
us. The palm was said, in the sixteenth century, to grow higher and
stronger as weight pressed upon it. In the emblems of Alciato – the
many versions and translations of which were perennial bestsellers
across Renaissance Europe – the image of the palm struggling against
resistance, but nonetheless growing upwards, was given the caption:
Obdurandum adversus urgentia – 'Stand firm against pressure'. Or as the
1549 French edition put it: *Il se faut endurcir contre les adversités présentes.*
'One must harden one self against present adversities.'

The palm stands, in other words, as an icon of endurance, a fitting
iconographical accompaniment to a woman defending herself from

An emblem about facing adversity, 1550

snarling boars and bears. She was a palm growing tall on a lonely island. It, like her, is singular among the vegetation.

Island life was rough. They clung to existence by hunting and foraging. As time went on, Marguerite could do less, encumbered by the island's third inhabitant growing inside her and with whom she had to share her meagre diet. As the seasons turned, the cold encroached for the winter. The way the icy air sliced through their clothes froze them to the core. They must have tended a continual fire to retain some residual warmth in the seemingly unending cold.

According to the reports of the time, bears would sometimes plod towards them through the trees, rising up on their haunches at the sight of danger. A shot from the arquebus with which they'd been left would send the creatures away, terrified by the unfathomable explosion, but other beasts came in the night, a rustle, a breaking twig, giving away the presence of another living creature, hostile, or just curious and hungry.

Months into their punishment, Marguerite gave birth. Labour was, in the period, a moment when life and death regularly met – mothers frequently died trying to bring new life into the world, even when help and the wisdom of previous births were at hand. Marguerite miraculously survived childbirth, evading the potential catastrophic loss of blood or possible infection. But as the days went by in the habitual exhaustion of life with a newborn – screaming, not sleeping – her child grew thinner and thinner; the soft fat of the baby dissolved, the tiny person became a looser, lighter load in her arms. Her child cried and cried, but Marguerite was so malnourished she barely produced any milk. And so her baby, devastatingly, left their harsh world not long after entering it.

A second tragedy shook Marguerite's life soon after that first death. Her lover died too, leaving her unimaginably alone. In her state of grief and exhaustion, each spadeful of dirt she dug for his grave exhausted her. She could scarcely scrape a pit broad enough for his body to fit into, and the peat was only a shallow layer over the bedrock, so he was not buried as deeply as he would have been in France. He was left there as a mound, loosely packed, lying just below a light covering of mossy soil. Bears, wolves and wolverines would come and sniff around the grave and she had to defend it, becoming the sentinel of this personal graveyard. She learned how to use the arquebus through trial and error. She had seen it fired countless times before, but actually loading and holding the long weapon felt awkward and unfamiliar. When it discharged, exploding in an angry outburst, the recoil made her close her eyes and tense her entire body just to remain standing. Each time, the blast frightened anything living in a wide circumference around her and almost knocked her flat onto the hard ground.

The delayed blows of her uncle, the deaths he had plotted, leaving his hands, at least in a literal sense, clean, decimated the tiny world Marguerite had constructed. Marguerite de Navarre, sister of François I and a writer and patron of the arts who was sympathetic to the Reformation, suggested that our stranded Marguerite, without anyone to speak to, turned inwards. The reformed faith preached a closer relationship with God and access to the scriptures in the vernacular. Now it was the only relationship she could have. The book in her hands, a tiny printing of the gospels, became her intermediary with the divine. She must have read and reread the pages, clinging somewhere inside herself, though perhaps she could not quite admit it, to the stories of the miracles, hoping that a New Testament wonder might happen to her.

Colony, Interrupted

Meanwhile, after abandoning Marguerite, Roberval made his way along the northern bank of the St Lawrence river, following Cartier's route closely. He eventually reached Stadacona in the third week of July 1542. There the crew quickly headed to the encampment left vacant by Cartier, eager to prepare themselves for the coming winter and perhaps a little wary of the Stadaconans. Roberval held back from making contact, busying himself and the colonists with work on their new home.

Roberval, whose goal was a stable settlement and earning a profit from its land, renamed the place 'France-Roy', to signal the change of government and a rupture from its previous – and less committed – inhabitants. Unlike Cartier, he was not obsessed with exploring upstream in search of gold. The upper citadel of France-Roy had a grand tower, private chambers, a hall, a kitchen and even an oven and mills, a far cry from Marguerite's miserable dwelling.

Still, despite their attempts to cultivate the land around the settlement, when they drew up an inventory of their stores in September, they concluded that their provisions would not see them through until the following summer. As archaeological and historical evidence has demonstrated, the colonists compensated by rationing their supplies, by adding the local animal and plant resources (cod, porpoise, wild fruit and berries, nuts, mushrooms, etc.) to their diet, and by bartering for fish, game and corn with the Stadaconans. Even when rationed, their meals sound more regular and more sustaining than those of Marguerite.

The spectre of scurvy soon swept through the fort. Over fifty of the inhabitants of France-Roy died during the winter of 1542–3. Cartier knew of an antiscorbutic concoction made from the bark of 'Annedda', the 'tree of life', which had been generously passed to him by the locals and which had saved him more than once from the ravages of the disease, but it seems he broke the chain of knowledge transfer and failed to relay anything about this essential cure to his countrymen. Ethnobiologists have investigated the botanical mystery of the

Iroquois brew and tried to identify which species of coniferous tree was the essence of this indigenous remedy. Was it the eastern white cedar, with its whispering leaves, or the robust white spruce? The black spruce, the towering eastern white pine, the red pine, the aromatic balsam fir, hemlock or the juniper? Recent research has gone further, revealing the bark and leaves of these trees not only contain vitamin C – the absence of which caused the dreaded scurvy – but are also a rich source of a particular set of amino acids. These compounds accelerate recovery because they are involved in bodily processes that support blood circulation and the healing of damaged tissue.[4]

André Thevet described scurvy as an awful plague: 'It begins with the legs, then rises higher and renders the mouth so stinking that it is impossible to endure the breath of a man attacked by this illness. The feet and legs swell, and [a person afflicted is] so feeble that they [cannot] move from one place to another.'[5] When a man was cut open to see what the disease had done to him, the inside of his body was found to have putrefied from within; his spleen and liver were spotted with blood and white blisters mottled his entrails.

The winter, its cold and plagues, eventually passed, and on 6 June 1543 Roberval set out with seventy men in eight smaller vessels to see if there was a route west. He also decided to try to establish a second settlement further up the river at Hochelaga, expanding their colonial presence in the St Lawrence region. The expedition did not bear fruit: eight men died and a boat was lost.

Just two days after Roberval returned to France-Roy, ships from France arrived to put an end to this phase of French colonial activity in North America. King François was again going to war with Charles V, who now had Henry VIII of England as an ally and was intending to attack France. Roberval had to return. The abandonment of the colony was not entirely due to failure, then, though it could hardly be described as an imperial success. Rather, this chapter was brought to an end because empire was suddenly bumped down the list of priorities due to what was happening back in Europe. In 1548, Charles V wrote instructions to his son, the future King Philip II, in case ill health got the better of him. He warned his son to watch out for the French as they might try to send ships across the Atlantic, threatening his dominion, encroaching on his territory. Although the monarch-to-be needn't be too worried, as the French 'have not shown much tenacity, and if a rigorous opposition is maintained, they give way at once and withdraw'.[6]

An Unexpected Catch

Some say Marguerite endured the island for a year, some more than two. She must have built a routine, finding where the black-and-white razorbills, or murres, nested so that she could catch her meals. Cod or tiny silver capelin might have been her choice on other days. Food was probably always the first concern of the day. At least water was plentiful, as the rain sits in pools on the island's granite bedrock. I imagine she selected a dip in the rock at the sea edge for her latrine, hidden from view, though there was, of course, no one to spoil her modesty. Later in the day, she would collect twigs in among the low shrubs, driftwood from the island's shore, or pile up clods of peat, all fuel for the fire to keep out the tyrannical cold.[7] On a day when the wind was not too harsh, she might walk along the granite edge of the island, jumping occasionally over pools in the rocks and casting a stone into the sea to hear its satisfying plop as it entered the water.

Perhaps it was such a day when her prayers for safe transport from that place were finally and miraculously answered. There, off in the distance – she had to look twice to make sure she was not imagining boats coming into view. Her heart began to race. Bedraggled, dirty, in torn and tattered clothing, she shouted and waved on the shoreline, desperate to be noticed by the passing vessels. She made as much noise as it was possible to summon from her malnourished body, willing with every bellow that her sounds would reach human ears. The fishermen at first could not quite believe their eyes: a spectre of a woman on the shore, urgently waving, crying words they could not yet make out. They took a rowing boat towards the shore, and as much as their eyes determined she must be a stranger, a wild thing, their ears now made them reconsider: she was speaking French. The Breton fishers took aboard this unexpected catch and shipped her back to France.

In Marguerite's story, in contrast to many of the others in this book, there haven't been the same disastrous navigational mishaps or sudden batterings by the weather which wreaked havoc on many early journeys that Europeans took across the oceans. She was flung ashore in an inhospitable place on purpose – and by a relative no less. These peculiar and cruel circumstances mean her voyage out across the Atlantic and back again is something of an anti-travel story. The conventional outcomes of travel – profit, transformation, knowledge – all fail to materialize from Marguerite's marooning. Everything was ventured, yet nothing tangible was gained. The island, a proxy for Roberval, stripped from her all that had come to enrich her life. She ended up with less than she had when she departed from La Rochelle in 1542.

Marguerite is in some ways the foil to Gonzalo Guerrero, who turned his back on the person he was before and decided he was better off not returning to Europe. Unlike Guerrero, whose shipwreck yielded an opportunity for a different life, Marguerite was cast away and left with a single wilting possibility: survival. Although she was cast out from Roberval's colony for her relationship with a man, she became a sort of Mary Magdalene, the biblical prostitute who turned pious. Her story, then, in time, became a way of thinking about how human nature, when challenged by the forces of the natural world, might be improved rather than degraded.[8] Her tale also encapsulates the fantasy of a self-sufficient colonizer who neither requires nor is changed by anything 'outside' them. This chimes with notions of Europeanness emerging in the sixteenth century which purposefully overlooked the ways in which 'European' knowledge has always been generated in relation – often obfuscated or violent relation – to ways of knowing elsewhere in the world:[9] 'No culture is immune to other cultures. No idea, invention, or technological device, whether in art, society, or science, is made by a single person or produced by a single sealed-off culture.'[10]

Marguerite's story of miraculous self-sufficiency contrasts so pointedly with what happened to Roberval's colony, which was ravaged by scurvy because he did not possess the indigenous knowledge of the St Lawrence Iroquois to stave it off. Roberval needed to be open to knowledge from elsewhere, but he was too wary of the people who had long thrived in the region, and so inadvertently let many of those he was responsible for suffer and die. His story is a fable illustrating the unavoidability of interdependence; hers is a fable of transcending that need.

Marguerite's endurance was remarkable, and not just in a physical sense. Although she has been the object of so much historical research, little has been found in the archives about her. Women's lives in the sixteenth century were not as regularly recorded in official documentation. Her story survived first by word of mouth and then in print, in the account by André Thevet but also in literary works, where it features in Marguerite de Navarre's collection of stories called the *Heptameron* and François de Belleforest's compendium, the *Tragic Histories*, which was an early modern bestseller and indeed retold the story of Enrique. What's more, even though Roberval was more powerful than Marguerite and was known to those who told her story, it is her tale, not his, to which they gave primacy. She usurped the narrative space of the swashbucklers in the typical travellers' tales of the age and highlighted the all too familiar brutality of those men. She suffered at the hands of one of them, but, in the end, did not become another casualty of their actions.

WORLD EVENTS

1542
Charles V establishes the
first Viceroyalty of Peru
– Lima, Peru

1543
Nicolaus Coper-
nicus publishes *On
the Revolutions of
the Celestial Spheres*
– Nuremberg,
Germany

1545
Council of Trent
begins, initiating the
Counter-Reformation
– Trento, Italy

1542
Bonne Aventure,
France

SHIPWRECKS

1547

Ivan the Terrible crowned
as the first Tsar of Russia
– Moscow, Russia

Death of Henry VIII,
succeeded by Edward VI
– London, England

1551

Ottoman empire captures
Tripoli - Tripoli, Libya

1554

São Bento, Portugal: Ran aground
at the mouth of the Msikaba river,
South Africa.

*Espiritu Santo, San Esteban, Santa
Maria de Yciar*, Spain: Wrecked off
Padre Island, Texas.

Bona Confidentia, Bona Esperanza,
England: stranded near the Kola
peninsula (Russia).

1552

São João,
Portugal

PART FIVE

Living with the Enemy

A letter to the King of Portugal from the coast of South America. It's dated 1 June 1553 and signed at the bottom by Tomé de Sousa, the first governor general of Brazil. After the usual epistolary ingratiation and diligent listing of the very important things he had achieved – look at all I have done fortifying defences, putting things in order, gathering information – Sousa relayed the story of a disaster:

> A fleet departed from Spain with approximately 300 individuals aboard, heading towards the River Plate. Part of this fleet landed on the Island of Príncipe along the coast of Guinea, while another part landed between the River Plate and São Vicente, approximately 60 leagues away, near the Rio dos Patos. Sadly, nearly all of the fleet was lost, and only around 60 people were saved, with almost half of them being women. Among the survivors was the wife of the governor, Fernando de Saraiva, who tragically passed away. Accompanying her were Saraiva's daughters and relatives, including nine or ten noblewomen, among others.
>
> Remarkably, when the indigenous people encountered these survivors, recognizing their similarity to us and learning they were considered our brothers, they showed kindness to them instead of harm, seeing them as helpless as they were. A captain from that group came named João do Sollazar, from the household of the Duke of Aveiro, who had made him a member of the Order of Santiago. When he arrived at São Vicente, I was already there, and he requested that I retrieve those lost men and women. I considered it a service to God and to Your Highness to organize their rescue by ship and bring them to São Vicente. It seemed to me that the women would arrive so exhausted from their hardships that they would marry whoever could provide them with sustenance, while the men would establish their own smallholdings . . .

A little further on in the letter, Sousa had some better news:

While journeying along this coast, I hear fresh rumours of gold among the natives, which I will believe, no matter how much I desire it to be true, only when I see it for myself. Nevertheless, I have ordered twelve men and a clergyman, a brother of the Society of Jesus, to go inland, and they are ready to go into the mainland following the route from Porto Seguro, and others have already been through Pernambuco. May Our Lord wish that these men bring news of some great treasure they might have found, given that Your Highness shares in whatever the Lord has.[1]

See how the ripples of shipwreck slowly make their way outwards from the site of catastrophe. A message first carried footstep by footstep from wreck to friendly settlement. Then written down, folded and sealed, and dispatched on a precious but flimsy piece of paper across an ocean. Sousa promises to be brief, but there is so much to tell: how he wishes he could have a proper conversation with his king and not be limited by pen and paper and time.

The fleet mentioned by Tomé de Sousa had departed Spain in April 1550 and did not have an easy voyage. The main ship became lost and was looted by French pirates from La Rochelle when they were sailing down the Guinea coast. One of the two smaller ships (caravels) was nearly wrecked, but succeeded in making its way across the Atlantic to the Portuguese settlement of São Vicente (present-day São Paulo state in Brazil) before bearing south to the island of Santa Catarina. Eventually the main ship in the fleet joined it. The other caravel disappeared without trace en route and was never heard from again. The bedraggled assembly of survivors decided to dispatch a group of people overland to Asunción in Paraguay (Spanish territory) to alert the Spanish of their arrival, while the rest remained at Santa Catarina and prepared to make the final leg to the River Plate by sea.

Fortune, however, had other plans for them: their largest ship, the *San Miguel*, sank in November 1550. Now not everyone could travel by sea, as there was not enough room on their only remaining vessel. They tried to decamp, some on land, some by sea, edging south towards the province of La Plata, but like all the other vessels

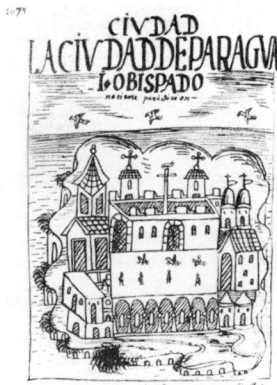

The city of Asunción (Paraguay), 1615

before it, the caravel sank, drowning their immediate hopes of reaching their destination.

The fleet was intended to carry the first of two waves of Spanish colonists associated with Don Diego Sanabria, who had succeeded to the governorship of La Plata after his father had died unexpectedly in Seville before he could travel to South America. Don Diego had stayed back in Spain to raise finance for and then accompany the second wave, but he had sent this trio of vessels in advance under the command of Juan de Salazar (who is mentioned by Tomé de Sousa in his letter). The colonists were intended to populate the city of Asunción; and to prevent Spanish men from marrying and having children with local indigenous women, there were more than fifty unwed or widowed women on board these first ships. They included Don Diego's stepmother, Doña Mencía Calderón y Ocampo, who had managed unusually to secure some of the gubernatorial privileges of her late husband and has since become known as the first *adelantada*, 'woman governor', of Spanish Latin America.

Stranded in a place known today as Laguna, the remaining group of Spaniards was fractured by conflict. Doña Mencía deposed the captain, Juan de Salazar, and placed Hernando de Trejo, her son-in-law, in charge. A second expedition now set off for Asunción, which lay around 1,000 kilometres away as the parrot flies, to let their fellow countrymen know what had happened to the fleet and to request help. These trekkers finally arrived in Asunción in July 1552,

at which point the marooned Spaniards in Laguna had been struggling for nearly two years to eke out an existence from the shellfish
and reptiles they could find on the coastline.

Meanwhile, the deposed captain, Salazar, and around a dozen
soldiers defected from the new leadership and headed not inland, as
the two parties headed to Asunción had, but northwards along the
coast to São Vicente. This breakaway party was the group mentioned
in Sousa's letter. They fashioned a small boat with the help of the
Guarani locals and a Spaniard who had 'gone native' among them.
Yet again, though, the waves treated them badly and their makeshift
craft fell apart, plunging them into the sea. Kicking, clinging to bits
of the broken boat, they tried to keep their heads above water. They
scarcely made it to the shore alive. They had to ask for the assistance
of the locals, who, promisingly, told them that they were not so far
from their desired destination. They were fifty kilometres away from
São Vicente, a trekkable distance. It was June 1553. They had left
Spain three years ago.

On board this fleet which had sunk mercilessly ship by ship into
the Atlantic was a man whom, if you'd been asked, you might have
labelled as the odd one out in the crew. Among those fortunate sixty
survivors of the serial wrecks, there was a gunner from northern

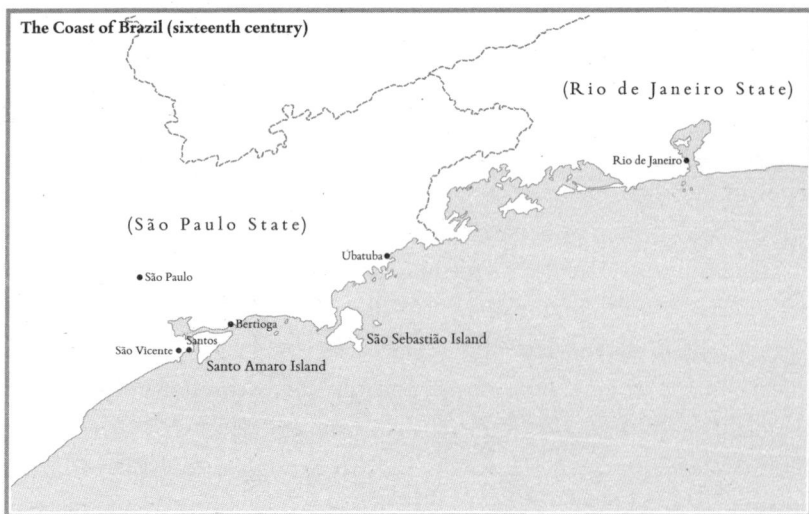

The Coast of Brazil (sixteenth century)

(Rio de Janeiro State)

Rio de Janeiro

(São Paulo State)

Ubatuba

• São Paulo

• Bertioga
Santos   São Sebastião Island
São Vicente •
Santo Amaro Island

Europe called Hans Staden.[2] He'd made it all the way to the picture-postcard coast of Brazil from the landlocked province of Hesse in present-day Germany. We do not know the exact reasons why Staden became a soldier or why he left Germany for Lisbon, but we do know that this unintended sojourn on Brazilian shores was not his first. Now in Spanish service, he had voyaged on a Portuguese ship to Brazil a few years earlier, in 1548, under the captaincy of António Martins Penteado. He was an itinerant gun for hire. This may, at first, seem surprising, but Germans skilled with artillery – be that cannons or more portable weapons – were the men of choice in many European fleets from the fifteenth century onwards. In the early sixteenth century, Germans constituted the majority of *bombardeiros* in Portuguese service and these migrant artillery experts were rewarded with yearly pensions from the crown. Under Portuguese regulations, *bombardeiros'* share of the booty if their ship captured another (as indeed Staden's vessel did off the coast of Morocco) was twice that an ordinary sailor, so they were not at the bottom of the nautical pecking order. When Staden ended up on the coast of Brazil for the second time, he was thus a seasoned interloper, ready to serve anyone who would pay him. The way he fell between the cracks of empires and states, and moved between languages, would lead both to the problems that beset his life and to their solutions.

9.   Frontiers of Hatred

Hans Staden's skills were put quickly to use by the Portuguese, there on the coast of Brazil where the success of the captaincy of São Vicente was precarious. Over the course of the 1540s, resistance to the Portuguese by groups of the local Tupi peoples had increased significantly as the Portuguese sought indigenous slaves to work the land or the six sugar mills that had been established in and around the towns of Santos and São Vicente. This culminated shortly after Staden's arrival in the formation of a fearsome coalition of indigenous groups under a pair of Tupinambá leaders, Aimberê and Cunhambebe.[1] During the ensuing series of conflicts known as the War of the Tamoios, Portuguese settlements were constantly under threat.

The coast of Brazil was inhabited by a complex mosaic of different peoples. They quarrelled, traded, told stories and gossiped in words belonging to more than forty different language groups.[2] Europeans, though, reduced them to simplistic catch-all categories: Tupi on the coast and Tapuia inland. The Tupi–Guarani peoples living close to the shoreline did speak related dialects and to an extent shared a common culture, but dealings between groups were often hostile. The Portuguese simply ignored most of the intricate interrelations between communities and subdivided the Tupi into broad groups that made sense to them in terms of their own political and military activities. They allied themselves with the Tupinikin, whose enemies were the Tupinambá to the north (who allied themselves with the French) and the Carijós to the south.[3] Imperial rivalries between European powers mapped themselves onto, and were consequently shaped by, the patterns of local frictions.

One thing above all stood out for European observers: these groups lived for war with their enemies. As the anthropologist Eduardo Viveiros de Castro has put it, if Europeans had wars of religion in the sixteenth century, then the Tupi had a religion of war.[4] Early modern

European representations of Tupi peoples often flattened their culture out to cannibalism alone, but the essential enmity at the heart of Tupi culture was not simply a thirst for blood. Anthropologists have worked hard to see the practice of anthropophagy and the culture of warfare related to it as part of how the Tupi conceived of themselves and how they made sense of their place in space and time. Rituals connected to the capture, killing and eating of enemies reveal an ontological openness among the Tupi: they needed people around them who were different in order to understand themselves. Cannibalistic rituals and the way that warriors acquired names as a result of their exploits represented a way of recording events, placing individuals within a cycle of past losses, present victories, future vengeance. This is not to gloss over the violence of Tupi society out of some misplaced and patronizing approval of any kind of cultural difference – that would be another form of exoticization – but rather to take seriously the complexity of indigenous ways of thinking.

While European observers struggled to grasp all that this desire for 'vengeance' entailed, they nevertheless tried to take advantage of the perpetual warring between groups. In contrast – and sometimes very stark contrast – to the enslavement of Africans, indigenous indenturing was formally outlawed in the *regimento* of 1548, which set out rules for the colonial administration of Brazil: the Portuguese were not supposed to raid villages simply in order to take slaves. There was, however, legal wiggle room, which permitted the enslavement of prisoners of war.[5] The Portuguese therefore incited skirmishes between the Tupinikin and the Tupinambá in order to acquire the prisoners as slaves. One issue, though, was that the captives thought it would be more honourable to die at the hands of their conquerors and refused to be sold. And the Tupinikin themselves were not always willing to pass on their prisoners: they wanted to ritually kill them in the traditional manner.[6] So Portuguese tactics encountered challenges that, to their way of thinking, were unpredictable and hard to understand.

Within the context of seemingly perpetual skirmishes between the Tupinikin and Tupinambá, the governor of Brazil had orders to bolster Portuguese defences along the coast. Indeed, the need for force to protect São Vicente and Santos, the two primary settlements of the captaincy, had been underlined in a letter to the Portuguese king in 1548.[7] After his arrival in 1553, Staden was sent to an outpost intended to reinforce the Portuguese presence – not São Vicente or Santos, where he would be surrounded by other Europeans, but rather a fort on the fringe of the captaincy at Bertioga.

Located opposite the eastern tip of the island of Santo Amaro and some fifty kilometres away from São Vicente by boat, Bertioga lay right on the embattled seam between Tupinambá and Tupinikin lands: it was on the front line, subject frequently to raids.

When Staden arrived in Bertioga, the fort was manned by a band of brothers whose father was Portuguese and whose mother was Tupi. Such blended individuals, fluent both in Portuguese and the Tupi languages, moved between worlds, brokering encounters, sharing knowledge. Bertioga had been burned down two years previously when some seventy canoes of men sprang on the dirt house and flimsy fortifications. The *mamelucos*, as mixed-race individuals were known, managed to withstand the attack, holed up in an adobe hut, but everything else needed to be rebuilt, and rebuilt better.

The captaincy of São Vicente in 1640

Still, the devastating attack confirmed the strategic importance of Bertioga as a first line of defence against the hostile Tupinambá. So the bulwarks were reconstructed. The Tupinambá's assaults were seasonal, synced with the bounty of the local environment: they came in November for the *abatí* (corn) ripening, August for the *paratí* (mullet) spawning. But as with the sudden downpours of the region, the Portuguese and the *mamelucos* never quite knew when arrows might rain down on them.

The improved defences at Bertioga certainly gave the Tupinambá second thoughts about attacking the fort directly, but they merely changed tactics: gliding in their canoes by night straight past Bertioga to São Vicente and seizing whatever hostages they could, making the most of a misplaced sense of security. To guard the mouth of the inlet, the Portuguese built a second bulwark, which squatted on the corner of Santo Amaro island facing Bertioga, its cannons trained over the blue mouth of the river towards the hump of forested mainland.

Staden went to inspect this tiny defensive outpost. No Portuguese gunner would take the risk of serving there: it was too flimsy, too exposed. Staden was not impressed, but he agreed to a four-month posting. They promised him some help and to pay him a good wage.

At the end of this initial stint, Staden was invited to stay longer by Tomé de Sousa, the governor general of Brazil. The outpost was upgraded to make it less vulnerable. Staden agreed to be stationed there for a further two years, on the promise that he would be able to depart afterwards without hindrance on the first Portuguese ship back to Europe and that he would receive his due recompense from the King of Portugal for his services.

And so Staden made a life for himself there, on the corner of Santo Amaro. The island slopes up from the water to forest, glossy green above and thick shade below. In among the palette of innumerable browns and greens are bursts of red: hibiscus flowers, the limbs of trees cradling tufts of bromeliad in crooks of bark. Humidity slumps over everything, all year, interrupted here and there by a stray breeze wandering in from the Atlantic and the heavy drumming of rain from above. The tangled roots of the mangroves, low, swampy, fertile, are a breeding place for birds and fish, but also for nuisance clouds of flies and gnats that must have bitten and bothered the German. For company he had a Carijó slave. For food he had the game that could be caught among the vegetation: armadillo, capybara, deer, wild boar. For work, his task was to watch, and watch, and fire at the sight or sound of prowling Tupinambá boats. It was work for the eyes, but also the ears; he trained himself to distinguish the rhythmic splash of paddles from the fish, and the birds, and the lapping of the water at the shore.

This was a far cry from Hesse where Staden had grown up. Throughout his youth, he moved between the small fortified towns of the region. Even though Hesse was relatively poor compared to other parts of Germany, they nonetheless would have had their markets and shops, the infrastructure of small-town life. Dense forest blanketed much of the region, rising up over the mountains. But now he had swapped those pine forests for mangroves and jungle.

Some time into his isolated posting, Staden received some surprise guests. A Spaniard, and a fellow German called Heliodorus Hessus whom he had first met in 1553 when he arrived in São Vicente on his last legs after his lengthy ordeal crossing the Atlantic. Staden's slave had set traps the night before, so Staden went to see what they might have caught. He walked through the undergrowth between the trees, his thoughts on whether they would find a boar or a fleshy armadillo for dinner together that evening.

The screams hit him first, slicing through the mottled shadows beneath the canopy. Then he saw them. On all sides, racing towards him, the people he was supposed to guard against. In the time it took to turn and see there was no way out, they were upon him. In a Christian reflex of helplessness, he petitioned God to take mercy on him. The blows pummelled him into the soil, pain seared through his leg as an arrowhead punctured his skin. His body was jerked every which way as the clothes were torn from him: jacket, hat, shirt all ripped off until he was naked in the dirt. They were arguing: I got him first. No, I did. Two men pulled Staden roughly to his feet. He was dragged hastily through the trees, sunlight making him close his eyes as he was hauled along to where their canoes were hidden. There were more of them there, waiting to see whether the ambush had yielded a prize. At the sight of Staden, naked, restrained, the waiting Tupinambá hurtled towards him, threatening that they would eat him. Their leader pronounced that they would avenge on him the deaths of their friends and family at the hands of the Portuguese. He would be ceremonially killed in a ritual feast to solemnize their victory over their enemy.

The arguments continued. Several of the Tupinambá each claimed to have captured him; they disagreed over who should take the glory. Unable to reach a consensus, some wanted to kill him there and then, and divide his body into spoils they could take to their villages. Staden did not know where the final blow would come from. He looked tentatively around, waiting for someone to strike. But the leader of the attack declared that he would not die that day. He would be brought home alive with them, and once they were back they would gather as a community, brew beer and prepare a feast. Then they would devour on him. Ropes were knotted around his neck and he was tethered to a canoe as they pushed off from the shore.

Staden had become the latest casualty in the long-standing cycle of vengeance and counter-vengeance between the Tupinikin and the Tupinambá. He was now both living enemy and spoil of war; he had been stripped and dragged into a different culture whose workings he had little sense of, but which he would, over his time as a captive, come to understand better.

History in Plumes

Near Santo Amaro, among the roots and rocks at the water's edge, the scarlet ibis nests. The blush of its feathers, their deep flame, meant that its plumage was highly prized. We tend to imagine Brazil in the colours of its flag, the green rainforest, the blue and yellow of sky, sea and sand. But back in the sixteenth century, Brazil was known for a different colour: red. It came from these feathers, exported as luxury rarities, and it came from the brazilwood that was felled all along the coast and transported back to Europe to make dye for cloth.

It was that wood which gave Brazil the name it still has to this day. It was not the first name imposed on the region by the Portuguese, however; they initially called the coastline of South America that they claimed 'Terra da Santa Cruz', the 'Land of the Holy Cross'. The new name quickly came to replace the initial one, and in referring to a natural resource that was taken by Europeans it remains inseparable from commercial exploitation, slavery and deforestation, the legacies of which are ever-present in contemporary Brazil. Back in the sixteenth century too, the change caused some consternation: the Portuguese royal chronicler João de Barros, who compiled one of the most extensive records of his country's imperial history, grumbled:

> It is as if the name of a wood to dye cloth were more important than the name of the wood that gave tincture to all the sacraments by which we are saved and that was spilled on it by the blood of Jesus

Christ . . . I advise . . . all those who read this, that they give to this land the name that was so solemnly bestowed upon it . . . [lest] we may be accused of being more devoted to brazilwood than to the cross.[8]

Staden warned the Tupinambá that the Tupinikin had already hunted that season where the scarlet ibises nested on Santo Amaro,

A Tupinambá feather mantle, 1689

but they still wanted to go and see if they could capture the grey fledglings and the bright-red adult birds. Hundreds and hundreds of feathers would be plucked and woven into mantles the length of ball gowns, which would envelop the wearer in vibrant plumage from head to toe.

The makers of these mantles would fasten each feather with delicate precision to a mesh of natural fibres. If you look at these cascades of vermilion in a museum today, you would be forgiven for thinking that you were staring at the taxidermy specimen of some mighty, extinct avian species. The French chronicler Jean de Léry described the craftsmanship as unmatchable, the result comparable to deep-napped velvet.[9] The capes made from these feathers were among the most important items in Tupi culture, worn during the most important ceremonial occasions: they were bridges to the ancestral realm during funeral rites, markers of power in festivities, and a kind of robe during cannibalistic feasts to celebrate triumph in war.[10] As Staden would later say of the Tupinambá: 'They know no treasures. Only feathers.' These were not mere costumes, as Europeans understood them, or luxuries for show, but spiritual objects that, when worn by shamans, enabled them to transform into birdlike creatures, crossing the barrier between the living and the dead. The scarlet ibises themselves, understood as mediators between realms, infused their feathers with their power.

Although these capes were not understood on their own terms, they were transported back to Europe to enter the collections of the wealthy who sought to gather so-called 'curiosities' from the world over. The demand for featherwork objects, interestingly, produced a bit of a market in artificially coloured plumes that looked like they came from rare birds but, in fact, came from more common species. After Europeans introduced domestic chickens to Brazil, their feathers were dyed red using brazilwood. To produce yellow feathers, like those at the top of some Tupinambá mantles, common parrots had their feathers plucked and then the feather follicles treated with a concoction made from the blood of a particular toad which made the bird's plumage grow back yellow in colour. Pêro de Magalhães Gândavo, in an early Portuguese account of Brazil, noted this technique for creating fakes and that it was explicitly used by the Tupi to deceive. He didn't specify who was being duped but we can surmise it was Europeans being taken in by the ersatz feathers.[11]

The eleven surviving capes from the early modern period were, until very recently, all in European collections; severed from their spiritual functions as part of Tupi life, they hang, for the most part, silently behind glass. In 2024, however, after more than two decades of negotiations between the present-day Tupinambá of Olivença in the state of Bahia and the Danish National Museum in Copenhagen, one mantle, 120 centimetres of scarlet plumage crowned with tufts of yellow, returned across the ocean to enter the National Museum of Brazil. In anticipation of the return, Chief Maria Valdelice said to *Piauí*:

> My grandmother used to say that the loss of the mantle weakened the Tupinambá people. I hope the relic will return soon to reinvigorate us. It doesn't matter if it arrives in Bahia or in Rio. The fundamental thing is that it returns. To date, no ordinance was issued recognizing our territory. The federal government has already identified the land as belonging to the Tupinambás, but has not yet ratified it. Meanwhile, the territory is invaded by resorts and sand mining companies. Without the ordinance, we cannot do anything. May the mantle bring new strength to the Tupinambás of Olivença! We need our land to be demarcated.[12]

The mantle's repatriation from Denmark shows that, alongside an overwhelming history of indigenous dispossession, genocide and enslavement, there is also incredible endurance.

What Kind of Stranger?

Staden and his captors did not find the scarlet-plumed *guará* (ibis) peacefully nesting. They found, instead, Tupinikin warriors and some Portuguese waiting to pounce and rescue him. Staden's slave had escaped when he had been ambushed and had gone to raise the alarm. The Tupinambá canoes were still safely two gunshots' distance from their enemies on the shore. At first they changed course to pull away, but the Tupinikin goaded them: they were cowards if they did not come and fight. Lead shot and arrows flew across the water towards the Tupinambá and their captive. The chief untied Staden's hands and thrust a gun and powder into them. He had firepower too, but he needed Staden to wield it. The German had no choice but to shoot at his friends. The exchange of fire did not last long, though, as Staden's captors did not want to risk their enemies taking to their own canoes and chasing after them, so they turned once more, and began to paddle off down the shoreline. As they passed the forts on either side of the river mouth, where Staden had been stationed, the chief forced him to his feet to humiliate him and to humiliate his friends watching from the ramparts. Two shots blasted towards them, but it was a waste of ammunition. The canoes had already moved swiftly out of range and the cannonballs plopped into the water far from them. Some of the Tupinikin took to their canoes and tore off in pursuit, but soon realized this was not a race they could win. Staden's captors rowed too quickly and had too much of a head start.

When they landed on another island later that afternoon, Staden took stock of his wounds. He could barely see; the bruises on his face had blossomed and swollen, forcing his eyelids shut. He was in agony from the arrow wound in his leg and could only hobble painfully around. He wept and wailed to his God. This incited no pity. The Tupi thought his moaning and his tears were dishonourable. He was not behaving as a captive should. In their world, an enemy prisoner should accept their fate: 'The Tupinambá wanted to be sure that the other they would kill and eat was fully defined as a man, who understood and desired what was happening to him.'[13]

They spent the night on the mainland. Staden had his first experience of sleeping in a net hammock and was mocked all evening. You are my pet, they said to him. The following day, they continued to make their way back home. Black storm clouds brewed on the horizon and the wind began to pick up. They turned to Staden, asking him to intervene with his God. He did so, praying for a sign that would show them that God was with him, that even if he seemed powerless, bound and unarmed, he had a supernatural ally looking out for him.

This would not be the last time that Staden played a shamanic role.

And every time he sought intercession from the heavens, it would trouble how his captors saw him. What kind of man was he? Was he truly an enemy? What would happen if he was harmed? Such doubts and questions were integral to his survival, but they were tied to moments, to phenomena like the weather, which he could not easily predict and which were ever-changing. In short, he sometimes seemed to have power, but any power he seemed to have was fleeting.

Bound in the canoe, Staden could not see what was happening to the weather as he muttered his pleas to God. The Tupinambá began to look back at the clouds, relief blowing over them. The storm was moving in another direction. Whatever the captives were saying seemed to work.

They spent the night again in hammocks, telling Staden that tomorrow they would arrive back in their country. Staden was not delighted to hear this. The journey was a prolongation of his life. The ritual, his death, would start once they arrived.

Not One of Them

Ubatuba was a small village on a hill with seven huts, or *malocas*: rectangular multi-family lodges made of wood and thatched with palm. Some were six metres wide and three or four times that in length. Tupi villages, like Ubatuba, were encircled by a protective wooden palisade to defend them from the frequent attacks of their enemies.

Just outside, each village cleared an area for cultivating vegetables, primarily manioc roots, which were an important component of their diet and which came to be an essential source of sustenance also for the French and Portuguese in Brazil. Manioc was remarkable for its versatility: it could be brewed into beer, or made into a range of different flours by grating, straining and drying the flesh of the root in different ways.

In today's Brazil, you can still consume it in myriad forms: boiled or fried, or the flour made into pancakes. It gives the famous Brazilian cheese bread, *pão de queijo*, its characteristic chewiness.

As Staden walked past the women pulling these tubers from the ground on his way up towards the village for the first time, he was

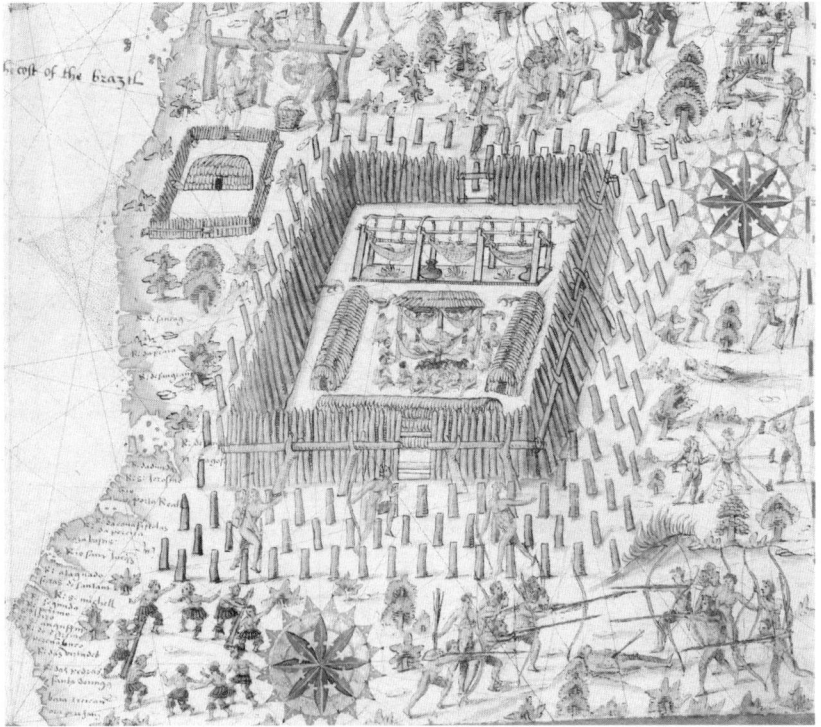

Map of the coast of Brazil, 1542

forced to declare to them: I, your food, am coming. The women ran up to him and thwacked him with their fists, saying repeatedly that they took revenge on him for those who had been killed. It was a humiliating welcome which emphasized the symbolic role that he would play as a captive, a body on which the rituals of vengeance would be played out.

Staden had acquired some fluency in the Tupi languages during his time in Brazil, so could understand what was being said around him, but his lack of familiarity with Tupi ceremony and protocol meant he could not foresee exactly what was in store. The hard task of comprehension for him was translating intentions, intuiting preoccupations, and the words he heard around him only gave a partial insight.

Two brothers, Nhaêpepô-oaçu and Alkindar-Miri, told Staden that he would be sent to their paternal uncle, Ipirúguaçu, who

Manioc roots as depicted by Albert Eckhout, 1640–50

would keep and then kill him. Rather than staying in Ubatuba, then, he was to be sent to reciprocate Ipirúguaçu's gift of a captive to Alkindar-Miri the previous year. Captives brought honour and prestige as their killer would take on new names that were a record, a memory, of those he had slain and the battles in which they were taken.

But first, the *poracé*: a dance. The women dragged Staden by the cords tied around him, yanking so hard at times that he felt strangled. In the middle of them all, exposed and powerless, Staden asked: are you going to kill me? The reply came back: not yet. No sooner was the reprieve granted than a woman grabbed hold of his head, the edge of something sharp glinting in her hands. She scraped it across his forehead, but not to make him bleed. She shaved off his eyebrows. As she went to remove his beard, he began to resist more violently. He writhed. He twisted. Too much movement to let the sharp edge do its work across his jawline. She left him alone, with the promise she would shave it off another day. His facial hair was the last frontier separating him culturally from the world in which he was now immersed. In the woodcuts that accompanied the original printing of his account, it is his beard that identifies him.

In language, the line between Staden and his captors will have been reiterated subtly but persistently each time they used the first-person plural, for in Old Tupi there are two forms of 'we', where English only has one: an inclusive 'we' (*oré*), which includes the person

The dance with the *araçoía*, as portrayed in 1557

Hans Staden at the Youngsters' feast, as portrayed in 1557

being addressed in the collective, and an exclusive 'we' (*îadé*), which holds them outside that 'us'. With you or without you.

Staden's difference was also marked with a dance in which he was made to participate in celebration of his captivity. As the village's women encircled him, he stepped in time, the rattle attached to his leg accentuating the rhythm of their movements.

The plumes of an *araçoía* on his head, he was the percussive and visual centrepiece of the dance. Once the music and movement had ended, Staden was handed over to Ipirúguaçu. It had been foretold that the villagers would capture a Portuguese, and now here he was, the manifestation of that prophecy. Staden questioned the accuracy of the prediction, seeing the possibility of disrupting the events beginning to unfold. It wasn't yet true, he protested, because he wasn't Portuguese. He was German, and Germans were friends of the French and thus of the Tupinambá too – but not of the Portuguese, who were allied with their enemies.

And so began a months-long game of mistaken identities. Staden had been found among the Portuguese, so was assumed to be one of them; at this stage, the Tupinambá had no time for the finer points of national identity, how and why he was where he was. Still, he told his captors how he had come to Brazil with the Spanish and been ship-wrecked. That bit of his story was corroborated by a man enslaved to a Galician at Bertioga, but unfortunately the man said that the

Castilians were allies of the Portuguese. Staden insisted that the next time the French came to Ubatuba to trade, they would recognize him as one of their German allies. His hope was that any European would take pity on his plight and play along with his story.

While Staden might have thought of himself as a mercenary without any national affiliation, in practice he was enemy or ally according to circumstance and by association. All he needed, though, was for a seed of doubt to germinate in his captors' minds over who he really was. Only enemies would be killed and eaten.

Lines Redrawn

Staden's claims were soon put to the test when a Frenchman who had integrated himself as a go-between in a nearby village came to visit. Staden's hopes lifted at the thought that a fellow Christian might corroborate his story. The Tupinambá dragged Staden to speak with Carautá-uára, as he had become known. An invisible barrier immediately rose between the two Europeans in spite of Staden's assumption of fellowship: the Frenchman spoke in his own native tongue, a language Staden could not understand. He'd learned Spanish and Portuguese by immersion, a polyglot from his adventures, but he did not know the language of Germany's closer neighbour. Conversation failed. Collusion was impossible. Staden simply could not grasp what he was saying. The Frenchman turned to his captors and spoke in Tupi: he's Portuguese. Eat him. That Staden understood very well and it sent searing panic through him. He begged, *begged* for the Frenchman to tell them not to kill him. Although he did not know the man, this felt like cruelty and betrayal. How could someone with whom he believed he had something in common act like that? He realized that he held somewhere deep inside the assumption that an instinctive bond of fellowship ought to connect anyone of the same religion. He should perhaps have inferred from his own story, however, that people often choose their loyalties based not on abstractions or ideals but on who has the most immediate power over them. And in Europe, of course, Christians warred with Christians more than anyone else.

Led back to his hut, Staden sat on the edge of his hammock and swung his legs round to lie back. Cradled in the netting, its cords and knots pressing into his back and rubbing uncomfortably against his sunburned shoulders, despair rampaged out of him. He screamed. He howled a hymn, the verses giving shape to his loud misery. Life is lived in a vale of tears. His thoughts turned to Jeremiah in the Bible: 'Cursed are those who trust in mortals.'[14]

The Frenchman stayed for two days longer and then departed, leaving Staden to the fate he had sought to ensure would be death.

In the conversation between the Frenchman – probably a *truchement*, a merchant living among the Tupi and facilitating trade – and the German gunner, the *lingua franca* was not a European language, not the Latin that we are taught was the pan-European idiom of cross-cultural exchange, but Tupi. It may not have been the conversation that Staden wanted to have, but it was made possible by a local language both men had learned through immersion.

Thus Spake Cunhambebe

Several days after the Frenchman called Staden Portuguese, thwarting his attempts to refashion himself as an ally, he was taken to the nearby village of Ariró, where the leader was Cunhambebe, renowned in the region and dreaded by Europeans as one of the most tenacious and effective warriors among the Tupinambá.

André Thevet described him as the 'most feared of the country's principals'.[15] Staden was being brought before Cunhambebe to be shown off as a spoil of war.

Drunk on manioc beer, the men of Ariró mocked him and asked whether he, their enemy, had arrived. This was another performative exchange, where questions and answers, if indeed they were expected at all, were scripted, the back and forth a consolidation of their hatred of each other, the enemy among them a symbol of the never-ending cycle of war. Staden did not respond with the expected affirmative, though; he said that he was not their enemy. Trying his luck, he approached Cunhambebe and attempted to flatter him.

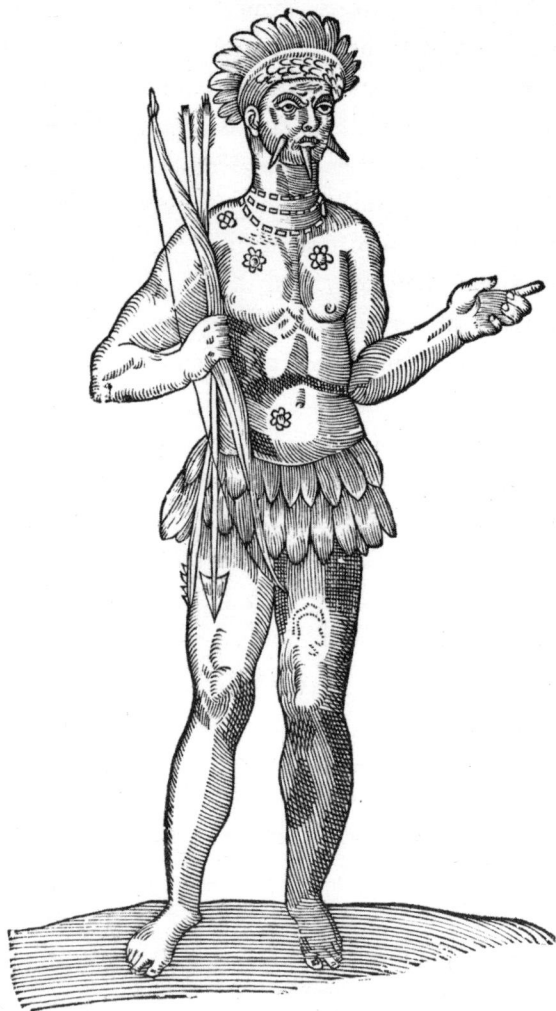

Portrait of Cunhambebe, 1642

The strings of shells around his neck and his piercings were signs of prowess and power, that he was someone to be reckoned with. Cunhambebe proved receptive to having his ego stroked. He stood up and strutted about, seeming to show off, then turned to interrogate Staden. Why had he shot at them when he was at Bertioga? What were the Portuguese up to?

This was Staden's chance to weave his tale and he grabbed the spools of possibility with both hands. He had, he said, been forced to man the fort at Bertioga by the Portuguese. Cunhambebe said that the Frenchman had told him that Staden could not understand a word of what he had said. I've been away from my home for a long time, Staden countered, and have forgotten the language. Cunhambebe remained unconvinced, as I think I would have been. What's more, Cunhambebe had previously captured five Portuguese and they had all tried to persuade him they were really French. What Staden thought was an ingenious tactic ended up being a tried and tested defence – one that was tried and tested and failed. And even this far from home, it turned out, there were people who could fact-check his statements and prove them to be lies.

Nevertheless, Staden went on with his story, flattering Cunhambebe with what he had heard about him among the Tupinikin. He claimed, shifting his tack a little, that the Tupinikin were preparing twenty-five canoes to come and attack the Tupinambá. Perhaps information like that would persuade them he had more value alive. As all the *cauim*, manioc beer, had been drunk, the villagers ceased their conversation and sought a new form of entertainment. Staden had his legs tied together and was made to jump awkwardly around. They mocked him as their hopping food. He was pinched all over as people claimed different parts of him for eating. They called his God a piece of dirt, *teõira*. Even as he left Ariró, they continued to harangue him. But, once more, it was not quite time for his death.

10.   Prophecies and Realities

The prediction that Staden had made to Cunhambebe came true. Twenty-five Tupinikin canoes did head for Ubatuba and attack the village. In the confusion of the surprise assault, as the villagers scrabbled to find their weapons to retaliate, Staden asked to be untied so that he too could take up a bow and arrows. He saw a chance to escape in the fray. He planned to break through the village's stockade and join the Tupinikin, who knew he had been abducted and would recognize him. Even while they were defending themselves, his captors watched Staden closely; no chink of opportunity opened for him to seize. The defence was vigorous enough to hold off the attackers, and the Tupinikin, seeing they would take no captives and make no rescue, retreated.

That evening, the chiefs gathered at the centre of the village. The moon hung bright above them as they discussed when they would kill and eat Staden. They dragged him out into the night air and once more mocked and menaced him as he stood crestfallen on the dirt. As insults and threats darted towards him, Staden looked up. He stared at the moon, seeing in its craters the contours of an angry face. In between their insults, they asked him why he was gazing at the moon. It's angry, he blurted. Who was it angry with? Nhaêpepô-oaçu asked, curious. It's looking at your hut, replied Staden. This was not what the chief wanted to hear. Staden's words flew like a spark towards tinder, instantly igniting his wrath. Hurriedly, Staden changed his story, trying to deflect the moon's and Nhaêpepô-oaçu's anger in a different direction. It's angry at the Carijó slaves. That calmed him.

The Tupinambá believed that the celestial bodies were involved in human affairs, so Staden's attempt to threaten his captors with knowledge of the supernatural's state of mind seems to have been a strategy informed by his observation of the people around him and their beliefs, but it nearly dangerously backfired. Shamans wielded power and authority in Tupi communities, to be sure, but as Eduardo Viveiros de Castro has noted, 'the Tupinambá did everything the prophets and priests told them to do – except what they didn't want to do'.[1] Staden needed to be careful.

Word arrived the next day that, after leaving Ubatuba, the Tupinikin had raided the village of Mambucabe. Although all but one boy managed to escape the attack, the Tupinikin had torched the huts, burning the whole village down to the ground. As the people of Mambucabe were Nhaêpepô-oaçu's allies, he went with his family to help rebuild the village. It took them two weeks to reconstruct the huts.

While these men were away, a Portuguese ship arrived from Bertioga. It fired a cannon to signal its presence and the wish of those on board to talk with the Tupinambá. Staden tried to persuade his captors that his brother – who was French, of course – was on the ship, and that was why the crew wanted to speak with them. The Tupinambá paddled close enough to the vessel to be able to have a conversation with its sailors. When the Portuguese enquired about what had happened to Staden, they gave nothing away but told them to leave and never ask about their captive again. The crew's questions had, to Staden's peril, reassured them that their human prize was valuable, worth keeping.

The two weeks while Nhaêpepô-oaçu was away were especially long and worrisome for Staden. He feared that when the chief returned, his time would be up. One day, during this anxious wait, he heard wailing from the hut of the leader's family. The brother of the leader came to see Staden, and told him that Nhaêpepô-oaçu and many others in his family had fallen very ill in Mambucabe, and Nhaêpepô-oaçu was convinced it was because Staden's God was angry with them. Perhaps his story about the moon hadn't been so miscalculated after all. Staden confirmed that it was true, because they had told him they were going to kill and eat him upon their return. Staden said Nhaêpepô-oaçu ought to come back to Ubatuba and then he would speak to his God and have them restored to health.

When Nhaêpepô-oaçu returned, he reminded Staden about the moon and asked him to cure them of this sudden epidemic. Over the coming days, however, the illness ravaged the chief's family and the wider village. First one of his children died, then his mother, then a brother, then a second child, then another brother. The toll frightened Nhaêpepô-oaçu. Staden reassured him that he would not die, but that when he recovered he had to give up on the idea of killing him.

The pestilence was probably an outbreak of one of the many diseases Europeans had brought to the Americas which decimated a population with no acquired immunity.[2] It served Staden by giving the impression that he had a powerful ally who could lay waste to the village. The whole community stopped threatening and insulting him, so as to appease the invisible forces at work. Such sickness had never happened before when they captured Portuguese, so perhaps he really wasn't Portuguese after all.

Then, one day, Staden's would-be nemesis, the Frenchman Carautá-uára came back to Ubatuba. He callously expected Staden already to be dead, but surprisingly found that far from the German being deceased, he was enjoying a new status in the village and was able to walk about freely. When Carautá-uára stepped into the hut where Staden was, Staden thought it was worth another attempt to persuade him to help. Giving the Frenchman a second chance might just give him a second chance too. Although he was being treated well at the moment, Staden lived with the ever-present worry that his current reprieve would end. He did not want to become the Tupinambá's meat. Staden pulled him aside, so their conversation would not be overheard. In Tupi, he said: I am not Portuguese. I am German; I was shipwrecked with some Spanish, and that was why I had ended up with the Portuguese. He asked the Frenchman to tell the Tupinambá that he wasn't an enemy but a friend, and that they should let the Frenchman take him to where the French ships docked for trade so that he could negotiate passage away from this place.

This time, in the privacy of a hut, Staden could speak candidly. Briefly he became an impromptu preacher, rebuking the Frenchman, reminding him of his faith and the punishments or rewards of the life to come. It was a simple commandment: one Christian should help another. His words seemed to strike home and begin to break apart the Frenchman's callousness. Having to face up to his former actions and look in the eyes the person he had refused to help, Carautá-uára proffered excuses and explanations. Because he was French, he'd had to treat the Portuguese like this; they stood in the way of him and his countrymen gaining a foothold in Brazil and profiting from it. In order to survive – and prosper – he'd had to learn how to adapt to the Tupinambá way of life, and especially to how they treated their enemies.

Now, out of pity or shame or a change of heart, he had been moved. After he left the hut, he went to tell the Tupinambá that Staden was indeed a friend of the French and should be treated as such. He said that he wanted to take him to where their ships docked, so that he could return home. But Staden's captors were not going to let him go so easily. They would release him only in return for a hefty ransom, a full shipload of axes and mirrors and knives and combs and scissors. He was a prisoner taken in enemy land. He would not be given away for free.

The Frenchman departed with a promise that next time a ship arrived from France, he would return for Staden.

Rehearsal Dinner

A few days after, the residents of Ubatuba congregated at a nearby village to celebrate the sacrifice and consumption of one of its captives. For Staden, it would be like watching a rehearsal of his own demise. One of the villagers came up to the foreign spectator and handed him a rectangular object with a smooth but tough exterior of animal skin and a ruff of beige within: a book which they had taken from a Portuguese whom they had captured with the help of the French. It was most likely a book of prayers. Staden spent most of the day, head bowed, leafing through the pages of this gift.

Later on the day before the feast, Staden approached the man about to be roasted and devoured to ask him whether he was ready to face his fate. To Staden's surprise, the man did not seem unduly bothered by what lay ahead. He spoke about what was happening to him with the lightness of somebody talking about going to something like a village fete. He quipped about the quality of the ropes that bound him, saying they were too short and inferior to those his own community made. Pride with a side of gallows humour. Staden, though, felt the need to comfort him. He said that he too was a captive and that he would not eat him. As for the others, he went on, well, they could only eat the man's body, the flesh of which he was made, but they could consume nothing of his soul. The man wasn't certain whether to believe this or not, but was engaged enough in the conversation to ask if it was indeed true. He couldn't be sure about what Staden was saying, because he had never seen God. The German said that he would in the next life.

That evening, the winds got up and violent gales swept across the village. Again, the Tupinambá supposed it was Staden who was to blame: their suspicions had been raised by the fact that he had spent the afternoon sitting and reading the book that he'd been given. They presumed that Staden was a friend of the man that they were going to kill and eat, and that in retaliation for the feast Staden had spoken to his God and summoned the winds. Ultimately, the storm had no effect on the course of events. The feast took place the next day and the captive was killed and consumed. The wind and the rain did stretch what should have been a day's journey back to Ubatuba into a three-day marathon. When the waves became too strong, they were unable to proceed any further in the boats and had to do the rest of the distance on foot. Once more, they blamed Staden for their meteorological struggles. He said it was because there was a boy in their group who kept gnawing away at a human bone while they made their journey.

Closer Encounter

Five months into Staden's captivity, another Portuguese ship sailed into view off the coast of Ubatuba. Although strictly the Portuguese and the Tupinambá were sworn enemies, from time to time they would trade; exchanges of momentary mutual benefit and need. The Portuguese offered knives and sickles, the Tupinambá would provide manioc flour to feed the growing population in and around São Vicente, including several thousand indigenous slaves forced to work the sugar mills. These moments of interdependence weren't without their suspicions. A single canoe would approach the Portuguese ship, goods would change hands as hastily as possible, while a cluster of other Tupinambá boats kept watch, their archers poised to shoot at the first sign of any hostility. There were no thank-yous or pleasantries. The Tupinambá usually brought the interaction to a close by releasing their arrows in the direction of the ship, as if to resume as quickly as possible the usual pattern of hatred and aggression.

On this occasion, the ship anchored off Ubatuba and fired a cannon to open the parley. The conversation that followed was not about the usual trade, but once again about the lost gunner. After the Portuguese had been pushed away last time, they knew they needed to promise something that would make the release of their friend worth the Tupinambá's while. They invented a brother, on board their ship, who would ransom him handsomely. This was all relayed to Staden, who said that if he could talk directly to his brother, the latter could get their father to send a ship filled with goods. The Tupinambá were worried, though, that if Staden was able to speak freely in a language they didn't understand, he would give away the plans they were hatching to attack Bertioga again. He assured them that he wouldn't.

It worked. Staden's captors agreed to take him close to the ship. He needed the Portuguese now to play their roles as he directed, so that the drama's lines would be intelligible to his Tupinambá spectators in one way when they really meant something else entirely. He was putting on a performance of both family and language. Let me speak with one person on their own, he instructed the ship's crew, and don't say anything about my not being French. It needed to look like he was speaking to his brother alone. A man called Juan Sanchez came forward who knew Staden from before. We came to see if you were still alive, Sanchez replied, and to see whether they would be willing to ransom you. If they aren't, we will try to capture some of them so that we can do a hostage exchange. Staden expressed how much peril he was in and that it was unlikely they would want to sell him. He asked for knives and fish hooks so that he could show he had got something out of his fictional brother.

The Tupinambá began to move closer and he sensed they were about to rip him away from the conversation. His parting words were a warning: they are going to attack Bertioga again, beware! As they rowed the canoes back to shore, Staden promised his captors that his brother would break away from the Portuguese and return with a whole ship filled with the implements they wanted. They liked the sound of that.

A Gamble

Preparations for war were commencing. The Tupinambá intended to revisit the place where Staden had been snatched and attack the Tupinikin and Portuguese once more. Canoes and weapons were fashioned and stored at Ubatuba. Staden kept hoping, as they assembled their equipment, that they would leave him behind during the expedition, so that he might have the chance to escape. Sooner than expected, though, an opportunity presented itself. A small French craft was scouting the area for pepper, long-tailed monkeys, and parrots. When it anchored nearby, Staden begged to be taken to it. Although he had not tried to make a break for it when the Portuguese vessel came by, his captors did not want to ferry him out to another European ship.

There had been too many failed attempts at freedom, too many chances of escape that had come and gone. Enough of wile and guile, playing the go-between, inventing stories and scenarios to get near to a vessel on which he could leave that place behind. This time, Staden decided, he would be a straightforward fugitive. He began to sprint to the shore. As he hurtled barefoot out of the village and across the beach, the village raced after him. He could hear his pursuers behind him, the sand rough on his feet as he willed his body forward. A hand grabbed his shoulder; he used the momentum of the man pulling him back to turn and strike. Free again, he pelted forward, splashing into the water until it was up to his waist and it was quicker to hurl himself into the waves and swim. Not thinking, committed to the risk he was taking, he kicked and clawed his way forward through the water. His hand clunked against the stern of the ship. Relief. Fingers grabbing onto the side, he pulled himself upwards. Half of his body was out of the water when something hit him from above and sent him crashing back down into the sea.

He surfaced, wiping the salt water from his eyes. He hadn't really thought what would happen when he got to the ship. Looking up, he realized: the Frenchmen had forced him back. They were not going to let him climb aboard. With the village watching from the shore, the Frenchmen had to make a quick calculation: was saving this man worth annoying their allies? Worth giving up foodstuffs, animals, objects they wanted to obtain and then sell or give to people in France? The cost of rescuing the captive outweighed the benefits.

As Staden swam back to shore, resignation to his fate slowed his strokes. More than at any time before, even that first time when Carautá-uára had told his captors to eat him, he thought he would never get away from that place. Now, in trying to leave, he might have sealed his fate. He paddled slowly, preparing his answers to the

The *Maria Bellete* refuses to let Staden board, as portrayed in 1557

inevitable questions. Why had he dashed off like that? Why had he come back? He opted for indignation in place of contrition: how dare you think I was running away! I was, of course, making sure that when the ship came back, it brought with it lots of goods.

Returning to Where It All Began

Ubatuba was now becoming a hub of war. Canoes arrived from other villages; among them was Cunhambebe. The gathered warriors wanted to take Staden with them. He made a pretence of not wanting to go, hoping that this would lead them to guard him less closely when in Tupinikin territory, and thus he would have a chance to steal away. There were thirty-eight canoes in total, with close to twenty men in each of them. It was going to be a significant offensive. If they'd left him behind, he would have tried to make for the French ship again.

They made camp on the island of Maembipe – São Sebastião, to the Portuguese – about a day away from where they planned to attack. Cunhambebe walked among the men, encouraging them now they were nearing their enemies. He said they should take note of what they dreamed that night in case it foretold good fortune for their campaign. The following day, the leaders gathered around a bowl of boiled fish and as they breakfasted they recounted their dreams. They intended to move closer to their objective and camp again, at a place called Boiçucanga. Staden thought he might be able to make a run for it from there, as it wasn't very far from the Portuguese settlements.

As the fleet made its way along the coast, more canoes appeared from around an island. It was the Tupinikin. Staden and his captors made to hide behind a rock, hoping their enemies would row past them. But the Tupinikin caught sight of them and promptly turned for home. Staden and the Tupinambá gave chase for four hours, trying to catch up with them. There were five Tupinikin canoes and Staden knew all of the people on board, including two *mameluco* brothers who had been with him at Bertioga. A battle ensued. For two hours, the Tupinikin fended off their attackers, firing guns and loosing arrows, but eventually their ammunition was exhausted and the Tupinambá could close in. Some were killed, others taken captive. The battle had been out at sea, so they rowed back to land with their captives to camp for the evening. The sun was setting as they pulled in, exhausted, to Maembipe. The severely wounded prisoners were killed immediately and their bodies chopped up and roasted; the others were taken to the huts of those who had captured them.

Staden went to speak with the two brothers, who had been his friends when he had been stationed on Santo Amaro. They asked whether they were going to be killed and eaten. Staden's response was less than reassuring: 'We have to be content with the things that Almighty God decides to do to us.' He told them that he had already seen one of the other men who had just been captured, a *mameluco* by the name of Jorge Ferreira, being eaten, but he hoped God would protect them. Staden's sympathy, despite their similar plight, was meagre. He said it was more horrifying for him to be in this predicament as he came from far away and was not accustomed from birth to what the Tupi people do. It wasn't so awful for them, he said. The brother told him that what he had suffered had hardened him.

The next day, after they decamped again, to a place called Ocaraçú, Staden encountered Cunhambebe, the fearsome Tupinambá ruler, with a basket of human flesh in front of him. Staden reproached him, saying that even a 'senseless animal hardly ever eats its fellow'. Cunhambebe took another bite and then replied: 'I am a jaguar.'[3]

As dusk fell, the captives were ushered into the heart of the camp, encircled by the watchful eyes of their captors. The air was thick with tension and the rhythmic sound of *maracás*, rattles made from dried gourds, through which the spirits could speak.[4] The prisoners, defiant and unyielding, raised their voices and spoke with indignation, proclaiming their readiness to embrace their fate. 'We shall be avenged,' they declared. 'Captivity cannot diminish our spirit. For the brave, it is an honour to die in enemy lands.' Their demeanour was fearsome, courageous, in stark contrast to Staden's tears upon his own capture, when he, in the eyes of the Tupinambá, had wept unheroically.

They were taken back to the villages of their captors the following day. In Ubatuba again, Staden found that the French ship, his potential salvation, was still lingering at anchor. But that was not to be his ticket home.

Two Departures

As you may have guessed from the existence of Staden's autobiography, his departure from Ubatuba eventually came. But it was not in the form he expected. Rather than being handed over directly to Europeans, he was first given to another ruler. Before he left the village, he told the two *mameluco* brothers to run away into the mountains, advising them of a route whereby they would not be caught. He heard later that they had been successful.

Staden was taken to the village of Taquaraçú-tiba and to a chieftain called Abatí-poçanga. His former captors advised that he should not be mistreated, as he was a man protected by a vengeful deity. Two weeks into this new chapter of captivity, the distant echo of gunfire was heard coming from Niterói, across the bay from what is now Rio de Janeiro. Staden's heart leapt when the news came that a French ship had dropped anchor there to trade with local villages. He asked to be taken to it, claiming his brother awaited him with a trove of goods. Meanwhile, the ship's captain had heard that a European man was being held captive in Taquaraçú-tiba and dispatched two of his men and some locals to the village to investigate. They asked to see Staden and when they saw him naked gave him some of their clothes out of pity. Disillusioned by the greed that had tainted all his previous interactions with the French, he could not quite believe it when they told him that they were there to rescue him. Seizing the moment, he instructed one of the Frenchmen to pretend to be his brother, who had brought some chests of goods to give him. In order to receive the goods, the Tupinambá were told that they needed to take Staden to the ship. The ploy worked, although after some time there, their chief, Abatí-poçanga, asked that Staden fetch the promised goods so that they could head back to the village. The French had not yet loaded their ship, however, so the captain asked Staden to stall.

Once their cargo had been loaded, the final deception unfolded.

The captain, through his interpreter, thanked the Tupinambá leader for his 'care' of Staden. Then ten of the crew all pretended to be Staden's brothers who would not let him be taken back to the village. Claiming he was outnumbered, and throwing in a reference to Staden's dying father for good measure, the captain managed to persuade Abatí-poçanga to allow Staden to leave, softening the blow with a gift of some trinkets. In the end, Staden's liberty was acquired for five ducats' worth of goods. A far from extortionate ransom – the equivalent of about two logs of brazilwood.[5]

Yet just as they were setting sail, a Portuguese ship appeared – the same one that had tried to rescue Staden before. The French, scenting an opportunity, readied their cannons. Staden, thrust into the role of go-between again, called in Portuguese for the ship to surrender. The confrontation escalated; the Portuguese resisted fiercely, fighting off the attack. They wounded several Frenchmen, and Staden too. He had survived the Tupinambá only to face death from European guns.

Finally, in October 1554, Staden's ship departed Niterói for Honfleur, where it arrived the following February. Staden secured a passport to go on to Le Havre and then Dieppe. There he encountered the families of the sailors who had refused to let him on board their ship. They had never made it back to France. Staden took his chance for payback and recounted their indifference to his plight, their abandonment of a fellow Christian, knowing what the Tupinambá would do to him. As wives and parents enquired about their loved ones, he hinted at divine retribution for the sailors' callousness. The crew's fate, the families' tragedy, all to his mind revolved around him and his extraordinary story.

To Be Continued . . .

In Hans Staden's narration of his time as a captive among the Tupinambá, one thing stands out: the resilience of Tupinambá culture as Europeans encroached on their territory. Although the indigenous groups of the Brazilian coastline were gradually displaced and decimated by disease and war, the story of indigenous communities in

Brazil during the sixteenth century and beyond is less about extinction and more about enduring against all odds.[6] Indigenous cultures of the myriad kinds found still today in Brazil may have been threatened for centuries, but they have continued. Indeed, it is worth remembering that maps give us a sense that everything is known about a place which is demarcated by a political border, yet in Brazil there were communities in the Amazon, for instance, that had had little contact with white people well into the 1990s. Brazil was not 'discovered' in 1500; Portuguese ships just knocked into the coastline of a particular section of the South American continent.

And so this narrative is far from concluded; it's a living history, continually renegotiated and reinterpreted. The colonization of Brazil is not a single event in the past but an ongoing process. As the indigenous thinker Ailton Krenak has said, the initial encounter between white people and indigenous people is relived every day in Brazil in the way that the environment and indigenous communities are treated by businesses and governments.[7] Yet there have always been resistance and response to that encounter, whereby the legacy of the 'merchandise people', as Davi Kopenawa Yanomami, a shaman and spokesperson for the Yanomami people, calls white people, is still being challenged through demands for the repatriation of objects and through legal claims to land rights.[8] Staden's story shows us just how tenacious that resistance to colonial rule was right from the beginning.

PART SIX

Sunken Aspirations

Meet Manuel. Manuel de Sousa de Sepúlveda. Noble. Captain. Profiteer. Lover. He was generous, which means to say he was rich, and he was successful as a military captain in Portuguese Asia, which means to say he had relatives in high places. He was the kind of man who chiselled his name above the portal of the fort he was commanding as a reminder that he was once there and in charge. If you were a viceroy in India facing a siege or seeking to quash a rebellion, you'd send for Manuel to skipper one of your ships. When he decided to cash in on his exploits, hang up his sword and head home, you'd write to the king lamenting his return to Portugal.[1] As it turned out, all those on board his ship heading west would regret that he captained it too. But for very different reasons. Manuel belongs to that class of imperial swashbuckler who served two seemingly contradictory masters: their country and their own greed. He might have borne arms as an old-fashioned soldier, but he also looked at the world, as many in the Portuguese empire did, with a merchant's eye for profit. This led to some disastrous decisions.

Manuel left Lisbon in 1537, almost forty years after the Portuguese empire in Asia had been inaugurated by Da Gama. At this point, the empire, after its initial growth spurt, had entered a period of consolidation. 'Consolidation' should not be taken to mean 'calm', however. No sooner had Manuel arrived in India than he was dispatched north with his cousin Martim Afonso de Sousa to Diu to extinguish the latest diplomatic fire. Diu had been in the sights of the Portuguese since the 1520s. An important waypoint between the Indian Ocean and the Arabian Gulf, it was a hub for the Gujarati merchants who made up one of the principal rivals to the Portuguese control of trade in the region. The 'illegal' trade in spices heading west to Arabia and North Africa, and then onwards to Europe, had Diu as one of its key entrepôts.

Diu was not an easy prize to seize, though, nor an easy one to keep. The Portuguese had the opportunity to take the city in 1509, after a decisive naval victory over the combined forces of the Sultan of Gujarat, the Mamlūk Burji Sultan of Egypt and the Samudri Raja of Calicut. But the then viceroy, Francisco de Almeida, declined to take it as a Portuguese possession, thinking it would be too expensive to maintain, and so signed a trade agreement with Malik Ayyaz, the governor of Diu for the Sultan of Gujarat. By the time that the Portuguese governor of the Estado da Índia, Nuno da Cunha, arrived in Asia in 1529, however, Lisbon had become obsessed with Diu, thinking that taking the port would plug this important hole in their mercantile operations in the Indian Ocean. Cunha's primary instruction from King João III as he departed from the Tagus was to conquer Diu, or adopt a scorched-earth policy until it fell under Portuguese control.[2]

It was not direct action by the Portuguese, though, that eventually won them this crucial asset. The Sultan of Gujarat, Bahadur Shah, came under pressure in the 1530s from the newly established Mughal empire as it advanced south. To bolster his position, he decided to seek an accord with the Portuguese. He conceded the fort of Bassein (Vasai) to them in 1534, but the ever-increasing threat from the Mughals led him in the following year to allow the Portuguese to occupy the fort at Diu. After the Portuguese sought a pact with the Mughal empire in 1537 to shore up their own position, Bahadur Shah changed his mind about their presence in his port and sought to push them out.

It was at this point in the fort's embattled history that Manuel swept into Diu. A diplomatic meeting between Martim Afonso de Sousa and Bahadur Shah did not go well and the sultan was killed. Manuel's first venture was thus something of a disaster. The power vacuum left after the death of Bahadur Shah was filled by an even more anti-Portuguese ruler of the Gujarat sultanate, which set about besieging the fortress the following year. The Gujaratis were aided in their endeavours by the Ottoman Turks, an alliance that really worried the Portuguese, who had tried to keep them out of the Indian Ocean. When we look at the fortunes of a single place like Diu, we see the vicissitudes of empire that stories at a global scale can miss.[3]

Over the next five years, Manuel built a sturdy reputation as a military captain. His career is emblematic of the tricky situation that the Portuguese found themselves in with such a dispersed set of holdings in Asia. During this period, he would scud around the Indian Ocean to Cochin to rescue the oft-threatened ruler there from the foes, such as the Samudri Raja of Calicut, who encircled him. He would help with the defence of Goa, the capital of Portuguese India, and travel as far as Aden on military operations, rushing back again to Cochin when the situation deteriorated there once more. A map plotting his career over these years, all angles and about-turns, would give a sense that the Portuguese spent much of their time on the defensive, trying desperately to hold on to their chain of ports. As essentially one long frontier, the empire had no secure centre. Its shape was consistently under threat from one corner or another. Allegiances shifted like the tides, putting at risk forts that were once thought safe. Pacts against the Portuguese might be made between local powers, but also with larger forces, such as Safavid Persia, the Mughals or the Ottomans. If, at the start of the sixteenth century, the Portuguese king Dom Manuel had imagined reaching the realm of Prester John and encircling the forces of Islam, then there was always the risk that Islamic allies could easily encircle his outposts of Christendom too, as they did later in the century during two famous sieges of Diu.

Empires on Water

In many ways, the Estado da Índia troubles our rigid ideas of empire, for when we think of empire, we tend to think only of soil. But that choppy space *between* lands, the sea, was just as important for the Portuguese. In the words of Sanjay Subrahmanyam, this was an empire 'written on water'.[4] As we have seen, what was critical to imperial operations was controlling who crossed the sea and with what. Indeed, Korean and Chinese chroniclers of the period describe the Portuguese as a peculiar species of 'frogmen', as much at home on the sea as on land.[5]

Manuel had not entered service out of straightforward patriotism

or an old-fashioned belief in the nobleman's duty to display prowess
in arms. He had been tutored in a world of chivalric values, yes, but
clearly saw the opportunities for enrichment that the empire offered
and pursued them. Indeed, for many – even those lower down the
pecking order – service in the empire was seen as something of a get-
rich-quick scheme. Poets, in particular, lampooned those who would
leave their homeland to make some money in the spice trade and then
try to get a pension on their return to Portugal for services rendered
to the crown. At least in the popular imagination, the classic career
paths of the ambitious and upwardly mobile – the church, service
with a noble, the law – seemed to pale in comparison to the profits to
be made in the Estado da Índia.

Manuel wrote to King João III in 1539, barely two years after his
arrival in Goa, to request a reward for being such a good captain. His
words, penned in a small, precise hand on paper folded four times into
a tight square, give us a sense of his expectations: 'I have faith in the
virtue of Your Highness that you will do for me that which is customary to do for men of my quality and with my record of service.'[6]
A study in pushy *politesse*. What he was looking for was a captaincy of
a fort, which, as the historian Charles Boxer once put it, came with
various 'perquisites and pickings' that made such postings lucrative.[7]
He got exactly what he wanted in 1542, when he was made captain of
Diu, a post he would hold until February 1545.

When Manuel returned to Gujarat, though, he found that there
was already someone in Diu who had been promised the same
position. Usually, captaincies would last three years, but letters of
engagement were issued rather more frequently than that. With Portuguese imperial possessions scattered far away across Africa and
Asia, no single body could keep consistent track of who was promised
what and when. As Manuel reached Diu, the captaincy was about to
be vacated by Diogo Lopes de Sousa, and a certain João Mascarenhas was waiting in the wings to assume it. A game of bureaucratic
Top Trumps ensued: Manuel held in his hand a letter addressed directly to him by João III pledging the captaincy to him as a reward.
Mascarenhas had something different: a so-called *carta patente*, a sort
of promissory note or certificate of entitlement and the more usual

statement of one's right to such a post. The king, who of course could not be consulted about any of this, was nonetheless invoked. Which expression of the royal wishes carried more weight? The answer, it turned out, was the more recent personal letter. Mascarenhas waved Manuel's letter above his head in frustration. He would have to wait his turn. But that didn't stop him complaining about his unfair treatment to all who would listen.[8]

A squabble over who got to do a job first might seem insignificant, but it highlights the remoteness and diffuseness of the Portuguese empire. A return voyage from India to Portugal and back, dependent as it was on the seasonal monsoon winds, took around eighteen months in total. Too long to check with Lisbon on any immediate issue. It was inconvenient even to consult the highest authority in the Estado da Índia itself, that is, the governor, as he was stationed hundreds of kilometres down the coast in Goa and was often away on some military expedition. Captains took advantage of this fact to do as they pleased.[9] And governors vented their frustration about it. Viceroy Afonso de Noronha complained in his report to the crown in 1552 about the power of the captains and the difficulty he had in bringing them into line. Their ability to siphon off money from the activities of the fort under their control, he wrote, gave them significant capital to pay people off who might oppose them. Noronha grumbled to the queen, Dona Catarina, that his authority to kick anyone out of office was limited as they would soon activate their family networks to petition the monarch in Portugal on their behalf, thereby making him look bad.[10] In theory, he was the most powerful Portuguese figure in Asia. In practice, as he confessed, his sway was limited.

To mitigate these problems, governors and other officials would attempt to place their own family members in key positions, who would collaborate with them for mutual gain. This was exactly the case with Manuel. In the same year he became captain of Diu, his cousin Martim Afonso de Sousa was appointed governor of the Estado da Índia. Each reinforced the other's power, prestige and ability to make private profits. If the word 'empire' conjures a juggernaut advancing implacably towards a single national goal, the reality, even with all its structures of bureaucracy and chains of command,

was a more human affair, where empire was skewed by the preju-
dices and desires of individuals who found themselves occupying
positions of localized power.[11] That is not to downplay the brutality
or exploitation of the enterprise taken cumulatively, just to acknow-
ledge the diverse energies that powered it. Manuel put some of his
money into expanding and shoring up the fort at Diu's defences. This
was what allowed him to leave his mark there: 'Manuel de Sousa de
Sepúlveda built this'. A nobleman's graffiti is called an 'inscription' or
a 'commemoration'.

· If Manuel's official record was more or less spotless up to this point,
he was later to become embroiled in scandal. The woman who would
become Manuel's wife, Dona Leonor de Sá, had been promised by
her father – the governor, Garcia de Sá – to one Luís Falcão, former
captain of Hormuz and captain of Diu between 1546 and 1548. In
1548, Falcão was murdered before the two could marry: he was shot
in the head while sitting with his son in front of the hearth. Even for
the brutal world of the Estado da Índia it was an unusual event, and
speculation abounds in the documents that mention the episode. One
theory, proposed by Simão Botelho, the crown's treasurer in Goa,
was that Falcão's men in Diu, miffed that their self-interested captain
had not paid their wages, decided to bump him off. A tidier solution to the mystery was to pin the murder on a man who was about
to die – and whom no one in authority would ever have listened to
anyway – as then there was not likely to be any comeback. This is the
version proposed in documents from the governorship of Francisco
Barreto, which stated that a man of no standing, one João Freitas,
confessed to the murder on his deathbed some years later.[12]

My favourite explanation has a more supernatural dimension. It
comes in Jerónimo Corte-Real's epic poem about the tragic events
of Manuel's life, which was first printed in 1592. The whole bizarre
episode, as it is described at length by Corte-Real, was masterminded
by Venus, goddess of love. Her son Cupid struck Falcão down with
a thunderbolt because Leonor had been promised to him and he was
therefore blocking the passionate affair between Leonor and Manuel.
Though Corte-Real's solution technically takes humans out of the
equation (and out of the firing line of blame), in his choice of deities he

obliquely points to an all-too-human motivation for Falcão's murder: desire. By turning Manuel and Leonor into ill-starred lovers, Corte-Real was trying to amp up the tragedy of the shipwreck that would end lives a few years later. One has to give Corte-Real credit for how he worked with the scanty historical materials that documented Manuel's career in Asia to achieve this. He was perhaps responding to rumours that Manuel and Leonor had married in secret, a fact that would come to light if things progressed any further with Falcão. Throwing my own detective's hat into the ring, this all makes Falcão's untimely end extremely convenient for Manuel and his relationship. The latter was well liked by the Portuguese in Diu and so the death might have been to the advantage of many, given that Falcão was not a generous leader. Whatever the motivation, though, this is an imperial whodunit that has never been solved.[13]

11.   The Weight of Greed

We know that Manuel had planned to depart India in January
1546 – some six years before he actually did set sail from Cochin
for Lisbon – because of a letter he wrote to King João III, which
stated that his time as captain of Diu had ended and that he would
like to return to Portugal, if things remained peaceful in Diu.[1] His
plans were scuppered, though, by another attack on Diu in April.
This time he was trapped inside the fortress as the Gujarat sultanate,
supported once again by Ottoman forces, attacked the Portuguese
stronghold. Against the odds, the defenders managed to endure seven
months of bombardment before the governor, Dom João de Castro,
arrived with reinforcements and routed the enemy. That 440 men
had held out against combined forces of near 10,000 was the stuff
of legend. God had protected this stronghold of Christians against
nefarious Islam, it was said. Stories from the blockade spread widely
back in Portugal. One of the most memorable was that of a Portuguese soldier who had run out of ammunition, but still had plenty of
gunpowder, who ripped out one of his own teeth to fire at an Ottoman soldier who was just about to breach the fortress's wall.[2]

Once more Manuel wasn't prepared to let his suffering for the
crown go unrewarded. He was granted a 'concession voyage' to
Bengal, an extremely lucrative venture that might secure him a profit
of thousands of cruzados (a Portuguese coin worth 400 reis).[3]

Manuel's voyage home to Portugal in 1552 was a final opportunity
to reap the private benefits of empire. He would have to fill the hull
of his carrack, the *São João*, with spices and other goods for the crown,
but would be given a share of the merchandise once he had arrived in
Portugal. The bulk of the cargo, as had been the case since the early
years of the empire, was pepper. Those teeny aromatic beads packed
into the hull of the *São João* made up approximately 80 per cent of
the merchandise by weight. The crown could derive a huge profit

from the sale of this pepper, as demand surged in Europe during the sixteenth century and prices remained high. The Portuguese sold it in Lisbon for almost four times the price they paid on the Malabar coast, hence the name 'black gold'. Even factoring in the expense of the shipping, wastage and other costs, the Portuguese stood to make much more than the Venetian merchants who had dominated the market in the previous century. The Venetians had always had to pay a higher initial price, as each successive trader in the chain leading from India across to Egypt added their own markup to the goods. No wonder the English and the Dutch wanted a share of the Asian trade and quickly followed where the Portuguese had led.

For someone whose first encounter with pepper was something resembling fine ash shaken from a plastic cylinder left for years on a sticky café table, it was tricky for me to understand, when I first heard about the spice trade, why empires would be launched in the search for this dried little fruit. But since ancient times, pepper has been in demand both for alimentary and medicinal purposes. Its aroma and gentle heat have made it a condiment for meat for centuries; indeed, as a devil in a Portuguese play all about food fraud suggests, its fragrance would allow a less than scrupulous butcher to convince you that a chewy old piece of mutton was, in fact, the tastiest morsel of lamb.[4] In the manuals drawn up in Asia by Portuguese botanists, pepper was said to get your juices flowing. Garcia da Orta, the renowned Sephardi plant expert, recommended pepper as a diuretic and advised that it would clear the head of phlegm.[5] It apparently helped with digestive problems, epilepsy and insect bites too. A more unusual use, noted by Cristóbal Acosta in his later botanical treatise, was as a form of contraceptive suppository.[6]

The procurement of pepper was not always straightforward, however. The Portuguese never took control of the inland regions of India where spices were grown. Although they had knocked out one set of intermediaries by opening up their sea route around the Cape of Good Hope, in India they were dependent on a series of go-betweens connecting producers with the ports where they purchased their stock. The autonomy of the pepper producers also meant that the Portuguese could never truly control who had access to their

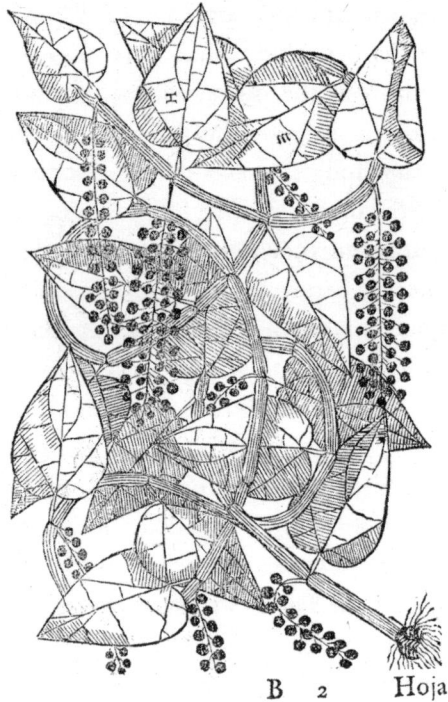

B   2   Hoja

Black pepper from Cristóbal Acosta's botanical treatise, 1578

goods. The Portuguese demanded lower than market prices and so growers would always seek out other merchants, such as those from Gujarat, who would pay more, even if this had been expressly forbidden by the Portuguese under their self-proclaimed monopoly on the trade. A further problem was cash. Growers wanted to be paid in gold. This was in short supply as Portuguese funds were tied up in their vast network of operations in Europe, Africa and the rest of Asia. Usually the ready cash to buy pepper arrived in India late in the year, towards the end of the harvest, and so the Portuguese had to make do with whatever they could get their hands on. This often meant that, even if they got the sheer quantities they sought, the pepper was damp and of poor quality.[7]

So there were fundamental issues with Portuguese operations even when the political situation was stable. Manuel departed, however, at a point when the regions inland, annoyed by the ruler of

Cochin, turned against him and, concomitantly, the Portuguese. The so-called 'King of Pepper' allied himself in 1549 with the Samudri Raja of Calicut, who was the sworn enemy of the Portuguese. The supply of pepper dwindled; for the next four years, as the Portuguese crown became embroiled in this conflict, it struggled, as did Manuel, to acquire the tonnes of spices that they sought.[8] In Manuel's case, he had to venture further south, to Coulão (Kollam), where he acquired 4,500 *quintais*, before returning to Cochin, where he purchased another 3,000 *quintais* of spices. The *São João*, the biggest ship yet constructed by the Portuguese, could carry some 12,000 *quintais*, or around 700 tonnes. In other words, Manuel filled less than two-thirds of its capacity.[9]

Cochin is encircled by water and the land sits so low that, over time, some of the vestiges of the Portuguese buildings in the city have become submerged. The whole lush region is broken into islets by a vast lattice of waterways. The first Portuguese building there was a fort, dug into the marshy ground of a palm grove, and constructed out of earth and wood. And the Portuguese presence in the city grew from there until it became one of the most important centres of trade in the early years of the Portuguese empire in India. The warehouses, which came later, were tucked inland where smaller boats would not be so much at the mercy of the strong tidal currents on the ocean side of the city.[10] For a sense of the spice trade, you can still visit the ginger warehouses built by the Dutch, who seized Cochin from the Portuguese in the latter half of the seventeenth century. The buildings form a rectangular U of whitewashed walls and tiled roofs, backing onto the water. As you walk from the courtyard into one of the double-height storerooms, your body feels an immediate change. The temperature drops in the shade and a different warmth, that of the earthy, almost sweet, aroma of ginger, subsumes you. Piles of knobbly, pale-beige tubers surround you, drying out slowly, releasing their scent, and waiting for export all around the world. It must have been headily fragrant work packing the pepper, and other spices, and lugging them to the ships.

Despite failing to get his hands on the desired quantity of this miraculous spice, Manuel did not let the spare capacity on his enormous carrack go to waste. He crammed any vacant stowage and all the deck space with packages of silks, bales of cotton, hardwoods, furniture and crates of Chinese porcelain. Strict guidelines issued by the monarchy prescribed limits for the total laden tonnage of ships. Captains persistently ignored these instructions, as Manuel also did. This was partly because the crown did not pay adequate wages to seafarers, choosing to remunerate them instead with space on board their ships. Above the hold, cabin and deck space was allotted to each crew member according to rank, which they could rent to merchants or use to store their own trade goods. Officers were permitted a certain number of 'liberty chests' in which they could import certain products entirely or partly duty-free, and so earn a greater profit on them. If the crew had their own stake in the cargo, the reasoning went, then they would be more likely to defend their ship vigorously against attack by pirates or other enemies of Portugal.[11] This thinking was lopsided, though. It paid too much attention to external dangers and none to the internal threat posed by the crew. Water barrels, essential to their survival on the long journey back, were often replaced with merchandise by greedy captains.[12] Contrary to the regulations, captains would even load boxes and bundles of goods on the outside of the ship by projecting planks out from the deck, or would simply let packages dangle from ropes over the side of the hull. Profit and prudence were thus squarely in opposition when it came to loading ships for the voyage back to Portugal.[13]

Things Fall Apart

The hulking carrack weighed anchor on 3 February 1552, laden with all its luxuries and some 600 souls. It is impossible to take a full roll call of everyone aboard, as most of them are never named in the sources. Bringing together all the evidence, however, we can figure out that Portuguese were in the minority. There were around 220 of them and almost double that number of enslaved people. The proportion of slaves aboard reminds us that transporting human chattels was not limited to the triangular Atlantic trade between Europe, West Africa and the Americas. Indentured people were forcibly conveyed across the Indian Ocean and the Pacific too, though that is a history of exploitation that has been neglected.[14]

Nothing about the *São João*'s journey would be easy. The ship dragged its keel sluggishly through the waters of the Indian Ocean because its sails were too tattered to harness the wind. It only neared the far side of the crossing towards the end of June. The vessel had only made a single voyage out to Asia from Portugal before then, so in carrack years (even if ships' life expectancy was low) it was still only just out of adolescence, but recklessness in maintaining it had taken its toll. Corners were cut and costs were saved in India; catastrophically, there were no spare sails. The ship was little more than a battered wooden hulk. Then the rudder fractured. The carpenter noticed that the pintles, the rods on which the rudder would rotate, had cracked and went to tell the pilot, who did not pass on this alarming news. Any rumour of damage to the rudder would trigger destructive panic in the crew.

Panic flared up anyway. Mounting gusts of wind ripped off the mainsail of the *São João*. The sailors hurried to take in the foresail before losing all means of propulsion. The hull pitched and lurched on the rolling ocean. The wind drove the ship side on to the waves, exposing its flank to their unmerciful lashing. The rigging and mast supports on one side were obliterated. The mainmast became a lever for the wind to exert strain on the ship, a crowbar forcing open the hull. The crew wanted to chop it down to ease the vessel's agony, but none of them could keep their feet for long enough while the *São João* reeled with the waves.

Some of the crew managed to start hacking at the mast. It did not take much effort to fell it: the storm sent it crashing down after a single blow from an axe. The gusts tossed the crow's nest into the ocean as though it were a bundle of twigs. The waves snatched half of the rotten and already damaged rudder away. Water gushed in from leaks in the hull below. Now the foremast threatened to prise the ship open from above. The crew went to hack it down, but the wind beat them to it. The deck became an emergency tailor's shop with sailors patching up new sails from any scrap of canvas they could find on board. Their hope was to try to repair the rudder and hoist something resembling a sail to carry them north to Mozambique, where they could get help, after the end of the storm.

They set to work and spent ten days constructing a rudder and trying to fashion some sort of mast. When they put the rudder in place, they realized that they had made it too short and too narrow to be able to steer the ship. On 8 June, they spotted the coast and decided that their only option was to wait for the *São João* to be carried closer to land, then they would launch the longboats and abandon ship.

A rowing boat was lowered and sent off to reconnoitre the coast. It returned having identified a lone stretch of sand amid the otherwise perilous rocks lining the shore of what is now South Africa. A first boat carried Manuel and twenty men ashore to guard the beach: in disaster, hierarchies are often sharpened, ruthless choices made about who must be saved first. On its third trip, the boat capsized, tossing those aboard into the sea.

Finally, the *São João* ran aground near what is now Port Edward, just north of the Mtamvuna river. Nearly 500 people were still aboard: 300 hundred slaves, 200 Portuguese. The jaws of the waves bit the ship in two and cast its human and material contents into

Shipwreck of the *São João* in 1552

the waves. Over a hundred who tried in vain to cling to the cargo to keep their heads above the surface perished in the water. Their desperate attempts to stay afloat are recorded in the woodcut that illustrated the account of the disaster when it was republished in the eighteenth century: people struggled in the waves, mingled with cargo and debris.

The timbers of the ship might help them to swim, but they were also a danger. Splintered wood and nails lacerated their bodies as they were swept to the shore.

Within a few short hours, the *São João* was ripped to shreds. No plank longer than a person remained of the giant vessel.

Anti-Discovery

When Europeans landed on foreign shores, no matter how desperate and depleted from their journey, they typically attempted some form of fanfare. They had concocted elaborate rituals to claim the lands they encountered. Besides a show of military force, they erected monuments, planted flags, made loud proclamations, and/or measured the stars to solemnize their arrival and to begin the process of claiming unceded land as their own.[15] Washing up on shore in the aftermath of a wreck, by contrast, marked a kind of anti-discovery: an unwanted arrival, the failure of a journey.

Lost and afraid, Manuel and those who survived the wreck immediately set about constructing defences for themselves in anticipation of impending hostility. If we look back at those names that Vasco da Gama foisted on this coastline in his journey to Calicut, they seem in hindsight painfully euphemistic. Not only an unwanted renaming in a new language, but too optimistic for the histories of disaster that would scatter these shores. The survivors had arrived in Christmas Land (in Portuguese, 'Terra de Natal') in June. A cause of celebration for Da Gama perhaps, but not for them. If we look at a map of the area and plot the many wreckages that occurred throughout the sixteenth century, we see it was along this shoreline that the Portuguese most frequently met with disaster. The Portuguese novelist Lídia Jorge has written of the *murmuring coast* of Mozambique, suggesting it still echoes with the violence of the Portuguese colonial regime.[16]

For those who made it to shore, it was time for a pep talk and to decide a course of action. Plan A, to build a new vessel from the remnants of the old ship, had washed away in the storm. Plan B, to walk hundreds of kilometres north to the Lourenço Marques river (today's Maputo river) where they might find help from Portuguese who stopped or traded there, really deserved to be further down the alphabet of options.

At this stage, though, it was their only choice. Manuel tried to lift the spirits of the survivors and encourage an *esprit de corps*. If we stick together, he said, we have the best chance of making it back to Portugal.

They stayed on the shore in a makeshift camp fashioned out of the wreck's debris for almost two weeks without sight of any inhabitants of that land. Brief excursions inland uncovered only abandoned

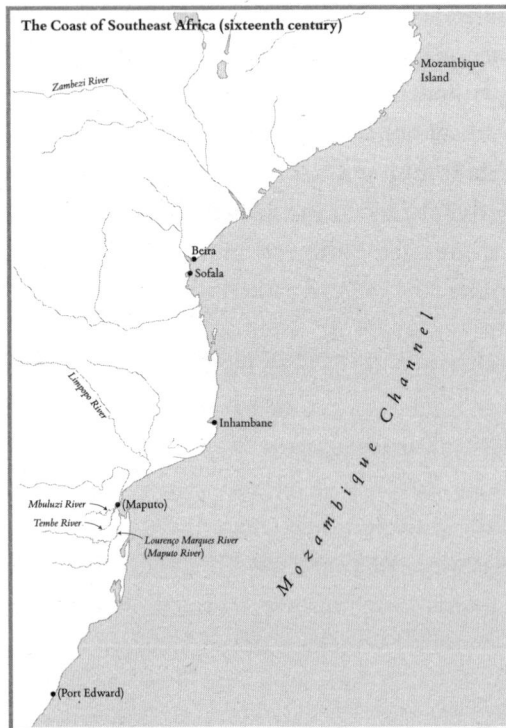

The Coast of Southeast Africa (sixteenth century)

houses. Eventually, though, a group appeared on the crest of a hill with a cow. Thank the Lord: a real meal. The survivors tried to barter for the beast with nails salvaged from the ship. This awareness of the metal's value in sub-Saharan Africa dated from the fifteenth century, when the Portuguese had shipped iron to West Africa, where it was used both as a currency and as a commodity to be reworked into tools.[17] On the Guinea coast, it was often sold for an impressive markup by Portuguese traders. Manuel and his crew seem to have carried that knowledge with them and extrapolated it to this unexpected setting. A workaday element that had held the ship together was suddenly more prized than the luxuries that the *São João* had been carrying. That is not to say that Africa lacked ore or the technology to extract it. Quite the opposite: Bantu-speaking communities had long-established technologies for smelting and smithing, and there was an existing trade in iron from the Swahili coast to India when the Portuguese arrived. Indigenous smelting traditions endured even with the arrival of colonial techniques, a sign of their resilience and usefulness. Indeed, this time the survivors didn't get their beef. Five more local men appeared on the hillside and shouted down to their compatriots to abort the deal. Clearly what the Portuguese were offering was not worth it. With dinner herded away from them, they prepared for their long journey north.

In tales of adventure, the promise to leave no one behind is usually made before things get really bad. In this story, it didn't take long to get to that point.

12.   A Trek to Tragedy

When the 500-strong procession set off on 7 July 1552, it was headed by the pilot, André Vaz, bearing a flag and a crucifix. The experience of hardship was not distributed equally. Leonor – Manuel's wife – did not have to walk at the beginning of the journey. Instead, she was carried in a litter by enslaved people. This probably consisted of two long poles attached to either a chair or a platform on which Leonor sat, with the slaves bearing the weight on their shoulders. Others carried Manuel and Leonor's young children on their backs.

One evening, during their first month of trekking, Manuel noticed that one of his illegitimate sons was no longer with the group. Scanning the line of exhausted marchers, dread began to flood his body. Darkness was encroaching. Knowing that separation from the group meant danger from predators or losing the rest of the group entirely, Manuel offered a desperate reward of 500 cruzados to anyone who would retrace their steps and rescue his boy. This figure was four or five times the average annual salary of a judge, let alone a sailor. It equated to some 200,000 reis, at a time when a mason in Lisbon earned in the region of 60–70 reis per day, and a labourer somewhere around 40 reis per day.[1] Yet no one took up the offer. Men who had risked their lives to get rich on the voyage were not willing to expend their limited energy to save another man's son. Manuel, weighing up the risks, was forced to leave his boy behind.

These moments of disappearance or abandonment became a cruel daily occurrence. Sustained only by a dwindling supply of rice salvaged from the ship and the occasional piece of scavenged fruit, individuals too weak to continue dropped by the wayside, begging those still able to walk to continue their grim march towards safety.

In the face of hunger and thirst, an economy of desperation established itself among the survivors. A jug of water would sell for ten cruzados, a cauldron holding two gallons for a hundred: a sign of scarcity and the danger involved in leaving the group to seek for sustenance. A snake's shed skin, desiccated and unappetizing, would fetch fifteen cruzados and would be dunked in water to make the discarded tube of scales at least chewable.

Three months into their trek, the survivors came across an old man who was the chief of two villages. They hoped that hospitality, not cruel opportunism, would be the custom there. Their host fed them and gave them a chance to rest. But when the time came to leave, Manuel learned that these kindnesses came with tacit expectations attached. A river lay ahead of them – most likely the River Tembe – and to avoid painfully extending their journey to find a crossing point, they asked to be carried across in the king's boats.[2] After some protests against their departure, the 'king', as the Portuguese account refers to him, said he would help them on their way if first the captain would dispatch some of his men with the king's warriors to attack a neighbouring settlement. Eventually, Manuel decided that he would allow twenty men to accompany the raid.

The word used in the account of the shipwreck to describe people in the region was *cafre*, which derives from the Arabic word *qafr*, meaning 'non-believer'.[3] In Portuguese usage it was a slippery term which brought together phenotype, geography and religion to designate black sub-Saharan East African non-Muslims (but was not always clearly distinct from other racialized terms with which it seemed to overlap). It is a case in point of the ways in which religion, skin pigmentation, language, geography, and more besides, came together in a classificatory system that generated hierarchies between people – one that we now call 'racialization'. The epithet and its equivalents in European languages have a long history; the K-word, in particular, was a derogatory term in Afrikaans before and during Apartheid. *Cafre* is one term in an early modern glossary of exclusion and racism which moved between languages, shifting its meanings and resonance in different contexts.

After five days, the band that had been dispatched to help the king returned and Manuel and the others were keen to be on their way. The king tried to persuade them to stay and issued a warning: beware my rival beyond the river – he will not treat you as well as I have done.

The company's desire to cross the river was a sign that they did not know where they were. They had, in fact, reached their destination: they were already in the vicinity of the Lourenço Marques river, where the Portuguese would stop to take on fresh water on their route between Portugal and India. They had also seen a red cap, a commodity frequently gifted or traded by the Portuguese on the coast of Africa, but ignored the sign that this was a place frequented by their compatriots.

With the king not keen for them to go, Manuel sent a group of men to assess whether they would be able to steal the king's canoes and thus cross the river on their own, but they were guarded day and night. He had to try negotiating again. Having little else to bargain with, he offered some of the group's weapons in payment for passage across the river. Concerned that the king might take advantage of the Portuguese being divided while they were being ferried in batches across the river and attempt something untoward, he also requested that the king and his people stay away, which they did. Manuel's paranoia was unfounded. The king accepted their offer and they were transported without an issue.

It took them five days to reach the next river, the Mbuluzi, which, like the Tembe, flows into the Espírito Santo estuary.[4] They walked along the bank of the river towards the estuary and set up camp there, but found the water salty and so some of them immediately had to double back on their route to find fresh water. The next evening, three canoes drew up at the camp. One of the women with the Portuguese group, who came from Sofala, was beginning to understand the local language and so could communicate with the visitors. She learned that a Portuguese ship had recently been in the area, but had now departed. A glimmer of hope. Through this interpreter, Manuel asked the men whether they would carry his company across the river. It was already nightfall, so they refused to do it there and then. But in exchange for a few nails, they promised to ship everyone over to the other side the following morning. As Manuel was being ferried across, however, he panicked. Fearing treachery, he drew his sword and began shouting at the men paddling him across the river, who leapt out of the boat in fear. Leonor tried to calm him down as he was putting everyone in the canoe in danger. He was not in his right mind. It was an outburst that cost him the respect of his followers. From that point onwards, he was no longer truly the captain.

The Final Struggle

The 120 men, women and children who remained from those that had set off on this trek all those months ago felt little relief on crossing this latest river. As a group of locals approached the dishevelled band, they scrambled to defend themselves. Through the woman from Sofala they communicated that they were shipwrecked Portuguese, looking for guides to take them to the river that they believed lay ahead and for supplies to sustain them in their now desperate plight. They were told that if they wanted shelter and supplies, they would have to go with the locals to the village of their king. They agreed, and accompanied their new associates for a league. Suspiciously, they were then told not to follow the locals into the village, but to wait by a cluster of trees and they would bring food out to them. Manuel did what he was told.

For five days they remained there, exchanging nails for provisions. Eventually Manuel entreated the king to shelter his wife and family. The king agreed, but informed Manuel that it would not be possible to take everyone into that one village because it would put an undue strain on its resources. They would have to divide themselves up between several other villages which would look after them. Furthermore, they would have to hand over their weapons for safe-keeping as they were making the villagers nervous.

Fatigue saw the last of Manuel's good sense evaporate. He relinquished the weapons. He let his followers be scattered. After insisting they must stick together, back when they were first cast onto shore, now he was the one to break the last survivors apart.

The first king had been right. As soon as they arrived at the villages, they were set upon. Exhausted and unarmed they could not fight back. They were robbed, thrown out and left to die. Manuel and around twenty others who had stayed with the king were pillaged of the gold and jewels they carried with them. It was then that Manuel realized how vulnerable he had left himself and all his followers.

The tragedy finally reached its climax with the scene that made the wreck of the *São João* unforgettable: the demise of Leonor, wife of the ship's captain. Stripped of her clothes by locals eager to snatch the fabric to sell, Leonor buried herself in the earth out of shame. Each handful of soil was an attempt to claw back the values and status that had been torn from her. Her husband's biblical reassurances – 'naked we came into this world . . .' – did not console her in this final humiliation. She never rose from her self-made grave. Her hair, grown long over the months of wandering, became a shroud over the half of her body she had left exposed. His wife gone, Manuel walked off and was never seen again.

Only twenty-five made it back to Portugal, seventeen slaves and eight Portuguese. Most of them were rescued by a Portuguese ship trading ivory in the region, after one of its crew heard rumours that Portuguese seafarers were wandering lost in the area. They sent out a search party, and offered a reward of beads to any locals who brought lost survivors from the *São João* to them.

The Debris of Disaster

In a macabre twist of fate, another Portuguese ship, the *São Bento*, was wrecked in the same vicinity two years later. Those survivors, knowing the story of Leonor and Manuel, saw terrible omens in the many haphazard graves they encountered along their path to safety. Later still, another set of shipwrecked Portuguese, from the *São Tomé* in 1589, encountered a king who wore rings that were said to have been taken from Manuel's fingers.

The skeletal remains may now have been scattered, but other fragments of Portuguese wrecks are still being recovered today. You can find pale shards of porcelain, corroded cannons, beads, gems and cowries from the ships in the KwaZulu-Natal Museum in Pietermaritzburg, South Africa. These objects have a strange fascination.

Shattered porcelain bowls with traditional inscriptions wishing 'good fortune and prosperity' take on a sinister irony in the wake of

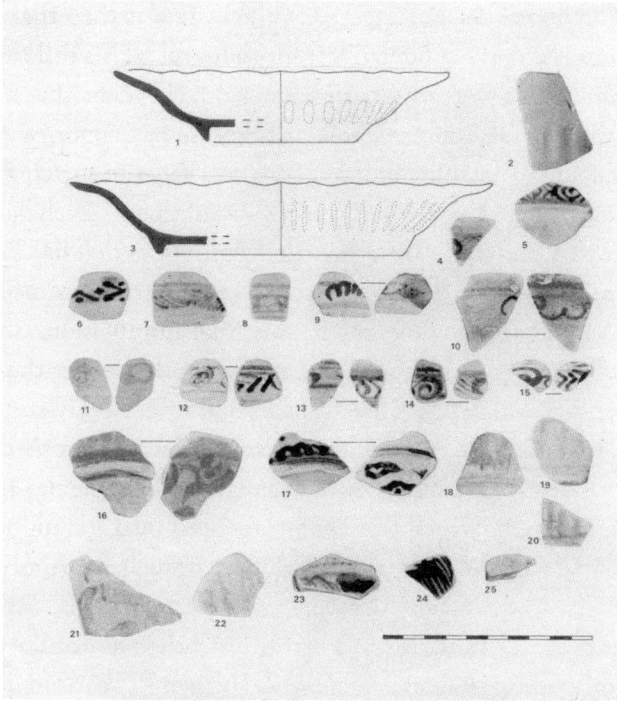

Fragments of porcelain from the *São João* wreck

the wreck. As items to be traded, prosperity was exactly what those goods were supposed to represent, but greed and mismanagement transformed them into both a cause and an index of disaster. Cowries found stuffed in a cannon tell of the movement of different kinds of currency around the globe. These shells could have been used to purchase slaves on the Guinea coast. That transaction was forestalled by the wreck, but this economic disturbance came at the expense of countless lives – most of which were enslaved people. While disaster must be included in our story of empire, we have to be careful that we do not gloss over too easily the loss of life that was entailed in this counter-story to imperial expansion. Sometimes I sense a feeling of anti-imperial schadenfreude when reading academic work on shipwrecks, that they are being celebrated for symbolically smashing apart the imperial ship of state. But we mustn't become too counterculturally complacent. Needless death is always needless death.

While Leonor and Manuel's story was held up as a cautionary tale even in the early modern period, the same mistakes kept being made. Shipwrecks were unsettling, but accounts of them didn't really change history's direction. It'll be different this time, people said. There is nothing like hindsight to give you a sense of superiority over other people's errors.

We are not entirely sure when the first edition of the story was printed, as it was not dated, but we do know that new editions in Portuguese appeared in 1564, 1592, 1614, 1625 and 1633. The story rapidly spread around Europe too, either as full translations or summarized in compendia as a warning of how fortunes could change in an instant. Giovanni Maffei included it in his widely republished history of the Portuguese in India (*Historiarum indicarum libri XVI*), printed in Florence in 1588, which was then translated into Italian by Francesco Serdonati in the next year, and into French by Arnault de la Borie in 1603. The most memorable reworkings, though, were for the stage. In Spain, Tirso de Molina wrote two plays about the disaster: one was called *Escarmientos para el cuerdo* (*Lessons for the Sane*; 1619); the other, which took Manuel de Sousa's name as its title, has in the past been attributed to the famous playwright Lope de Vega. In France, Nicholas Chrétien des Croix transformed the narrative of the wreck of the *São João* into *Les Portugais infortunés* (*The Unfortunate Portuguese*) in 1608. Misery seemed to migrate easily across genres and languages.

In the eighteenth century, the story was reprinted in Portugal along with several other shipwreck tales from the sixteenth century as an anthology entitled the *História trágico-marítima* (*Tragic History of the Sea*). This collection resurfaced, interestingly, at the beginning of the 1970s, when Portugal was still a colonial power and under the rule of the Salazar regime (Europe's longest twentieth-century dictatorship). It was republished as part of a subversive series which mobilized texts from the past to criticize the present. One of the most notorious books in the series was an anthology of satirical and erotic poetry: a historical rejoinder to the conservative sexual mores of the Estado Novo which landed its editor, Natália Correia, in trouble with the state censors. The publication of the *Tragic History of the Sea* — with an afterword by the Marxist writer José Saramago, who would become Portugal's (as yet) only Nobel laureate for literature – was seen as a way of questioning the triumphalist versions of Portuguese history that were peddled in schools at the time and found material form in the monuments that still stand in the country's capital. Shipwrecks represent the limits of empire; the cracks in the hull a sign of the fracture lines that existed from the beginning in Portugal's imperial enterprise. Yet, these stories of catastrophe have tended to sink beneath the surface of national consciousness.

Part of this forgetting comes from our collective addiction to historical beginnings and endings, firsts and lasts, which means we tend to skip over the long and messy bits of history in the middle. The wreck of the *São João*, along with the stories of Hans Staden and Marguerite de Roberval that preceded it, make up the uncomfortable middle of the sixteenth century and the uncomfortable middle of this book. All three stories underline that this was a century of persistent turmoil: disaster, resistance and, as we will also see in the next chapters, European nations taking inspiration from the worst of each other.

WORLD EVENTS

1558
Elizabeth I becomes
Queen of England –
London, England

1556
Deadly earthquake
strikes Shaanxi, China
– Shaanxi, China

Akbar the Great begins
his rule over the
Mughal empire –
Agra, India

1559
Treaty of Cateau-Cambrésis
ends the Italian Wars –
Cateau-Cambrésis, France

1556
*Nossa Senhora
da Ajuda*,
Portugal: Hit
a shoal near
Alagoas,
Brazil.

1558
San Sebastian,
Spain: Ran
aground on
the coast of
Chile.

1561
San Pedro, Spain: Part of Pedro de
Ursúa's expedition in search of El
Dorado, the ship was wrecked near
the Huallaga river, Peru, due to a
mutiny led by Fernando de
Guzmán and subsequent harsh
conditions.

1555
Ascenção,
Portugal:
Foundered in
the Bay of
Angra,
Terceira
Island, Azores.

1557
Abrigada, Portugal

1559
*Nossa Senhora da
Graça*, Portugal:
Foundered and
sank between
Mozambique and
Cochin, India.

San Juan, Spain: Another ship in
Pedro de Ursúa's expedition,
overtaken by Lope de Aguirre,
faced internal conflict and was
wrecked along the Marañón river
(Amazon river), contributing to
the collapse of the expedition.

SHIPWRECKS

1562
French Wars of Religion
begin – France

1566
Death of Suleiman the
Magnificent – Szigetvár,
Hungary

1572
St Bartholomew's Day
Massacre of Huguenots in
France – Paris, France

1565
First permanent European
settlement in what is now
the United States at
St Augustine – Florida, USA

Siege of Malta, the Knights
Hospitaller defend against the
Ottoman empire

1571
Battle of Lepanto, Holy
League defeats
Ottoman fleet – Gulf of
Patras, Greece

1570
Victoria, Spain:
Foundered on a
voyage from Seville
to the Antilles.

PART SEVEN

Not Quite Drake

England looked on while Spain and Portugal encompassed the globe, shipping silver and spices back to their shores from Africa, Asia and America. England's merchants, save for some spasmodic attempts to encroach on Portuguese interests along the west coast of Africa, had to satisfy themselves with the limited markets they could reach across the Channel or the North Sea. In trade, England's overriding emotion was envy.

If only England could find its own route to Asia, find its own way to the once-mythic and now very real riches of China, India and the Spice Islands of the Pacific. The problem with this imperial daydream was that each of the compass quadrants that might represent a potential passage beyond Europe had been steadily ticked off by successful rivals or by failed home-grown adventures. The southeast went to Portugal as Da Gama rounded the Cape of Good Hope, that route on which Manuel de Sousa de Sepúlveda's ship had sunk. The southwest became Spain's with Magellan's crossing into the Pacific around the southern tip of the Americas. To find a passage free from the diplomatic wrath and cannon fire of their competitors, the English had to look away from Africa and South America, turn their attentions northwards and plot a course above the known continents. A disastrous voyage to the northeast led by a man named Sir Hugh Willoughby shattered hopes of an ingress to Asia around Russia.[1] Small recompense was found in the establishment of a new market for English goods in Russia, known at the time as Muscovy, but it offered a sputtering stream rather than a torrent of profits. All that remained by the second half of the sixteenth century was the compass's top left quadrant: the northwest.

Interest in this route had begun early in England, but exploration was not concerted or systematic. The Italian Giovanni Caboto, better known by his anglicized name, John Cabot, had supposedly grazed the coast of North America near Newfoundland in Canada at the end of the fifteenth century.

His son Sebastian boasted to the Venetian compiler of travel information Giovanni Battista Ramusio that his prow had entered the fabled Arctic strait to Asia in 1507–9, but there is little evidence to corroborate this. In 1527, John Rut took two ships, with Henry VIII's support, to the coast of Labrador, lost a ship en route, and returned without adding any clear new knowledge about what would become known as the northwest passage. Almost ten years later, Richard Hore tried again, but his expedition ended, if reports are to be believed, in the crew drawing lots for who would be eaten when their provisions ran out.[2]

It wasn't really until Sir Humphrey Gilbert, the explorer and soldier, pitched the idea of the northwest passage to the Privy Council in 1566 that momentum began to gather around the idea of sailing through the cold of the Arctic to the South Sea. Gilbert conjectured that the northwest passage offered an easy shortcut to Asia which the English would be foolish not to exploit. Given that England lay at a similar latitude in the northern hemisphere to the places that Europeans sought in Asia, the thinking was that a route to the north would prove shorter than those followed by the Iberians, which required sailing far to the south before climbing north again. In 1583, on the final voyage of several that Gilbert made in his lifetime, he claimed the harbour of St John's in Newfoundland for Queen Elizabeth I (remember Marguerite passed by there) but died in a shipwreck off the Azores on his return journey.

Maps of the far north in the age were largely based on speculation and misinformation, but gave credence to the idea of a nautical yellow-brick road, the Strait of Anian. In some cartographic wishful thinking, the world map published by the Venetian printseller Giovanni Francesco Camocio in 1567 depicts an 'unknown northern sea' (*mare septentrionale incognito*) above Canada, with imaginary ships already sailing through it down to the South Sea.

Not everyone was convinced, though. Richard Grenville, a privateer who happened to be Gilbert's cousin and more interested in exploring warmer, southern latitudes, raised sensible doubts about

The northwest passage depicted by Giovanni Francesco Camocio, 1567

whether the sea would remain liquid long enough for a ship to sail all the distance west. In those frozen parts, would not a ship be choked by ice? Gilbert's proposal came to nothing. The Privy Council referred him to the Muscovy Company, which had the sole rights to trade involving regions to the north of Britain. The company refused to cede its privileges and support the venture. Too many costs. Too many risks. Too much to lose if the venture worked out as Gilbert hoped and they had let their monopoly go.[3]

13. Albion's Would-Be Columbus

Over the years following Humphrey Gilbert's proposal for exploring a possible northwestern route to Asia, however, the Muscovy Company's outright opposition began to soften, perhaps because their principal trade with Russia delivered such underwhelming profits. And so things turned out differently when a new proposal to seek the northwest passage came before the Privy Council in 1574. The adventurer seeking permission and assistance to navigate the waters that connected the Atlantic and the Pacific through the Arctic was a man named Martin Frobisher.

Frobisher fancied himself Albion's Columbus and Cortés combined – hubris not lost on those who later chronicled his voyages and described his inflated ego as a 'monstrous mind'.[1] Exploration was a very sixteenth-century way to win a fortune and be written into the history books, and Frobisher wanted to make a name for himself. The idea of sailing through the northwest passage had supposedly entered his head during a conversation between inmates in a Lisbon jail. Historians have dismissed this anecdote as fanciful, the product of his contemporaries' imaginations, but – and forgive me for succumbing to the story – it seems fitting that his poorly conceived plan would have gestated while he languished in prison, egged on no doubt by inmates' bravado.

Frobisher had ended up behind Portuguese bars after a bungled bid by an English fleet to encroach on the lucrative Portuguese trade on the west coast of Africa in 1555. This already gives you a hint of the kind of man he was: his professional life was lived in that zone at the edge of the law and often in contravention of international diplomatic agreements. Frobisher had been apprenticed as a merchant under the watch of his successful uncle, Sir John Yorke, after he had been orphaned at a young age. Martin seemed to show no talent for licit profit-making, however, and slid over time into a related, but rather more dubious, occupation: privateering.[2] The distinction between privateer and outright pirate was fine, sometimes blurred. Privateers officially launched their vessels armed with a licence to recoup losses suffered by someone or other, in a crude form of international reparation. But most used these letters as flimsy excuses for more indiscriminate sea banditry, where diplomacy and protocol were quickly forgotten when the opportunity for individual gain bobbed on the horizon.[3] These were men who made their money by seizing the fruits of others' diligence. With their raids, they regularly rocked the unsteady boat of relations between England and Spain. Frobisher frequently attacked ships he shouldn't have, which led to several run-ins with the Admiralty Court, which dealt with crimes and offences involving English ships. Blind eyes, though, were often turned to these plunderings, as Frobisher and his ilk provided cheap naval coverage for the crown and an off-market supply chain of hard-to-get goods for people in high places.

In spite of Frobisher's distinctly grey – if not downright black – reputation, the Privy Council referred him to the Muscovy Company, as it had done before with Gilbert. While the company was still not making use of its rights to exploit northwestern regions, it remained protective of them and rebuffed Frobisher's first approach. It was still wary of kicking itself in the future. Just two months later, in February 1575, however, his persistence changed the company's mind and a permit was made out to Frobisher and his newly acquired partner, Michael Lok, to seek out the northwest passage. It was the intervention of this second man that made the difference to Frobisher's fortunes.[4] Lok, who was London agent of the Muscovy Company and a well-respected merchant, became a key backer. His networks provided much of the investment in the enterprise over the coming years. He was seemingly lured by the prospect of getting rich from intercontinental trade, as had happened with Spain and Portugal. He knew too that some of the Muscovy Company were hungry for more sizeable profits than their adventures in Russia had afforded them. Lok was no uninformed gambler. He was a geography enthusiast with an extensive personal collection of maps and travel narratives. His professional life as a trader had taken him to France, Spain and Portugal, then further east to Venice and the Greek islands, and eventually as far as the Levant. He was fluent in a range of Romance languages, Latin, Greek and possibly even Arabic. Exploration brings with it an inherent fumbling in the dark, but Lok had at least done his homework.

With Lok on board, the pair gradually secured the backing of a number of Privy Councillors: Lord Burghley, the Earls of Warwick, Leicester and Sussex, and Sir Francis Walsingham. From the Muscovy Company, one of its two governors, Lionel Duckett, signed up, along with one of its founding members, William Bonde, plus its former ambassador to the Russian court, Thomas Randolphe, and Anthony Jenkinson. Two prominent mercers from the City of London, William Burde and Thomas Gresham, each put in £100. This was substantially more than most of the other backers, who invested the minimum share of £25. These were important people, and so, as well as financing, their backing brought credit of another sort. Ultimately, for men of their means these were sums they could afford to lose. The slim chance to win big was worth trying one's luck.

The Company of Cathay was born, at least in name, if not in legality – the papers of incorporation were never signed by Elizabeth I. It was an ill-fated precursor to the more bloodily successful East India Company, in which empire, profit and violence would be fused.

The promised profit from the venture was, however, not large (or likely) enough to attract sufficient investment. The total amount raised by Lok and Frobisher came to £875, not nearly enough to pay for the ships and crew required. As we will see, it was Frobisher's bombastic character, quick temper and lack of serious long-range oceanic experience that seem to have given investors pause for thought.

An Oceanic Gamble

The springtime window for a voyage north in 1575 came and went. It was not to be their moment. Our duo, however, proved disastrously persistent. A year's delay had not put off the initial investors and when the pair reapproached those who had signed up for the venture in 1575, they recommitted the same sums. Provisions were made, however, to curb Frobisher's control of the voyage. Lord Burghley was particularly keen for his involvement to be limited. William Borough, a seasoned mariner of the Muscovy Company, was chosen to take charge of hiring the crew and deciding the course they would sail.

No new investors, though, put their money on the table to support the venture in 1576. The enterprise thus remained well shy of its intended budget. What happened next has long surprised historians by how out-of-character it seemed for an otherwise cautious and well-respected merchant. Lok went in deep. He shouldered half the risk of the entire project himself by lending the balance of the funding required for it to go ahead. It was an investment that would make or break him.

Still, even with Lok's surprising gamble, without hefty further investment they could not acquire hefty ships. Lok went to Matthew Baker, one of the leading shipwrights of the age, and commissioned a new vessel of between twenty-five and thirty tons, the *Gabriel*, and a pinnace of around seven tons. These were tiddlers compared to the great Portuguese *naus* of 600 tons or more which ploughed the seas between Europe and Asia laden with goods. Another ship, the *Michael*, of similar size to the *Gabriel*, was purchased for £120 from two of the shareholders in the voyage, Christopher Andrews and Robert Martin.

Lok knew from the Muscovy trade that men needed extra fuel if they were to toil in frosty seas. The ships' stores were thus packed with provisions enough to stave off the cold despite the damp and microbes that would inevitably spoil some of their stock. On the menu: beef, salted and dried fish, Suffolk cheese, wheat, oats and dried peas. They'd have meat every other day. Historians have suggested that the provisioning was ample in brute calorific terms. Yet there was nothing in the barrels to ward off the onset of disease caused by a diet devoid of fresh vegetables.

Besides their edible provisions, the hold jingled with several hundred bells and a pile of cloth and ribbons: items to be traded with or given to any humans they might meet. This seemingly superfluous stock, however, would soon become significant. To help them find their way, they took an abundance of compasses. Reading these devices was a subtle art, and plenty of spares were needed as the delicate dials, like the sailors who used them, could lose their sense of north on the lurching waves. Frobisher and the master of the *Gabriel*, Christopher Hall, took a six-week crash course in the rudiments of oceanic navigation and northern geography from England's doyen of maps and instruments for measuring the stars, John Dee. But, as soldiers and sailors liked to complain, although Dee's theories were all well and good, practical experience was a different matter entirely.[5]

Icy Peril

June 1576: departure. It was supposed to be the start of an epic odyssey but the voyage commenced with a frustrating little farce. Barely out of the docks, the pinnace crashed into another boat near Deptford and had to be repaired at Greenwich before the expedition could make its way in earnest. The queen waved at the fleet from her palace window in Greenwich, bidding Frobisher to come and see her and take his leave. She handed him letters of recommendation in Latin and Greek, missives designed to secure safe passage and a warm reception wherever the ships might end up. More recently, Elizabeth II also issued such letters. Open a recent British passport and on the front flyleaf her late majesty still requests and requires that the bearer be allowed to pass freely without let or hindrance. And just like the Passport Office, Elizabeth I charged Frobisher for the trouble of such a declaration: £1, for a letter that most of the world probably couldn't read.

Finally exiting the Thames estuary, the ships turned to port and began tracking their way north up the English coastline. After a day's sailing, contrary winds drove them into Harwich and stranded them there for a few days before the gusts decided to blow in a more favourable direction. They reached Shetland a fortnight after setting out, on 26 June, where they stopped to repair a leak that had sprung in the side of the *Michael*'s hull and to fix the faulty caulking of the water casks, which only became evident after a few days at sea. It was now time to head out into the Atlantic for their great crossing. For three days it was plain sailing until, as we learn from the logbook of Christopher Hall, stormy weather bore down on them for over a week. The small fleet had to take in their sails, a kind of nautical surrender to the weather. It would have been reckless to attempt to ride out the unruly winds. They would tear the sails apart or snap the masts in two.

Progress was fitful during the storms. They were too far north to read their latitude from the pole star, that stalwart index of location for the sailor, and had to wait for the curtain of storm clouds to part to be able to measure their latitude from the height of the sun, adjusting their course each time the weather gave them the chance to get their bearings. They had been instructed to use a technique known as 'westering', tried and tested by the fishing vessels that sought their catches in the northern seas. They had headed due north from England until they reached their desired latitude, and then turned west and tried to hold a steady course. A simple right-angled route that, despite the difficult weather, did take them across the Atlantic until . . . Land ho! The coast of Greenland. Not that they knew this. Legend led them to believe they had reached the fabled island of Friseland. The sight of the snowy shoreline did not arouse straightforward relief, however. It rose up in forbiddingly sharp protrusions 'like pinnacles of steeples'.[6] Everywhere was white and cold. And before they could reach this jagged place, they had to pass through a set of floating dangers. Titanic bergs of ice stalked these waters.

The sight of this new landscape mesmerized and perturbed the English. Thomas Ellis, who went on and wrote a report of Frobisher's third voyage in 1578, gives the clearest impression of how strange this drifting ice seemed. He struggled to describe a single, enormous iceberg, and even sketched it from different angles as though it were a piece of fantastical natural architecture, ungraspable, immeasurable. Some of these 'monstrous' islands of ice that floated around Greenland were so tall they had clouds about their tops.[7] Fog swept over the ships. They had to retreat to open sea to avoid a deadly collision with a roving berg. For days, the fleet tried to reconnoitre this land, but each attempt to move coastwards was thwarted by the conditions. The crew took soundings, but their leads never touched the bottom of the sea. Abandoning this coastline, the trio of ships resumed their course west. Another storm blew in, this time too violent for the pinnace, a small boat, which sank into the depths of that bottomless ocean. The tempest separated the two principal ships. Each was now alone. The *Michael* persisted for a few days but the prospect of ice fields along the coast of what its crew took to be Labrador persuaded them to turn back, to head for home.

The tiny fleet was thus reduced to a single vessel. Peril soon struck Frobisher's lonely ship. Waves breaking over the *Gabriel* flooded it with water until it lay on its side. Many took to prayer. Gallons of ocean sloshing in the hull, Frobisher took action. He cut away the mizzenmast in order to help right the ship, then heaved on one of the sails, rocking the boat violently enough to toss the water out the way it had come in. It saved the *Gabriel* from going the way of the pinnace. The crew pushed on, trusting that the sea would finally end at some point and land would begin again.[8]

A few days later, land did indeed appear on the horizon. Once more, though, a ring of ice blocked their approach. They steered south, spotting land again after another two days. Once more, they thought it was the coast of Labrador, but they were much further north than that. What they saw before them was, in fact, Resolution Island, at the southern tip of Baffin Island. They called it Queen Elizabeth's Foreland, though as yet they had met no one to whom they could present her letter. The deep water, rapid currents and large amounts of ice prevented them from disembarking here. They headed briefly north in search of safe harbour. Time and again, they met the same problems. After several more tense days, Hall eventually managed to drop anchor by an islet off the eastern coast of Baffin Island. One of the men who went ashore on what became known as Little Hall's Island picked up a black rock the size of a halfpenny loaf as a 'token of possession'.[9] It was a lumpen souvenir, heavy but uninteresting, and taken as a tourist takes a pebble from a beach, almost without thinking. But this simple act was to prove the most consequential action of the whole voyage.

Frobisher decided to explore an opening of water that lay close by, suspecting, hoping that it might offer a passage west, that it might be the rumoured Strait of Anian. He named it Frobisher Strait, in emulation of Magellan, who sailed a different passage into the Pacific.

It was, in fact, a bay to the south of Baffin Island. He gave his own name to a geographical dead end, which perhaps tells you all you need to know about the success of this voyage as a reconnaissance of foreign lands. They sailed into the bay, where islands speckled the sea to either side, and as they sighted them, began to name them. On 19 August, a small group decided to go ashore on one of them, named Burche's Island after John Burche, the mariner who first spotted it.[10]

They climbed to the highest point of the island and, from there, they had a better view of the forbidding landscape. Sharp rocky points crested the horizon, with few trees to soften the outlook. All around, the earth was hard and little grew but lichens and mosses that crouched in cracks and clung to the rocks as winds ripped across the strait. Dionyse Settle, who joined Frobisher on his second voyage to the region, commented that the land yielded little that sprang forth from roots. He did note, however, that deer roamed about, with antlers larger than those he had ever seen back home, and the islands, though ostensibly barren, were home to hares, wolves, 'fishing bears' and flocks of seabirds.[11]

The islands were also home to people. From their vantage point, the Englishmen spied kayaks on the horizon travelling from the other side of the strait towards them. Hall and Frobisher sped immediately back to their ship; but, curious about the local inhabitants, sent a boat out to try to draw the Inuit in. They came in close to the English ship but eventually turned their kayaks away and put in at the island. Alone, Hall went to try to talk to them. He offered gifts of sewing needles. An Inuk man came back with him to the *Gabriel* and was offered dinner, but did not much like the mariners' meal. This show of hospitality on the part of these incomers seemed to allay immediate fears and suspicions about these new arrivals. The rest of the Inuit came aboard the English ship.

Hall's description of these people tried to slot them into a known category: the Tartars. He said that they had long black hair, broad faces, flat noses and 'tawny' skin. Both men and women wore sealskins, but the women were distinguished by blue streaks on their cheeks and around their eyes, the Inuit practice of *kakiniit*, or facial tattooing.[12] Women received these lines, chevrons and dots across

forehead, chin and cheeks when they first menstruated. These mark-
ings were said to outlast death and allow ancestors to recognize a
woman's face in the afterlife.[13]

Incommensurable Values

It was by then 20 August, the evanescent summer dimming and slipping away with each passing day. The *Gabriel* went east around the
island and found a huddle of dwellings on the shore. This enticed them
to drop anchor, but they soon withdrew when they realized they had
been seen by the locals. The Inuit waved the Englishmen back and let
them explore their homes. An Inuk man returned to the ship with them
and was given a bell and a knife. He was then escorted back to shore by
five of Frobisher's men. They were instructed to land well away from
the rest of the Inuit, but didn't. All five were captured and never seen
again by their compatriots. But their story endured. The story of their
arrival and their living out their days among the Inuit was passed down
for generations, eventually reaching the ears of the American explorer
Charles Francis Hall during his expedition to the region in 1860–62.[14]
An alternative history hidden from European records for centuries.

After the capturing, two days passed and kayaks were spotted
again. Most kept their distance. Frobisher at this point wanted to
retaliate and seize a captive. He needed the Inuit to come closer. He
threw clothes into the water. An Inuk man drew near to retrieve
the apparent offerings. Frobisher held out a bell. He dropped it in
the water. Then he held out a second. The Inuk drew closer still. He
reached out for the bell, and Frobisher yanked him aboard.

Historians have often written of this episode that Frobisher 'lured'
the man towards the boat. But we cannot be sure that he was duped.
Perhaps it wasn't naivety. Though dismissed as 'toys' or 'trinkets',
worthless nothings in English accounts of the voyage, it is clear that
these so-called 'trifles' were more like commodities, items that had
been carefully chosen to be traded or offered as gifts; in previous
interactions with those outside Europe, bells in particular had proven
valuable. Perhaps the man had taken a calculated risk, or indeed was

continuing the sequence of gift exchanges that had marked their previous interactions. The scholar John Haines has pointed out that, in the Arctic context, cooperation was key to survival, so the Inuk may have approached the situation with quite a different set of expectations from Frobisher and his men.[15]

Europeans at the time liked to think they were always ripping everyone off to score a profit for themselves. But as we have seen in some of the shipwreck stories in this book, all value depends on context, and gold would be discarded for the most basic provisions in certain circumstances. So here we should not assume things are as simple as some have led us to believe. Indeed, for the man who reached out his hand to take one, bells had a very different meaning. Haines again: 'what Frobisher had let fall into the water was not a commodity or even trinket. It was to the Inuk a celestial sounding object, controlled by its person (*inua*). When foolishly thrown into the water, the bell along with its guardian spirit (*tu·rŋaq*) had been defiled.'[16] Two different value systems were meeting.

What the chroniclers are right about is pinning down the English attitude. George Best, a gentleman-soldier who travelled later with Frobisher and wrote an account of his voyages, called this hostage their 'new prey'. The English were predators. Abducted and exiled, this man showed what he thought of his captors and their actions by biting his tongue in two in 'choler and disdain'.[17] Body trapped, his will would not submit.

Snow had blanketed the deck of the *Gabriel* with a thick layer of white on the day that their men had been abducted. The season was swiftly turning. They had lost their other ship, their pinnace, many of their men; they were, by now, a skeleton crew of thirteen with cold and fatigue in their bones. By 23 August, they were unanimous: it was time to go home. Their journey east proved mostly smooth, unlike their voyage west. Save for another ambush by an Atlantic storm, which flung a man overboard. Miraculously, his cold fingers clinging to a sheet, he was hauled back on deck. There were no more losses until they reached English soil.

Frobisher received a hero's welcome when he got back at the beginning of October 1576. The Inuk and his boat made a particular stir. He was a breathing emblem of a strange place, living proof of the voyage. He didn't survive many days in England, however, but died quickly of a cold that he had caught on the voyage back.[18] His fleeting presence was recorded in oil paint, just as Frobisher was also commemorated with a portrait. A wax death mask was even taken of the Inuk so that Cornelius Ketel, the painter, could continue to make likenesses of the man after he perished. They have all now been lost, but one life-size portrait of the Inuk was sent to Queen Elizabeth I, its size itself an attempt to convey the importance of Frobisher's voyage and what he had found.[19] It was as if, at last, the English had their own Columbus. That Frobisher was so readily praised suggests a deep desire for a hero in the mould of the Iberian adventurers, whether or not their own version truly measured up. Beyond making a spectacle with a captive, what had he actually achieved? As Michael Lok would say rather sourly some years later: 'the passage of Cathay is by him left unto us as uncertain as at the beginning, though thereupon hath followed great charges to the Company'.[20] In other words, his voyage had been expensive and fruitless.

In the meantime, Frobisher set about trying to assure people that he had indeed found a passage to Asia, but had simply not managed to sail far enough into the strait to reach the Pacific. A second attempt, he said, was needed.

All for a Rock

Another visit to the northeast of America would indeed be made, but it was not Frobisher's geographical claims that would secure it. It was the unassuming black rock that a man had taken from Little Hall's Island which would guarantee the continuation of the northwest venture. Frobisher passed this lump to Lok as a keepsake and as hard evidence of his travails on the other side of the Atlantic. Holding this piece of the New World in his hands, Lok began to ponder its value. It was heavy. It glistened. Might it be ore? Lok chipped off some small samples and sent them to specialists at the Royal Mint and the Mines Royal to assess its worth. Despite its sparkle, each returned pessimistic assessments. It was of no value. Rubble. Scree. At the beginning of 1577, Lok gave a sample to the Venetian goldsmith Giovanni Battista Agnello, hoping that he might have a different opinion. From this lump of rock, Agnello wrested gold. He urged Lok to send ships to fetch more of this ore and bring it back to England for refining. It would, in Agnello's view, make them all rich.[21]

Lok informed the queen and his investors of this precious surprise. Further, if inconclusive, examinations of the ore were made. Eventually, Lok followed Agnello's suggestion and requested a licence to ship more of the ore across the sea and to process it back in England. Unbeknown to Lok, however, Agnello had also been consulting with other men about this special ore. These whispers reached William Winter, a naval administrator who had mining interests and later became an investor in Frobisher's voyages. Winter engaged a metallurgist from Saxony – Saxons were reputedly the best metallurgists – called Jonas Schutz to assay the rock. With Schutz's intervention, the value of the ore skyrocketed, now being regarded at eight times the initial estimate of its worth. Pots of gold may not lie at the ends of rainbows, but they seemed to lie in the ground on the opposite side of the ocean. It was a venture that should have seemed too good to be true.

For much of this time, Frobisher had been kept in the dark about the experiments on the rock. In March 1577, Walsingham of the Privy Council, however, instructed Lok to inform Frobisher about its potential value as the commission for organizing the second expedition was about to meet. News of the miraculous bounty that lay waiting to be dug up in the north quickly spread more widely across London. And the purpose of the second expedition now shifted away from finding a passage to the Pacific to quarrying more of the ore. Walsingham increased his stock in the enterprise fourfold. William Winter also went in for £200. The queen herself joined with stock worth £1,000, partly paid for by the donation of one of her own ships, the *Ayde*, valued at £750. By the time the fleet was due to depart, the value of the expedition's assets had increased to £4,275.[22]

In context, the pivot from exploratory voyage to mining expedition is not quite as surprising as it might seem. Mining was an important and growing industry. Gold extraction was one of the earliest and most important imperial industries and, as we have seen throughout this book, the precious metal was often on the minds of Europeans as they sailed to distant shores. In his translation of Iberian accounts of the growth of their empires, Richard Eden, the sixteenth-century alchemist and translator, even appended an extract from an Italian treatise on mining, an inclusion that clearly signalled the twinning of imperial expansion with the search for deposits of metals and minerals.[23] Mining was a key part of imperial enrichment; it was a sign of the times. As George Best wrote in the preface to his account of Frobisher's first voyage: 'Solomon himself, with all the precious metal of Ophir . . . cannot be comparable to the great store of gold, and all other metals, which daily are digged out of the bowels of the earth, almost in all parts of the world, and now lately in the supposed hard and congealed frozen lands, almost under the Poles.'[24] It ran against the suppositions of the age that frozen lands could foster gold. But the promise of riches has always overridden people's caution and better judgement. This desire to cross into the Arctic and dig for minerals marks the beginning of an ongoing story about the poles. Nowadays, the metals and minerals may have changed, but nations still try to claim the snow-capped bits of the planet for their untapped resources.

Prospecting for metal from Agricola's treatise on metals, 1556

14.   Second (and Third) Time Unlucky

The amount of money ploughed into Frobisher's second voyage was not sufficient for the greed of its leaders and backers. The fleet would be made up of the queen's ship, the *Ayde*, plus the *Gabriel* and *Michael* from the previous voyage. The merchandise left over from the 1576 journey was loaded back onto these ships in light of the focus not on trade but on the extraction of ore: they were not heading for Asia any longer, so they did not need items for trade, just those goods they could use for negotiations with the Inuit. Better efforts were made to clothe the mariners and miners than on the previous trip, with thick woollen garments included in the stores. Convicts were added to the personnel, with the intention of marooning them on Friseland so that they could observe the changing seasons and explore the area, in order to inform any future designs that England might have in the region. But they never had to endure their frozen punishment. Frobisher left them behind on English shores, as he had too many men on board his ships. When he was ordered to offload some of the men on board, he chose not his own men but the criminals that had been foisted on him by others. He never really liked following anyone else's orders.[1]

The fleet bade Harwich farewell on 31 May 1577. This time around, the journey out was less arduous. In just a matter of weeks, Frobisher entered that same region of frosts and snows he had visited the previous summer. Once more he tried to make land on the southern tip of Greenland, but mist colluded with the bulwark of icebergs to force the fleet to keep its distance. Storms now descended on the three ships as they made their way west across the stretch of water between Greenland and Baffin Island, but they held their course, finding their way to Little Hall's Island, their destination, this time all together.

It was 17 July.

Frobisher and Schutz, the metallurgist, scoured the island for evidence of the ore. They searched for hours. They found no piece of

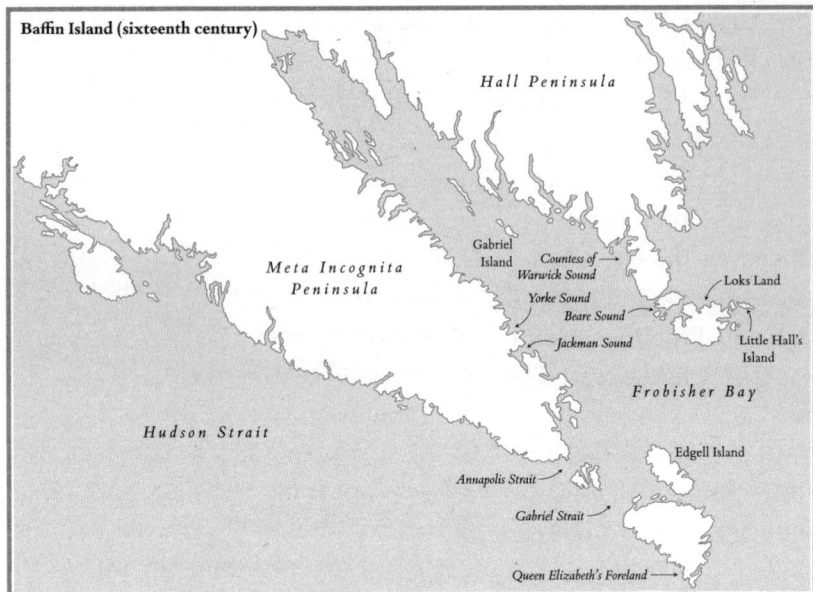

Baffin Island (sixteenth century)

Hall Peninsula

Meta Incognita
Peninsula

Gabriel
Island   *Countess of*
              Warwick Sound
          Yorke Sound
            Beare Sound
          Jackman Sound

Loks Land

Little Hall's
Island

Frobisher Bay

Hudson Strait

Edgell Island

Annapolis Strait

Gabriel Strait

Queen Elizabeth's Foreland

that shimmering rock larger than a 'walnut'.[2] Nothing of the 'loaf'-sized proportions that one of Frobisher's men had picked up the year before. It's curious that they kept comparing the rock to foodstuffs, perhaps revealing something about their hunger to find more of it.

A few days later, Frobisher and a large party of his men trekked across the neighbouring Great Hall's Island to its peak. He christened it Mount Warwick, after one of his patrons, and there had erected a column of stones as a sign of England's claim to the territory. As they began to descend the hill, several Inuit came to examine this new assemblage atop the island. They waved to the Englishmen to suggest they wanted to talk to them. Perhaps animosities had been forgiven or forgotten over the intervening months since their last encounter. Each group dispatched two men as their temporary ambassadors and they exchanged gifts: the Inuit gave two bow cases, the English gave pins.

The swap went smoothly, but Frobisher had instructions to bring back humans to England along with the ore. By then, Europeans who ventured across the Atlantic frequently abducted people they found, often to be paraded and shown off as symbols of conquests made in the name of European rulers. The next day, Frobisher and

Christopher Hall thought they had found their opportunity. They stumbled across two men who appeared to be unarmed. The English pair feigned the same protocol as the day before, pretending to offer an exchange of gifts, but then jumped on the two men when they neared, and tried to take them hostage. Frobisher and Hall miscalculated. The Inuit wrestled themselves free as their would-be captors slipped on the ice. The two Inuit retrieved their bows from behind a nearby rock and took aim at their aggressors. Their arrows drove Hall and Frobisher back to their boat. Scrambling away, Frobisher was struck in the rear. Their compatriots, hearing the noise, came to their aid. A caliver was fired. The Inuit retreated, and as they pulled away, one was tackled by a Cornish wrestler named Nicholas Conger.

The Inuk man, whose name has been recorded as Kalicho, would become another forced exile.

He is the best known and best documented of the Inuit to be brought back to England, and famously gave a demonstration of his prowess in hunting birds to the Mayor of Bristol. He paddled in a kayak on the River Avon and hit several ducks with his bird dart, amazing the English onlookers with his impeccable aim.[3] He did not survive many months in England, however, and appears to have died as a result of the broken ribs and a punctured lung he suffered when he was captured. He was buried in Bristol on 8 November 1577.[4]

John White's drawing of an Inuk, c. 1585–93

More domestic perils also hit Frobisher's fleet. A careless cook let a galley fire get out of hand, which threatened to incinerate the queen's investment in the enterprise. Smoke plumed out of the flagship. Luckily, a ship's boy spotted the smoke and sped to put out the flames. But just as this internal threat was extinguished, an external one presented itself. It was the weather's turn to try to destroy them. A storm broke out that evening which threw the ships violently about. The masters of the ships fought to stop them from being turned into driftwood. All around them they could see their enemies, the icebergs. They could no longer stay in such a treacherous anchorage. They had to move.[5]

Over the next few days, they sailed about the bay that they had called Frobisher Strait, seeking a safe place of harbour and the ore that was the raison d'être of their expedition, but had hitherto proven elusive. They looked first to the south, then to the north, eventually finding, close to what is today's Lefferts Island, a promising vein of minerals. They quarried ten tons of ore. Promising though this island was for their mining, it was no place to moor. The *Michael*'s hull was almost crushed by an iceberg against which the sailors had tied up.

On another island, they discovered a large fish preserved in the ice. This strange creature, a novelty to their eyes, was calqued onto an old and more familiar myth of a horned animal: they called it a 'sea unicorn'. It was probably a narwhal. The beast was de-tusked, like the walruses, elephants and rhinoceroses that were the other mammoth obsessions of the Renaissance. Its horny part passed into the queen's collection and was, we are told, prized like a jewel.[6] An image of the creature ended up in Best's account of the voyage.

A unicorn fish as depicted in George Best's account of Frobisher's voyages, 1578

It smirks, as if it knows something that we don't.

At last, they found a sound that was broader than the perilously narrow channels that had proven to be traps rather than havens for their vessels. Here they could safely anchor, protected from ice floes. They named this bay 'Countess of Warwick Sound' and found an island there, today's Kodlunarn Island, which was rich with seams of ore. It promptly became their base camp.

As they explored the surrounding area further, they came upon some abandoned Inuit roundhouses. Here Kalicho explained through gestures the use of objects that were found in the settlement. Then he wanted to communicate something else. Staying behind, he pushed five sticks into the ground in a circle, and placed a bone in the middle. He called the Englishmen back to see. At first, they worried that it was witchcraft and they were about to be cursed. But then they supposed he was trying to tell them something. Their best conjecture was that it was a message to his own people that he had been taken in exchange for the five men they had captured the previous year.[7]

Deadly Encounter

Meanwhile, Frobisher dispatched the *Michael* with its captain, Gilbert Yorke, to fetch the *Ayde*, which had been left across the bay in Jackman Sound. On arrival, Yorke reported that the previous day he had, much to his surprise, found traces of the five men who had been lost the year before: 'a doublet of canvas made after the English fashion, a shirt, a girdle, three shoes for contrary feet, and of unequal bigness, which they well conjectured to be the apparel of our five poor countrymen'.[8]

In direct contradiction of Frobisher's orders, Yorke sent the ships to the leader of their fleet, but took two pinnaces towards the shore with designs to talk to the Inuit or else capture some of them. Those tents had been removed, but as the Englishmen marched across the land, they spotted an Inuit settlement in a valley. The Inuit sought to escape in their boats, but the English fired off their calivers to signal to their comrades guarding the pinnaces to row and trap them. The

English forced the Inuit back ashore, who broke their oars so that their kayaks would not be taken. Then the Inuit set upon their attackers. In the fray, those Inuit who were mortally wounded launched themselves into the sea.

In Best's eyewitness account, this behaviour was troubling for the English. It flew in the face of their expectations. People weren't supposed to choose death over surrender. As Best recorded, it constituted a surprising act of defiance:

> And when they found they were mortally wounded, being ignorant what mercy meaneth, with deadly fury they cast themselves headlong from off the rocks into the sea, least perhaps their enemies should receive glory or prey off their dead carcasses, for they supposed us belike to be Cannibals, or eaters of man's flesh.[9]

This episode reads subtly differently in Dionyse Settle's account that was printed as part of Richard Hakluyt's monumental compendium of travel writings, the *Principal Navigations*, in 1599. Spot the difference:

> perceiving themselves thus hurt, they desperately leapt off the rocks into the sea and drowned themselves; which if they had not done, but had submitted themselves . . . we would both have saved them, and also have sought remedy to cure their wounds received at our hands. But they, altogether void of humanity, and ignorant what mercy meaneth, in extremities look for no other than death.[10]

Settle's version denigrates the Inuit and casts the English as benevolent. The Inuit here are not defiant, but ignorant. The insinuation of English cannibalism perhaps proved too much and had to be expunged. The Inuit refusal to submit was turned into an incontrovertible sign of their 'inhumanity'. It is worth remembering here that mercy is never a straightforward kindness. As a form of supplication, begging for mercy required abasement. It was a form of submission that crystallized an asymmetry of power and depended on a set of specific cultural norms. While the accounts of this episode do not give us direct access to the rationale of the Inuit, the English chroniclers worried about what they did. The need to dismiss their actions caused them to be registered as unruly and unexpected, a departure from the script that the English expected those they encountered to follow, a script that reinscribed their values, their superiority.

'Five or six' were killed. One of the English was injured. The survivors fled, but an older woman and a mother with a small child, who had been injured, were left behind. Ageism and misogyny have often imagined witchery and devil-work around old women. Here the men sought to verify this. They stripped her and pushed her to the ground. She had ten toes, not the cloven hooves of their paranoid imagination. But deemed too ugly, she was left behind. Youth was a better prize in their eyes. The younger woman and her child became the next English captives. The child had been injured in the arm by an Englishman's arrow, but rather than accept the salves that the surgeon offered, the mother removed them from her child's arm. She healed the wound with her own method, by licking it clean. This pair would be called Arnaq (the word for 'woman') and Nutaaq (the word for 'child'); and just like Kalicho, whom they now joined, they would also have their portraits taken after they were transported to England.

With blood on their hands and new captives in their boats, Yorke and his group of Englishmen returned to the rest of the fleet.[11]

An Ersatz Success

After mining for around a week on Kodlunarn Island, 160 tons of ore had been clawed from the earth and piled onto the ships, but the fleeting summer was fast beginning to wane. Frobisher's fuse was shortening too. On one occasion, Hall's forgetting to doff his hat when speaking to the captain sent Frobisher into a rage: 'being in a furious humour of temper, he openly reviled him with outrageous speeches and swore by god's blood he would hang him.'[12] A little extreme for a momentary lapse in courtesy. But hot-headedness – and vainglory – were Frobisher's defining traits. He was the foil throughout the venture to Hall's calm and caution.

The English dismantled their base camp as the snows began to settle in and took to their ships for the return journey. The *Michael*, detached from its consorts once more, had to make its own way to England, but docked safely in Yarmouth, while the *Ayde* and the *Gabriel*, although separated en route, both eventually reached Bristol.

On the expedition's arrival back in England, Elizabeth named the land which was not hers but which Frobisher had claimed on her behalf. She did not name it after herself or another person, though, as was the custom, but after an idea. She called it 'Meta Incognita', the 'Unknown Limits'. It is a peculiar – and alluring – name. It sounds a little romantic now, but its emphasis on the unknown was as much strategic as mysterious: if this place was 'unknown' from a European perspective, none of England's rivals could declare any real prior title to it. English commentators, like their French counterparts, rubbished the presumption that the world was divided up between Spain and Portugal after the Treaty of Tordesillas, arguing that no single nation could lay claim to such vast portions of the world.

News spread quickly about Frobisher's second voyage, and publications reporting on the expedition declared it a triumph. The fleet had broadly achieved what it had set out to do, but it could not truly announce that its endeavours were a complete success until the dark ballast in the ships had been assayed and precious elements coaxed from the rock. The extraction was becoming all the more pressing too as the bills were stacking up. Even while the expedition was out in the Arctic, the Privy Council had encouraged new investors to join the enterprise in order to shore up its finances. Not a single person came forward. Lok had also sought loans to cover the costs, but he was losing credit and had little collateral to secure his borrowing. In October 1577, then, there was no other option for raising capital but to impose levies on the existing investors at the rate of 20 per cent of their existing stake. Alas, in for a penny, in for a pound. Frobisher himself was still waiting to be paid for his services in November.

Over the course of several months, Schutz tried his hardest to tease some value out of the stones. The rubble refused to yield any gold. After an assay in October, Schutz revised his estimate of its value, reducing it to £40 a ton, which was somewhat less than the £240 a ton promised before Frobisher embarked on the second expedition. The result was the same when more of the ore was fed into a furnace again in the following month. The problem, supposedly, was that the facilities lacked the firepower to smelt the ore effectively and that there was gold still stuck in the slag. But you know what they say about bad workmen and their tools. For the moment, the rock piled up in Bristol and London remained 200 tons of promise rather than profit.

Another expert in metallurgy was consulted: Burchard Kranich. You'd think that bringing in another specialist would have swiftly proved that the ore was worthless, but the immediate rivalry and animosity that set in between the two Saxon metallurgists had exactly the opposite effect. It prolonged the blind faith in the value of the ore even after Kranich was found to be tampering with the samples by adding silver salts when melting them down, thereby giving the impression that there were more precious metals in the ore than was actually the case.[13] The fact that both Schutz and Kranich were so desperate to win the right to be the sole assayer made everyone else involved sure that the ore was worth fighting over, even if hotter furnaces were needed to extract its true worth.[14]

Colonial Designs

Further experiments in 1578 continued to suggest a low value for the ore, and the recommendation remained that larger facilities were needed to extract the gold effectively. The business model had to change. The investors needed to double down on their investment. Bigger furnaces, more ore, that was how they would see a profit. Meanwhile, as news of the venture spread abroad, a threat began to loom in the minds of the English that another nation might jump in and steal their gold mine from under their noses. So the preparations that began to be made for, yes, a third voyage grew to include not only mining and freight-carrying on a much larger scale than before, but also the establishment of a permanent English colony in Nunavut. It would be the first English colony across the Atlantic.

To provide for this English usurpation of territory on the other side of the ocean, a prefabricated building was planned for the men to live in, its timbers, bricks and mortar to be ferried across the ocean. A flat-packed invasion. Doubtful of how easily a hundred men could sustain themselves through agriculture or hunting in the harsh conditions, enough meat, dried fish, bread, biscuit, wheatmeal and dried peas for a year would be transported to feed those who lived in the prefab until ships would return the following summer with further provisions.

These supplies were loaded onto a much larger fleet than before. In addition to the vessels that had already made their way across the Atlantic under Frobisher's command, one ship was purchased in return for shares in the venture, and seven others were chartered for the voyage. For Frobisher, the larger the fleet the greater the glory. And, for the investors, the bigger the liabilities. According to Lok, Frobisher was very concerned about his reputation and evidently decided to go big as he arranged for an additional four ships to join from among his old privateering friends.

It was the largest ever expedition to the north and would remain so for centuries. But Frobisher had a rival as England's number one explorer. In December 1577, Francis Drake had set out to find the supposed southern continent, referred to as Terra Australis. He would return nearly three years later, having been all the way around the globe. And he would thus completely overshadow the calamitous and expensive failure that Frobisher's venture turned out to be.

Trouble at Sea

On each of the two previous voyages, Frobisher and his fleet had followed the same navigational tactic: head due north to the desired latitude, then head due west. But this time, rather than sailing up through the North Sea, they went west first. It turned out to be a good decision as they reached the southern tip of Greenland more swiftly than before. They were even able to go ashore where ice had repeatedly resisted their earlier attempts. Frobisher claimed the land for his queen and took a whelp from some Inuit tents they found nearby. Such territorial claims still feel alive today, as Greenland is still subject to a European power, Denmark, and has in recent years been negotiating its independence.

The fleet set out to explore the rest of the coast but familiar fog soon submerged them in grey. Deprived of one sense, they kept in touch through their ears rather than their eyes. Trumpets and drums reassured them that they were still together. This acoustic tether proved enough to keep most of the fleet close. One ship, though, the *Michael*, drifted away from the rest. It would be four lonely and difficult weeks before its crew saw their compatriots again.

The majority of the fleet glided away from the fog across Davis Strait. Here the *Judith* also became separated from the rest of the fleet by ice floes. The other thirteen ships pressed on. Eventually, they spotted land, but they were still more than 150 kilometres away from Countess of Warwick Sound, their destination. That distance would multiply through navigational error and would not prove an easy final leg.

Seeing a huge iceberg in the strait that lay ahead of the fleet, the expedition's chief pilot, Christopher Hall – who was sailing with Gilbert Yorke – begged caution. But no one heeded the warning of the Cassandra of the voyage. At this point in previous years, they had encountered very little ice, but this time was different. The seasons had set an unexpected trap. Those who followed Frobisher ended up in a polynya, an oceanic lake bordered with banks of ice. The ships had to furl their sails to avoid being blown into a collision course with the encircling ice. The *Denys*, however, failed to take in its sails and crashed. In half an hour, the ship had sunk. The crew were all rescued, but key components of the blockhouse were swallowed by the icy waters along with the expedition's hopes of founding a colony.

Surrounded by the unmerciful ice, some of the ships moored themselves to the larger icebergs, hoping thereby to find some shelter from the smaller ones. Others, attacked by encroaching ice, had to improvise defences. They formed makeshift buffers out of all they could lay their hands on. They slung beds, masts, planks and cables over the sides of the vessels to cushion against impacts. With poles and bits of timber, other men stood guard on deck, manually fending off the ice. The ships were besieged. Thick boards snapped like matches with the force of the impending ice, but they did successfully defend their hulls from being crushed.[15]

On 3 July, the ships finally broke free of their prison. Back out in the safety of the open ocean, the crew made urgent repairs. Below the surface, though, the currents were dragging them south. Under-estimating the strength of the sea's pull, Frobisher determined that they must be near the northern shore of his strait and close to their desired destination. Low visibility prevented them from taking their latitude from the height of the sun, so they could not be sure. Hall, by far the wisest of the mariners, correctly inferred from soundings and observations that they were some distance further south than Frobisher thought. But the captain persisted in his error. Hall even took his pinnace over to the captain's ship to reason with him. Frobisher exploded. He swore on God's wounds that he would take his own life if they were not where he said they were. Unable to make Frobisher listen to him, Hall returned to his own ship, mistreated, but still sure in himself. He held his vessel back as Frobisher took most of the fleet into the strait that lay before them. Four other ships lingered behind with Hall; together they turned east in search of Countess of Warwick Sound. It wasn't complete desertion, but it was certainly somewhere near the edge of mutiny.

Hall was right about the mysterious strait. Frobisher and the bulk of the fleet wasted several precious days of the already short summer sailing in the wrong direction. To commemorate the error, they dubbed the channel 'the Mistaken Strait' (today's Hudson Strait). Having retraced their course back east again, they spotted Queen Elizabeth's Foreland and headed north. But again they miscalculated, and on 18 July ended up in another channel (today's Annapolis Strait), menaced on every side by ice and jagged rocks. Some of the fleet had to claw its way out laboriously by kedging – dropping the anchor ahead of the ship, then hauling on the cable to move the craft in the desired direction. Frobisher was beginning to lose patience. They battled against ice and wind for nearly two weeks, trying to find their way to and enter Frobisher's eponymous strait. Five ships left Frobisher's *Ayde* and another four vessels behind and charted their own course to the agreed meeting point. By 30 July, Frobisher was close enough to Countess of Warwick Sound to take a pinnace into it and make his final approach to the expedition's destination.

To his surprise, Frobisher found the *Michael* and the *Judith* already waiting at the rendezvous, despite the ordeals the two ships had individually endured. But while he was away in the pinnace, the ice was busy causing problems for the rest of his fleet anchored on the other side of the bay. His flagship, the *Ayde*, had just hoisted its anchor clear of the water when the vessel was struck by ice and one of the anchor's flukes punctured the hull. The pumps had not been standing by, and so could not counter the water flooding in. The sailors reached for anything that they could get their hands on to plug the hole, including a side of beef. Over a metre of water entered in just an hour. They spent the night bailing it out with buckets until they could bring the ship into harbour the following morning, when they heeled it over on one side and fixed the hole temporarily with lead.

Digging for Profit

On 1 August, the men of the expedition finally began their work of excavating the riches of the earth. They set to digging in various locations, not just on Kodlunarn Island, seeking the perfect seam – rich in ore, but close enough to the shore to make loading the ships easy. Over the course of the month, they excavated a total of 1,370 tons of ore from ten sites. As they laboured, they faced ever-present perils from the ice and the rocks. There was a steady stream of casualties caused by fatigue and the cold.

On 9 August, Frobisher held a council to discuss establishing the colony. They had lost some of the key components of the planned blockhouse with the sinking of the *Denys* and they could not build something from scratch in the time they had remaining. The ships that had not followed the captain into Frobisher Strait were still absent, and so they lacked further key provisions for construction and their sustenance. (Four of the ships eventually made it to Countess of Warwick Sound later in the month; the fifth, unbeknown to Frobisher, had deserted and sailed for England.) The council decided, then, not to leave any men behind on Kodlunarn Island over the winter; instead they constructed a small dwelling, a house ready for them to return to the following year (but to which they never would). Inside this cottage they left freshly baked bread and a selection of items, supposedly 'the better to allure those brutish and uncivil people to courtesy, against other times of our coming'.[16] The house and its offerings constituted a ghostly and hollow form of hospitality. Gifts and a welcome meal left in an abandoned building. They were also born of misplaced arrogance. The Inuit had long endured the harsh winters; these English accoutrements weren't going to change their ways of living and surviving.

By the end of August, it was the familiar story of the changing seasons. Snow had begun to cover the earth and the ships in white. Frobisher and his men needed to flee the incoming cold. They decided to set sail in their ships laden with rock.

Epic Failure?

In the expedition's absence, huge smelting works had been constructed at Dartford in Kent, ready to process its bounty. After the ships returned to England in dribs and drabs in September and October, two assays were made of the ore they brought back, but nothing of value was extracted. Frobisher was no Midas with a golden touch. It later emerged that, like the whole enterprise, the furnaces were poorly conceived – their design was so bad that they could not refine any ore, and certainly not that containing only imaginary gold. The ore was sold off to repair roads and buildings as an exotic, but cheap, form of aggregate. You can still find this dark debris in walls around Dartford today. The furnaces were abandoned, just as mills and mines and factories have often been abandoned in the shifting economic landscape of England. In hindsight, the very first assessments of the ore were the most accurate. It was indeed rubble.

To meet the massive outstanding balances for crew wages and freight charges, the expedition's backers had to suffer another levy, assessed at an eye-watering 85 per cent of their existing investment.

Some, including the queen, did cough up, writing off the disaster. None of the Privy Council members, however, paid their dues. Consequently, Lok ended up in debtors' prison eight times as the company failed to pay its creditors.

Frobisher luckily escaped any formal reproach. In later years, he was involved in abortive ventures to the Moluccas and to North America once more, but was never trusted with a commercial enterprise again. Serving as Drake's vice-admiral in a raid on the West Indies in 1585 brought him back into good repute. Where violence and a lack of caution were assets, he was welcomed. Where money was concerned, he was not. Frobisher found his way into a printed album of English heroes in 1620. This *English Heroology – Heroologia Anglica* – was a sort of printed Hall of Fame. Like any form of commemoration, though, it was somewhat selective. Frobisher's failures received no mention at all in the blurb biography that accompanied his portrait. Rather amusingly, his name in the border around his portrait noted that he was a knight bachelor, or *eques auratus* in Latin. More literally, *eques auratus* means 'gilded' or 'golden knight'.

Frobisher's and Lok's story is one where proverbial prudence – all that glisters is not gold; do not throw good money after bad; the bad workman blames his tools – begged to be heeded, but it never was.

Posthumous portrait of Martin Frobisher, 1620

It epitomizes so much that we have explored throughout this book. Frobisher and the English were just like the Spanish, Portuguese and French in looking everywhere for the glitter of precious metals. But, like Vasco da Gama and Jacques Cartier, Frobisher returned to Europe at the end of his voyages with less than he'd hoped for. Greed overran his good sense, just as the hunger for profit made Manuel de Sousa de Sepúlveda overload the *São João* and cause the death of almost everyone it carried. The Inuit resisted European intrusions into their territory around Baffin Island just as Enrique did on Hispaniola, Guerrero and the Maya did in Yucatán, and as the Tupinambá did in Brazil. The ambitions of Frobisher and his queen to found a colony in Nunavut were as ephemeral as those of Cartier, Roberval and Marguerite in another part of the territory we now know as Canada. Magellan might have found his passage west, unlike Frobisher, but he was defeated by Lapulapu in Mactan, so never returned home. It is striking that Kalicho, the Inuk abducted by Frobisher, died within a few months of being brought to England, while Gonzalo Guerrero, who washed up in Yucatán after his ship was wrecked, built a long and fulfilling life for himself in another culture (even if most of his Spanish comrades were killed on the shores of Mexico before they could emulate his happy fate).

Europeans did not simply arrive and conquer only to be ejected during the anti-colonial struggles of much later centuries. Rather, resistance and blunders were both persistent occurrences. From the beginning, questions were raised about the morality of European actions and even whether, in economic terms, they were worth it. Stories of disaster spread across Europe, retold in different languages and transformed into different genres. The ripples of a shipwreck like Manuel de Sousa de Sepúlveda's spread far and wide. In seeing how explorers failed to reach their intended destinations and were laughed at, shot at and argued against along the way – not to mention how the weather and terrain often thwarted their progress – we see that empire was not inevitable. We are reminded that the cumulative exploitation that got us here led to just one possible present; things could have, and often did, go a different way. The past is open for renegotiation. We can go back to European sources and see how they conflict with one another and how, overlooked within them, there are dimensions of indigenous knowledge and defiance. We can see too that, whether it is the repatriation of a red feather mantle to its ancestral home or an art installation that casts a wry eye over the iconography of 'discovery', there are now new ways of looking at the past and new creative, legal and political approaches to redressing the injustices of history, at least in part.

Typically, we associate the first century of European intercontinental voyages either with somehow exemplifying the pinnacle of human tenacity or with inaugurating an unmitigated descent towards the untrammelled exploitation of peoples and nature. Overall, the pessimistic view is more clear-sighted about the wholesale impact of European empires. Yet if we hold back on the broad brushstrokes for a moment, we can see – as I have shown in the stories I have told – that there is a more intricate picture to look at, one which qualifies 'great achievements' with the details of what went wrong, and which accommodates the agency of those who challenged the arrival of empires and their later imperial impositions. That picture does not classify resistance, misunderstanding, misjudgement, incompetence or even the effects of bad weather as mere setbacks or inconsequential details that can be skipped over in our rush to look forward and plot history along the familiar arc of the rise and fall of civilizations. Instead, it is a picture that gives space to Enrique and the Taíno, Gonzalo Guerrero and the Maya, the Tupinikin and Tupinambá, Marguerite de Roberval and, yes, even a chancer like Hans Staden, and sketches truer to life portraits of figures such as Vasco da Gama, Ferdinand Magellan, Jean-François de la Rocque and Martin Frobisher. Following the lives of the individuals in this book gives us vivid snapshots of the complex realities on the ground and on the sea in the fifteenth and sixteenth centuries, and leads us to see that as much as this was the age of so-called 'discovery', it was also the age of wreckers.

WORLD EVENTS

1577
Francis Drake begins
his circumnavigation of
the globe – Plymouth,
England

1582
Oda Nobunaga, unifier
of Japan, is assassinated
– Kyoto, Japan

1590
Roanoke Colony, the
'Lost Colony' found to have
disappeared – Roanoke
Island, North
Carolina, USA

1578
Battle of Alcácer
Quibir, forces led by
Sultan Abd al-Malik
defeat the Portu-
guese – Ksar el-Kebir,
Morocco

1588
Defeat of the
Spanish Armada
by the English
fleet – English
Channel

1580
*Santa
Catalina*,
Spain

1587
São Salvador,
Portugal:
wrecked near
Hormen, Iran.

1591
Penelope,
England:
wrecked in Algoa
Bay, South Africa.

1583
HMS *Delight*,
England: Ran
aground on
Sable Island,
Nova Scotia.

HMS *Squirrel*,
England:
Foundered
near the
Azores.

1585
Santiago,
Portugal:
Wrecked on
Bassas da India,
Mozambique
Channel.

1578
Marigold, England:
Wrecked in the
Strait of Magellan.

SHIPWRECKS

1592
Japanese
invasions of
Korea begin
– Korea

1596
Dutch explorer Willem
Barentsz reaches Spitsbergen
– Spitsbergen (Svalbard),
Arctic Ocean

1598
Edict of Nantes
grants religious
freedom to Protest-
ants in France –
Nantes, France

1595
Santa Magharita,
Spain: Lost off
Florida.

1593
Santo Alberto,
Portugal: Sank
near Umtata
river, South
Africa.

1597
Amsterdam,
Dutch Republic:
Damaged then
set on fire near
Bawean Island
(Indonesia).

1605
Hoop, Dutch
Republic: Lost in
the Pacific Ocean
during a storm.

1596
San Felipe, Spain:
Wrecked on
Shikoku, Japan.

San Pedro, Spain:
Wrecked near
Bermuda in a
hurricane.

Notes

Unless otherwise specified, all translations of quotations are my own.

Introduction

1 Galeano, *Open Veins*, p. 171.
2 Duffy, *Shipwreck and Empire*, p. 63.
3 Arteaga, Desierto, Koyama, 'Shipwrecked by Rents', p. 11.
4 See *Journey without Return*, https://www.shipwrecks.es/.
5 Cressy, *Shipwrecks and the Bounty of the Sea*, p. 23.
6 See McCarthy, 'Gambling on Empire', pp. 71–4.
7 Havard and Vidal, *Histoire de l'Amérique française*, pp. 27–51.
8 See, respectively: Lyon, 'Spain's Sixteenth-Century North American Settlement'; Cervantes, *Conquistadores*, p. 84; and Bobb, 'Pedro Sarmiento de Gamboa'.
9 For a broad overview of later struggles in the Portuguese empire, see Newitt, *History of Portuguese Overseas Expansion*, pp. 203–34.
10 See Oberg, 'Tribes and Towns' and *The Head in Edward Nugent's Hand*.
11 Abulafia, *Discovery of Mankind*, pp. 168–9.
12 Cervantes, *Conquistadores*, pp. 30–31.
13 Cervantes, *Conquistadores*, pp. 43–7, 50–53.
14 Colón, *Textos y documentos*, pp. 317–18.
15 As you will see in later chapters, decolonial methods and practices are manifold. Some important works that have inspired my approach include: Azoulay, *Potential History*; Biedermann, *(Dis)connected Empires*; Gopal, *Insurgent Empire*; Hartman, 'Venus in Two Acts'; Mignolo, 'Epistemic Disobedience'; Sharpe, *In the Wake*; Trouillot, *Silencing the Past*.
16 Trouillot, *Silencing the Past*, p. 116.
17 Trouillot, *Silencing the Past*, pp. 113–15.
18 Azoulay, *Potential History*, p. 43.

Part One: The Explorer Who Asked for Directions

1 Smith, *Wealth of Nations*, II, 235.
2 For an excellent biography of Da Gama, from which I have drawn in this chapter, see Subrahmanyam, *Career and Legend*.
3 For information about the construction of Da Gama's fleet and the sourcing of its timber, see Barros, 'O Porto e a construção dos navios de Vasco da Gama'.

1. Into the Unknown

1 Camões, *Os Lusíadas*, IV.94–104.
2 Details of the voyage are all taken from the surviving ship's log: Velho, *Roteiro*. To avoid too many notes, hereafter I only note information not provided in the log itself. An English translation is available as *A Journal of the First Voyage of Vasco da Gama*, ed. Ravenstein.
3 Quoted in Subrahmanyam, *Career and Legend*, p. 124.
4 On the question of what the words 'discovery' and 'to discover' encompassed in the early modern period, see Godinho, *O papel de Portugal*.
5 Middleton, *The World of the Swahili*, pp. 46–7.
6 *Livro de Duarte Barbosa*, pp. 25–6. See also Burton, 'Urbanization in East Africa'.

2. The Portuguese Are Discovered

1 Subrahmanyam, *Career and Legend*, p. 120.
2 See Biedermann, 'Global Navigations', especially pp. 24, 39–40.
3 Saraiva (ed.), *Ditos portugueses*, p. 113.
4 For an overview of the history of the Portuguese empire in this period, see Newitt, *History of Portuguese Overseas Expansion*.
5 Quoted in Subrahmanyam, *Empires between Islam and Christianity*, pp. 32–3.
6 Moura Hue, *Antologia*, p. 153.
7 For this episode, see Flores and Marcocci, 'Killing Images', pp. 463–8.

Part Two: Double Treachery

3. Two Worlds in One Person

1 Cervantes, *Conquistadores*, p. 27.

2 Cervantes, *Conquistadores*, p. 27.

3 Colón, *Textos y documentos*, p. 141.

4 Leyes de Burgos, XVII, F.614 v, cited in Altamira, 'El texto', p. 35.

5 Stone, *Captives of Conquest*, pp. 61–3.

6 Stone, *Captives of Conquest*, p. 213 n. 63.

7 Cervantes, *Conquistadores*, p. 60.

8 Las Casas, *Historia de las Indias*, I, 358–9.

9 Carrasquillo, 'La creación', p. 70.

10 For more on the evolving legal status of different indigenous groups in the Caribbean and the constant Spanish violence against them, see Stone, *Captives of Conquest*, pp. 46–53.

11 Las Casas, *An Account*, p. 6; see also pp. 64–5 for equally vivid imagery describing the Spanish in Venezuela.

12 For more on Montesinos's sermon denouncing the Spanish treatment of indigenous groups and on the Laws of Burgos, see Stone, *Captives of Conquest*, pp. 58–60.

13 On the *repartimiento* of Albuquerque, its objectives and effects, see Stone, 'America's First Slave Revolt', p. 204.

14 For more on the architecture of colonial Santo Domingo, see Niell, 'Colonial Gothic', and Pérez Montás, *La ciudad del Ozama*.

15 Oviedo, *Coronica*, fols. 58v–59r.

16 Ponce Vásquez, *Islanders and Empire*, pp. 28–30.

17 Las Casas, *Historia de las Indias*, III, 261.

18 Las Casas, *An Account*, p. 15.

19 Cervantes, *Conquistadores*, p. 62.

20 Stone, 'America's First Slave Revolt', p. 204.

21 Lane, 'Africans and Natives in the Mines of Spanish America', p. 166.

22 See Stone, *Captives of Conquest*, p. 144.

23 Parry and Keith (eds.), *New Iberian World*, II, 329–34.

24 Altman, 'The Revolt of Enriquillo', p. 601.

25 Utrera, *Polémica de Enriquillo*, p. 185. See also, Guitar, 'Cultural Genesis', pp. 353–4.

26 The sentiment was expressed by the royal treasurer of Hispaniola, Miguel de Pasamonte, in 1529. See Guitar, 'Cultural Genesis', p. 361, and Utrera, *Polémica de Enriquillo*, pp. 480–81.

27 Guitar, 'Cultural Genesis', p. 366.

28 'Ha sido mui grande el gasto desta guerra', in Marté (ed.), *Santo Domingo*, p. 331.

29 Marté (ed.), *Santo Domingo*, p. 365.

30 See Crosby, *Ecological Imperialism*, pp. 173–6.

31 Las Casas, *Historia de las Indias*, iii, 268.

32 Las Casas, *Historia de las Indias*, iii, 268–9.

33 Marté (ed.), *Santo Domingo*, pp. 296–7.

34 Utrera, *Polémica de Enriquillo*, p. 144.

35 For a succinct summary of the peace negotiations over time, see Altman, 'The Revolt of Enriquillo', pp. 602–8.

4. The Lost and the Found

1 Martínez (ed.), *Documentos cortesianos*, pp. 47–8.

2 López de Gómara, *Cortés*, p. 26.

3 Clendinnen, *Ambivalent Conquests*, p. ix.

4 Díaz de Castillo, *True History*, pp. 93–5.

5 Thomas, *Conquest of Mexico*, p. 162.

6 Romoli, *Balboa*, p. 47.

7 Romoli, *Balboa*, pp. 119–20.

8 An excellent summary of the various versions of Gonzalo Guerrero's history can be found in Adorno, *Polemics of Possession*, pp. 220–45.

9 Seler, *Die Ruinen*, p. 91; Tozzer, *Landa's Relación*, p. 91. See also Houston, Taube and Stuart, *Memory of Bones*, pp. 18–22, and Lukach and Dobereiner, 'The Painted Body', pp. 46–50.

10 Finegold, 'Vitality Materialized', p. 75.

11 Adorno, *Polemics of Possession*, p. 232.

12 Martínez (ed.), *Documentos cortesianos*, pp. 47–8.

13 Clendinnen, *Ambivalent Conquests*, pp. 139–40.

14 Tozzer, *Landa's Relación*, pp. 192–3.

15 Clendinnen, *Ambivalent Conquests*, p. 152; Ardren, *Everyday Life*, p. 28.

16 Clendinnen, *Ambivalent Conquests*, p. 152.

17 Roys and Hoil, *Book of Chilam Balam*, p. 83.

Part Three: Around the World in 150 Deaths

1 Las Casas, *Historia de las Indias*, III, 175.

2 Garcia, *Fernão de Magalhães*, pp. 21–5.

5. Beleaguered Beginnings

1 A very full and detailed biography of Magellan in English is provided by Fernández-Armesto, *Straits*. In Portuguese there is Garcia, *Fernão de Magalhães*. Garcia's article 'Documentos existentes em Portugal' catalogues many of the sources available for the voyage. Stanley, *The First Voyage*, is now rather old but includes a number of documents in English translation, including the accounts of Antonio Pigafetta and Maximilian Transylvanus.

2 Garcia, *Fernão de Magalhães*, pp. 100–107.

3 Garcia, *Fernão de Magalhães*, pp. 137–8.

4 On the possible sources of information that Magellan had to hand for planning his journey, see Loureiro, 'As fontes'. For the idea that Magellan intentionally headed for the Philippines, see Field, 'Revisiting Magellan's Voyage', p. 314, and Fernández-Armesto, *Straits*, pp. 92–4.

5 Oliveira, *Viagem do Magalhães*, p. 78.

6 Pigafetta, *First Voyage*, p. 12.

7 The comment is made by Maximilian Transylvanus, in Stanley, *The First Voyage*, p. 194.

8 Herrera, *Historia general*, II, 237.

9 Barros, *Ásia, Década Terceira, parte primeira*, p. 645.

6. Adverse Endings

1 Pigafetta, *First Voyage*, p. 24.

2 Rodriguez, 'Juan de Salcedo', p. 160.

3 Adapted from the translation of Castanheda provided in the forthcoming Pinto, *Philippine History Retrieval*.

4 Adapted from the translation of Correia in Pinto, *Philippine History Retrieval*.

5 Pigafetta, *First Voyage*, p. 57.

6 For a detailed study of how Filipino indigenous perspectives on battle differed from those of the Iberians, see Angeles, 'The Battle of Mactan'.

7 Camões, *Os Lusíadas*, VIII.3.

8 For discussion of how colonization of the Philippines was incomplete, see Mawson, *Incomplete Conquests*.

9 Acabado, 'Archaeology of Pericolonialism', pp. 1–4.

10 Stoler, *Along the Archival Grain*, p. 181.

Part Four: False Diamonds and True Survival

1 *Voyages of Jacques Cartier*, p. 10.

7. Convicts, Captains and Lovers

1 Knecht, *Rise and Fall of Renaissance France*, p. 252.

2 Knecht, *Rise and Fall of Renaissance France*, p. 249.

3 *Voyages of Jacques Cartier*, p. 142.

4 The report by the Cardinal of Toledo's spy was discovered in the Imperial Archives at Vienna, and is reproduced in translation in *Voyages of Jacques Cartier*, pp. 152–5.

5 *Voyages of Jacques Cartier*, p. 132.

6 See Allaire, *Rumeur dorée*, pp. 35–47.

7 See Johnston, *Beard Fetish*, p. 65. See also Fisher, 'The Renaissance Beard', p. 156.

8 Details of the sketch are provided in Zvereva, *Les Clouet de Catherine de Médicis*, pp. 135–8.

9 Allaire, *Rumeur dorée*, pp. 152–3.

10 Allaire, *Rumeur dorée*, pp. 69–71.

11 See Borges, 'Aspetos do quotidiano'.

12 Léry, *History of a Voyage*, p. 8.

13 Casimiro and Borges, 'Life on Board Portuguese Ships', p. 2028.

14 Léry, *History of a Voyage*, p. 208.

8. The Lady's Isle

1 Schlesinger and Stabler (eds.), *André Thevet's North America*, p. 15.

2 Borges, 'Aspetos do quotidiano', p. 210.

3 *Voyages of Jacques Cartier*, p. 111.

4 See Durzan, 'Arginine, Scurvy and Cartier's "Tree of Life"'.

5 Schlesinger and Stabler (eds.), *André Thevet's North America*, p. 60.

6 Quoted in Biggar, *A Collection of Documents*, p. 34.

7 See Boyer, *Colony of One*, pp. 121–7.

8 Ferguson, *Dido's Daughters*, p. 255.

9 See Gopal, 'On Decolonization and the University', pp. 878–80.

10 Ramanujan, 'Some Thoughts', p. 331.

Part Five: Living with the Enemy

1 Dias et al., *História da colonização do Brasil*, III, 365–6.

2 What follows in Chapters 9–10 draws largely on Hans Staden's account. There is a useful translation into English with excellent contextualizing material: *Hans Staden's True Story*, ed. by Whitehead and Harbsmeier. My notes below are reserved for information not covered by Staden's own account.

9. Frontiers of Hatred

1 Monteiro, *Blacks of the Land*, p. 22.

2 Monteiro, 'Crises and Transformations', pp. 976–7.

3 Monteiro, 'Crises and Transformations', pp. 973–4.

4 Viveiros de Castro, *Inconstancy of the Indian Soul*, p. 36.

5 See also Hemming, *Red Gold*, pp. 150–52, and Monteiro, *Blacks of the Land*, p. 23.

6 Monteiro, *Blacks of the Land*, pp. 20–21.

7 Dias et al., *História da colonização do Brasil*, III, 259.

8 Barros, *Ásia*, I, III. English translation from Sadlier, *Brazil Imagined*, p. 19.

9 Léry, *History of a Voyage*, p. 60.

10 Buono, ' "Their Treasures Are the Feathers of Birds" ', p. 180.

11 See the discussion on the dyeing of feathers in Buono, 'Feathered Identities', pp. 112–20. For the passage in Gândavo, see Gândavo, *A primeira história do Brasil*, pp. 112–13.

12 Roxo, 'The Return of the Tupinambá Mantle'.

13 Viveiros de Castro, *Inconstancy of the Indian Soul*, pp. 65–7.

14 Jeremiah 17:5.

15 Thevet, quoted in Sadlier, *Brazil Imagined*, p. 36.

10. Prophecies and Realities

1 Viveiros de Castro, *Inconstancy of the Indian Soul*, p. 45.

2 For outbreaks of smallpox and measles in Brazil during the period and their effect on indigenous populations, see, for instance, Monteiro, *Blacks of the Land*, pp. 25–6, and Schwartz, 'Indian Labor', p. 58.

3 The response has been talked about at some length by anthropologists: see Agnolin, 'Antropofagia ritual e identidade', pp. 138–44.

4 For an extensive discussion of *maracás*, see Tomlinson, *The Singing of the New World*, pp. 110–20.

5 Duffy and Metcalf, *Return of Hans Staden*, p. 70.

6 Monteiro, 'Crises and Transformations', p. 980.

7 Krenak, quoted in Novaes (ed.), *Outra margem*, p. 25.

8 Kopenawa, quoted in Novaes (ed.), *Outra margem*, p. 19.

Part Six: Sunken Aspirations

1 *Documentos sobre os portugueses*, VII, 292.

2 See Jesus, 'O segundo cerco de Diu', pp. 29–30, and D'Silva, 'Nuno da Cunha', p. 215.

3 Jesus, 'O segundo cerco de Diu'.

4 Subrahmanyam, 'Written on Water'.

5 Flores, 'Floating Franks', p. 37.

6 Arquivo Nacional do Torre do Tombo, Corpo Cronológico, Parte I, mç. 66, n.º 40.

7 Boxer, *Portuguese Seaborne Empire*, p. 300. For more on how salaries were supplemented in various ways by captains, see Subrahmanyam, *Portuguese Empire in Asia*, p. 82, and Cruz, 'A viagem de Gonçalo Pereira Marramaque'.

8 Couto, *Ásia*, v.2, 197.

9 Biedermann, 'The Portuguese Estado da Índia (Empire in Asia)'.

10 *Documentos sobre os portugueses*, III, 260.

11 Subrahmanyam, *Across the Green Sea*, p. 79.

12 For details on the various reports about Falcão's death, see: Mendes, 'Luís Falcão', pp. 33–4.

13 Corte-Real, *Naufrágio e Lastimoso Sucesso*, Cantos II and III.

11. The Weight of Greed

1 Arquivo Nacional do Torre do Tombo, Corpo Cronológico, Parte I, mç. 77, n.º 70.

2 Sousa Coutinho, *História do cerco de Diu*, pp. 214–15.

3 Baião, *História quinhentista*, p. 312.

4 See the anonymous *Auto da Padeiras* (*Play of the Baker Women*), ll. 464–71, in Camões (ed.), *Teatro português do século XVI*, 1.3.

5 Orta, *Coloquios*, pp. 171–7.

6 Acosta, *Tractado*, pp. 21–9.

7 See Thomaz, 'A questão da pimenta', and Pearson, *The Portuguese in India*, pp. 41–9.

8 See, for instance, the complaints by the crown's treasurer in Goa, Simão Botelho, in the year of Manuel's departure: *Documentos sobre os portugueses*, VII, 286–8.

9 The story which follows is another that comes to us from a single source. The account of the wreck of the *São João* was first printed as a pamphlet, probably between 1555 and 1564, although it is not dated. The story is more widely known from the version which was reprinted in the eighteenth-century compendium of Portuguese shipwreck

stories known as the *História trágico-marítima*. This was partly translated by the historian Charles Boxer as *The Tragic History of the Sea* (1959–68), which was reissued in 2001 with the addition of a translation of the *São João*'s story by Josiah Blackmore. Other notes relate to information not derived from this account.

10 See *Património de influência portuguessa*, https://hpip.org/pt.

11 Boxer, *Portuguese Seaborne Empire*, p. 216.

12 Casimiro and Borges, 'Life on Board Portuguese Ships', pp. 2027–8.

13 Boxer, *Portuguese Seaborne Empire*, p. 218.

14 On the slave trade in the Indian Ocean, see, for instance, Allen, *European Slave Trading*, and 'Ending the History of Silence', as well as Pinto, 'The Forgotten Community'.

15 See Seed, *Ceremonies of Possession*.

16 Jorge, *A costa dos murmúrios*.

17 Evans and Rydén, ' "Voyage Iron" '.

12. A Trek to Tragedy

1 For data on prices and wages, see *Prices, Wages and Rents in Portugal 1300–1910*, http://pwr-portugal.ics.ul.pt/.

2 Welch, *South Africa under John III*, p. 334.

3 The etymology of the word *cafre* is noted by the sixteenth-century historian João de Barros in Barros, *Ásia*, 1.2, 206.

4 Welch, *South Africa under John III*, p. 334.

Part Seven: Not Quite Drake

1 Andrews, *Trade, Plunder, and Settlement*, pp. 64–75.

2 Hakluyt, *Principal Navigations*, iii, 130–31.

3 For a counter-argument to Gilbert's proposal, see the transcription of Richard Grenville's discourse provided in McDermott, *Martin Frobisher*, pp. 100–101.

13. *Albion's Would-Be Columbus*

1 Michael Lok, 'Testimony', in McDermott (ed.), *Third Voyage*, p. 84.

2 For a more detailed account of Frobisher's early life, see McDermott, *Martin Frobisher*, pp. 7–47.

3 Lane, *Pillaging the Empire*, pp. 2–3.

4 McDermott, *Martin Frobisher*, pp. 108, 115.

5 For the voyage's preparations, see McDermott, *Martin Frobisher*, pp. 120–35.

6 Christopher Hall, 'The First Voyage of M. Martine Frobisher', in Hakluyt, *Principal Navigations*, III, 30.

7 Thomas Ellis, 'A True Reporte of the Third and Last Voyage into Meta Incognita', in McDermott (ed.), *Third Voyage*, p. 198.

8 McDermott, *Martin Frobisher*, p. 138.

9 The phrase is from Dionyse Settle, 'The Second Voyage of Master Martin Frobisher', in Hakluyt, *Principal Navigations*, III, 34. For the taking of the rock, see Lok, 'Testimony', in McDermott (ed.), *Third Voyage*, p. 72.

10 Hall, 'First Voyage', in Hakluyt, *Principal Navigations*, III, 31.

11 Settle, 'Second Voyage', in Hakluyt, *Principal Navigations*, III, 38–9.

12 Hall, 'First Voyage', in Hakluyt, *Principal Navigations*, III, 31.

13 Engelhard, 'Marks of Belonging', p. 24.

14 Hall, *Life with the Esquimaux*, II, 78–9.

15 Haines, 'Frobisher's Bells', pp. 837–8.

16 Haines, 'Frobisher's Bells', p. 842.

17 Best, *A True Discourse*, I, 50.

18 Best, *A True Discourse*, I, 50.

19 Blackwood, 'Meta Incognita', pp. 36–7.

20 Lok, 'Testimony', in McDermott (ed.), *Third Voyage*, p. 72.

21 Lok, 'Testimony', in McDermott (ed.), *Third Voyage*, p. 72.

22 McDermott, *Martin Frobisher*, pp. 153–64.

23 Eden, *Decades of the Newe Worlde*.

24 Best, *A True Discourse*, I, 2.

14. Second (and Third) Time Unlucky

1 McDermott, *Martin Frobisher*, pp. 168–73.

2 Best, *A True Discourse*, ii, 8.

3 Cheshire et al., 'Frobisher's Eskimos', pp. 30–31.

4 For the details of the injuries sustained by Kalicho, see Cheshire et al., 'Frobisher's Eskimos', p. 40.

5 Best, *A True Discourse*, ii, 12–13.

6 Lok, 'Testimony', in McDermott (ed.), *Third Voyage*, p. 82.

7 Best, *A True Discourse*, ii, 19.

8 Best, *A True Discourse*, ii, 21.

9 Best, *A True Discourse*, ii, 23.

10 Settle, 'Second Voyage', in Hakluyt, *Principal Navigations*, iii, 35.

11 See Andrea, ' "Travelling Bodyes" ', pp. 145–8.

12 Transcribed in McDermott, *Martin Frobisher*, pp. 186–7.

13 Lok, 'Testimony', in McDermott (ed.), *Third Voyage*, p. 81.

14 McDermott, *Martin Frobisher*, pp. 199–202.

15 Ellis, ' A True Report', in McDermott (ed.), *Third Voyage*, p. 197.

16 Best, *A True Discourse*, iii, 51.

Bibliography

MSS

Arquivo Nacional do Torre do Tombo, Portugal
Corpo Cronológico, Parte I, mç. 66, n.° 40
Corpo Cronológico, Parte I, mç. 77, n.° 70

Printed Sources

Abulafia, David, *The Discovery of Mankind: Atlantic Encounters in the Age of Columbus* (New Haven: Yale University Press, 2008)

Acabado, Stephen, 'The Archaeology of Pericolonialism: Responses of the "Unconquered" to Spanish Conquest and Colonialism in Ifugao, Philippines', *International Journal of Historical Archaeology*, 21.1 (2017), 1–26

Acosta, Cristóbal, *Tractado delas drogas, y medicinas de las Indias Orientales* (Burgos: Martin de Victoria, 1578)

Adorno, Rolena, *The Polemics of Possession in Spanish American Narrative* (New Haven: Yale University Press, 2008)

Agnolin, Adone, 'Antropofagia ritual e identidade cultural entre os Tupinambá', *Revista de Antropologia*, 45.1 (2002), 131–85

Alcântara, Rodrigo d', *Sensing Tupinambá Mantles: From Colonial to Contemporary Brazilian Featherwork* (Montreal: Centre for Sensory Studies/ Concordia University, 2023)

Alegria, Maria Fernanda, and others, 'Portuguese Cartography in the Renaissance', in David Woodward (ed.), *Cartography in the European Renaissance*, The History of Cartography, 3, 2 vols. (Chicago: University of Chicago Press, 2007), I, pp. 975–1068

Allaire, Bernard, *La Rumeur dorée: Roberval et l'Amérique* (Montreal: Éditions La Presse, 2013)

Allen, Richard Blair, *European Slave Trading in the Indian Ocean, 1500–1850* (Athens: Ohio University Press, 2014)

——, 'Ending the History of Silence: Reconstructing European Slave Trading in the Indian Ocean', *Tempo*, 23.2 (2017), 295–313

Altamira, Rafael, 'El texto de las Leyes de Burgos de 1512', *Revista de Historia de América*, 4 (1938), 5–79

Altman, Ida, 'The Revolt of Enriquillo and the Historiography of Early Spanish America', *The Americas*, 63.4 (2007), 587–614

Amundsen, Karin Alana, 'Metallurgy, Mining, and English Colonization in the Americas, 1550–1624' (unpublished doctoral dissertation, University of Southern California, 2017)

Andrea, Bernadette, '"Travelling Bodyes": Native Women of the Northeast and Northwest Passage Ventures and English Discourses of Empire', in Ania Loomba and Melissa E. Sanchez (eds.), *Rethinking Feminism in Early Modern Studies: Gender, Race, and Sexuality* (Abingdon: Routledge, 2016), pp. 135–48

Andrews, Kenneth R., *Trade, Plunder, and Settlement: Maritime Enterprise and the Genesis of the British Empire 1480–1630* (Cambridge: Cambridge University Press, 1984)

Angeles, Jose Amiel, 'The Battle of Mactan and the Indigenous Discourse on War', *Philippine Studies*, 55.1 (2007), 3–52

Antenore, Armando, 'Somos tupinambás, queremos o manto de volta', *Folha de São Paulo*, 1 June 2000 <https://www1.folha.uol.com.br/fsp/ilustrad/fq0106200006.htm> [accessed 14 February 2024]

Ardren, Traci, *Everyday Life in the Classic Maya World* (Cambridge: Cambridge University Press, 2023)

Arnold, Torsten, 'Shipwrecks of the "Carreira da Índia" (1595–1623): Sources for the Study in Portuguese Maritime History' (unpublished master's dissertation, University of Lisbon, 2014)

Arteaga, Fernando, Desiree Desierto and Mark Koyama, 'Shipwrecked by Rents', *Journal of Development Economics*, 168 (2024), 103240

Auret, Chris, and Tim Maggs, 'The Great Ship São Bento: Remains from a Mid-Sixteenth Century Portuguese Wreck on the Pondoland Coast', *Annals of the Natal Museum*, 25.1 (1982), 1–39

Azoulay, Ariella Aïsha, *Potential History: Unlearning Imperialism* (London: Verso, 2019)

Baião, António, *Historia quinhentista (inedita) do Segundo cerco de Dio* (Coimbra: Imprensa da Universidade, 1927)

Barbosa, Duarte, O *Livro de Duarte Barbosa*, ed. Neves Águas (Mem Martins: Europa-Ámerica, [n.d.])

Barros, Amândio Jorge Morais, 'O Porto e a construção dos navios de Vasco da Gama', in *Estudos em homenagem ao Professor Doutor José Marques*, vol. 1 (Porto: Universidade do Porto, 2006), 131–41

Barros, João de, *Da Ásia*, 24 vols (Lisbon: Regia Officina Typografica, 1777–88)

Beck, Lauren, 'Introduction: Firsting and the Architecture of Decolonizing Scholarship on the Early-Modern Atlantic World', in Lauren Beck (ed.), *Firsting in the Early-Modern Atlantic World* (New York: Routledge, 2019), pp. 1–22

Belleforest, François de, 'Histoire troisiesme', in Hervé-Thomas Campangne (ed.), *Le Cinquiesme Tome des histoires tragiques* (Geneva: Librairie Droz, 2013), pp. 133–77

Best, George, *A True Discourse of the Late Voyages of Discouerie, for the Finding of a Passage to Cathaya, by the Northvveast, Vnder the Conduct of Martin Frobisher Generall* (London: Henry Bynnyman, 1578)

Bideaux, Michel, *Roberval, la Damoiselle et le Gentilhomme* (Paris: Classiques Garnier, 2009)

Biedermann, Zoltán, *(Dis)connected Empires: Imperial Portugal, Sri Lankan Diplomacy, and the Making of a Habsburg Conquest in Asia* (Oxford: Oxford University Press, 2018)

——, 'Three Ways of Locating the Global: Microhistorical Challenges in the Study of Early Transcontinental Diplomacy', *Past & Present*, 242, Supplement 14 (2019), 110–41

——, 'Global Navigations and the Challenge of World-Making: Introducing the Study of Spatiality in the Portuguese Empire', in Hilary Owen and Claire Williams (eds.), *Transnational Portuguese Studies* (Liverpool: Liverpool University Press, 2020), pp. 23–42

——, 'The Portuguese Estado da Índia (Empire in Asia)', *Oxford Research Encyclopedia of Asian History* <https://oxfordre.com/asianhistory/view/10.1093/acrefore/9780190277727.001.0001/acrefore-9780190277727-e-329> [accessed 28 October 2024]

Biggar, Henry Percival, *A Collection of Documents Relating to Jacques Cartier and the Sieur de Roberval*, Publications of the Public Archives of Canada, 14 (Ottawa: Public Archives of Canada, 1930)

Black, Charlene Villaseñor, and Tim Barringer, 'Decolonizing Art and Empire', *Art Bulletin*, 104.1 (2022), 6–20

Blackwood, Nicole, 'Meta Incognita: Some Hypotheses on Cornelis Ketel's Lost English and Inuit Portraits', in Thijs Westeijn, Eric Jorink and Frits Scholten (eds.), *Netherlandish Art in its Global Context* (Leiden: Brill, 2016), pp. 28–53

Bleichmar, Daniela, *Visual Voyages: Images of Latin American Nature from Columbus to Darwin* (New Haven: Yale University Press, 2017)

Bobb, Bernard E., 'Pedro Sarmiento de Gamboa and the Strait of Magellan', *Pacific Historical Review*, 17.3 (1948), 269–82

Borges, Marco Oliveira, 'Aspetos do quotidiano e vivência feminina nos navios da carreira da Índia durante o século XVI: primeiras mulheres, buscas e sexualidade a bordo', *Revista Portuguesa de História*, 47 (2016), 195–214

———, *Entre o Céu e o Inferno: vida e morte nos navios da expansão portuguesa (1497–1655)* (Lisbon: Planeta de Livros Portugal, 2023)

Bottineau, Yves, 'L'exotisme en Haute-Normandie dans la première moitié du XVIe siècle', *Études Normandes*, 27.3–4 (1978), 63–83

Bourrilly, Victor-Louis, and Nathanaël Weiss, 'Jean du Bellay, les protestants et la Sorbonne (1529–1535): les poursuites – l'affaire des placards', *Bulletin de la Société de l'Histoire du Protestantisme Français*, Études historiques, 53.2 (1904), 97–143

Boxer, Charles Ralph, 'The Naval and Colonial Papers of Dom Antonio de Ataíde', *Harvard Library Bulletin*, 5.1 (1951), 24–50

———, 'The Principal Ports of Call in the Carreira da Índia', *Luso-Brazilian Review*, 8.1 (1971), 3–29

———, *The Portuguese Seaborne Empire, 1415–1825* (Harmondsworth: Penguin, 1973)

———, *The Tragic History of the Sea* (Minneapolis: University of Minnesota Press, 2001)

Boyer, Elizabeth, *A Colony of One: The History of a Brave Woman* (Novelty, OH: Veritie Press, 1983)

Brito, Bernardo Gomes de, *História Trágico-Marítima* (Lisbon: Afrodite, 1972)

Buono, Amy J., 'Feathered Identities and Plumed Performances: Tupinambá Interculture in Early Modern Brazil and Europe' (unpublished doctoral dissertation, University of California Santa Barbara, 2007)

———, 'Tupi Featherwork and the Dynamics of Intercultural Exchange in Early Modern Brazil', in Jaynie Anderson (ed.), *Crossing Cultures: Conflict, Migration, Convergence: The Proceedings of the 32nd International Congress in the History of Art* (Melbourne: Melbourne University Press, 2009), 291–95

———, ' "Their Treasures Are the Feathers of Birds": Tupinambá Featherwork and the Image of America', in Alessandra Russo, Gerhard Wolf and Diana Fane (eds.), *Images Take Flight: Feather Art in Mexico and Europe (1400–1700)* (Munich: Hirmer, 2015), pp. 179–89

Burger, Elizabeth, 'Reinvestigating the Wreck of the Sixteenth Century Portuguese Galleon São João: A Historical Archaeological Perspective' (unpublished master's dissertation, University of Pretoria, 2003)

Burton, Andrew, 'Urbanization in East Africa, circa 900–2010 CE', *Oxford Research Encyclopedia of African History* <https://doi.org/10.1093/acrefore/9780190277734.013.31> [accessed 12 July 2024]

Cabral, Diogo de Carvalho, 'The Alphabetic Colonization of Amerindian Oral Ecologies in Early Brazil', in *Oxford Research Encyclopedia of Latin American History*, 28 June 2017 <https://oxfordre.com/latinamericanhistory> [accessed 14 February 2024]

Caetano, Gabriel Fernandes, 'Devouring Brazilian Modernism: The Rise of Contemporary Indigenous Art', *E-International Relations*, 24 February 2022 <https://www.e-ir.info/2022/02/24/devouring-brazilian-modernism-the-rise-of-contemporary-indigenous-art/#google_vignette> [accessed 14 February 2024]

Camerarius, Philipp, 'Chapter XII: Of the Doubtfull, Uncertaine, Inconstant, and Miserable Condition of Mans Life', in *The Living Librarie; Or, Meditations and Observations Historical, Natural, Moral, Political, and Poetical*, trans. by John Molle (London: Adam Islip, 1621), 34–45

Camões, José (ed.), *Teatro português do século XVI*, vol. 1, part 3 (Lisbon: Imprensa Nacional-Casa de Moeda, 2010)

Campangne, Hervé-Thomas, 'Framing the Early Modern French Best Seller: American Settings for François de Belleforest's Tragic Histories', *Renaissance Quarterly*, 71.1 (2018), 77–113

Carrasquillo, Rosa Elena, 'La creación del primer paisaje colonial español en las Américas, Santo Domingo, 1492–1548', *Antípoda. Revista de Antropología y Arqueología,* 1.36 (2019), 61–84

Casimiro, Tânia Manuel, and Marco Oliveira Borges, 'Life on Board Portuguese Ships in the 16th–18th Centuries: Theorizing Households through History and Archaeology', *Heritage,* 6 (2023), 2020–37

Castro, Aníbal Pinto de, 'O relato do naufrágio do galeão grande São João e o texto d'*Os Lusíadas*', *Santa Barbara Portuguese Studies,* 7 (2003), 17–28

Castro, Filipe Vieira de, *The Pepper Wreck: A Portuguese Indiaman at the Mouth of the Tagus River* (College Station: Texas A&M University Press, 2005)

Cervantes, Fernando, *Conquistadores: A New History* (London: Allen Lane, 2020)

Charité, Claude La, 'Les questions laissées en suspens par le *Brief recit* (1545) de Jacques Cartier et les réponses de la nouvelle 67 de *l'Heptaméron* (1559) de Marguerite de Navarre', *Œuvres & Critiques,* 36.1 (2011), 91–109

Cheshire, Neil, et al., 'Frobisher's Eskimos in England', *Arquivaria,* 10 (1980), 23–50

Clendinnen, Inga, *Ambivalent Conquests: Maya and Spaniard in Yucatan, 1517–1570,* 2nd edition (Cambridge: Cambridge University Press, 2003)

Coates, Timothy J., *Convicts and Orphans: Forced and State-Sponsored Colonizers in the Portuguese Empire, 1550–1755* (Stanford: Stanford University Press, 2001)

Colley, Linda, 'Going Native, Telling Tales: Captivity, Collaborations and Empire', *Past & Present,* 168.1 (2000), 170–93

Colón, Cristóbal, *Textos y documentos completes: relaciones de viajes, cartas y memoriales,* ed. by Consuelo Varela, 2nd edn (Madrid: Alianza, 1984)

Corte-Real, Jerónimo, *Naufragio e lastimoso sucesso da perdiçam de Manoel de Sousa Sepulueda & Dona Lianor de Sá* (Lisbon: Simão Lopes, 1594)

Coutard, Nicolas, 'Les sculptures amérindiennes en Normandie dans la première moitié du XVIe siècle', *Histoire de l'art,* Voyages, 51 (2002), 65–72

Couto, Diogo de, *Da Ásia,* vol. 5, part 2 (Lisbon: Regia Officina Typographica, 1780)

Cressy, David, *Shipwrecks and the Bounty of the Sea* (Oxford: Oxford University Press, 2022)

Crosby, Alfred W., *Ecological Imperialism: The Biological Expansion of Europe, 900–1900,* 2nd edition (Cambridge: Cambridge University Press, 2015)

Cruz, Maria Augusta Lima, 'A viagem de Gonçalo Pereira Marramaque do Minho às Molucas ou os itinerários da fidalguia portuguesa no Oriente', *Studia*, 49 (1989), 315–40

D'Silva, R. D., 'Nuno da Cunha the Founder of the Portuguese Bassein', *Proceedings of the Indian History Congress*, 42 (1981), 214–23

Davies, Surekha, 'Depictions of Brazilians on French Maps, 1542–1555', *Historical Journal*, 55.2 (2012), 317–48

———, *Renaissance Ethnography and the Invention of the Human: New Worlds, Maps and Monsters* (Cambridge: Cambridge University Press, 2016)

Dias, Carlos Malheiro, Ernesto de Vasconcelos and Alfredo Roque Gameiro, *História da colonização portuguesa do Brasil: edição monumental comemorativa do primeiro centenário da Independência do Brasil*, 3 vols. (Porto: Litografia Nacional, 1924)

Díaz del Castillo, Bernal, *The True History of the Conquest of New Spain*, ed. by Genaro García, trans. by Alfred Percival Maudslay (Cambridge: Cambridge University Press, 2010)

Documentos sobre os portugueses em Moçambique e na África central: 1497–1840, vol. 7 (Lisbon: National Archives of Rhodesia; Centro de Estudos Históricos Ultramarinos, 1971)

Domingues, Francisco Contente, *A carreira da Índia* (Lisbon: Clube do Colecionador dos Correios, 1998)

Duffy, Eve M., and Alida C. Metcalf, *The Return of Hans Staden: A Go-Between in the Atlantic World* (Baltimore: Johns Hopkins University Press, 2012)

Duffy, James, *Shipwreck and Empire: Being an Account of Portuguese Maritime Disasters in a Century of Decline* (Cambridge, MA: Harvard University Press, 1955)

Durzan, Don J., 'Arginine, Scurvy and Cartier's "Tree of Life"', *Journal of Ethnobiology and Ethnomedicine*, 5.1 (2009), article: 5

Eden, Richard, *The Decades of the Newe Worlde or West India* (London: William Powell, 1555)

Engelhard, Michael, 'Marks of Belonging: Inuit Traditional Tattoos', *Above & Beyond*, 3 (2018), 23–5

Evans, Chris, and Göran Rydén, ' "Voyage Iron": An Atlantic Slave Trade Currency, Its European Origins, and West African Impact', *Past & Present*, 239.1 (2018), 41–70

Ferguson, Margaret W., *Dido's Daughters: Literacy, Gender, and Empire in Early Modern England and France* (Chicago; University of Chicago Press, 2003)

Fernández-Armesto, Felipe, *Straits: Beyond the Myth of Magellan* (Oakland: University of California Press, 2022; London: Bloomsbury, 2022)

Field, Richard J., 'Revisiting Magellan's Voyage to the Philippines', *Philippine Quarterly of Culture and Society*, 34.4 (2006), 313–37

Finegold, Andrew, 'Vitality Materialized: On the Piercing and Adornment of the Body in Mesoamerica', *Latin American and Latinx Visual Culture*, 1.4 (2019), 55–75

Fisher, Will, 'The Renaissance Beard: Masculinity in Early Modern England', *Renaissance Quarterly*, 54 (2001), 155–87

Flores, Jorge, 'Floating Franks: The Portuguese and Their Empire as Seen from Early Modern Asia', in Robert Aldrich and Kirsten McKenzie (eds.), *The Routledge History of Western Empires* (London: Routledge, 2014), pp. 33–45

Flores, Jorge, and Giuseppe Marcocci, 'Killing Images: Iconoclasm and the Art of Political Insult in Sixteenth and Seventeenth Century Portuguese India', *Itinerario*, 42.3 (2018), 461–89

Floyd, Troy S., *The Columbus Dynasty in the Caribbean, 1492–1526* (Albuquerque: University of New Mexico Press, 1973)

Galeano, Eduardo, *Open Veins of Latin America: Five Centuries of the Pillage of a Continent*, trans. by Cedric Belfrage, 25th anniversary edition, foreword by Isabel Allende (New York: Monthly Review Press, 1997)

Gândavo, Pêro de Magalhães de, *A primeira história do Brasil*, ed. by Sheila Moura Hue and Ronaldo Menegaz, 2nd edn (Rio de Janeiro: Zahar, 2004)

Garcia, José Manuel, 'Documentos existentes em Portugal sobre Fernão de Magalhães e as suas viagens', *Abriu*, 8 (2019), 15–33

——, *Fernão de Magalhães: herói, traidor ou mito: a história do primeiro homem a abraçar o mundo* (Lisbon: Editorial Presença, 2019)

Ghobrial, John-Paul A., 'Moving Stories and What They Tell Us: Early Modern Mobility between Microhistory and Global History', *Past & Present*, 242, Supplement 14 (2019), 243–80

Godinho, Vitorino Magalhães, *O papel de Portugal nos séculos XV–XVI* (Lisbon: Ministério da Educação, 1994)

Gopal, Priyamvada, *Insurgent Empire: Anticolonial Resistance and British Dissent* (London: Verso, 2020)

————, 'On Decolonisation and the University', *Textual Practice*, 35.6 (2021), 873–99

Gordon, Alan, 'The Sixteenth-Century World and Jacques Cartier', in *The Hero and the Historians: Historiography and the Uses of Jacques Cartier* (Vancouver: University of British Columbia Press, 2010), pp. 10–28

Guiomarino, Hailton Felipe, 'Jauáraichê: sobre a devoração do ser', *Prometeus*, 40 (2022), 147–65

Guitar, Lynne, 'Cultural Genesis: Relationships among Indians, Africans and Spaniards in Rural Hispaniola, First Half of the Sixteenth Century' (Ph.D. dissertation, Vanderbilt University, 1998)

Haines, John, 'Frobisher's Bells: Commodities or Gifts?', *Sixteenth Century Journal*, 47.4 (2016), 819–45

Hakluyt, Richard, *The Principal Navigations, Voyages, Traffiques and Discoveries of the English Nation*, 3 vols. (London: George Bishop, Ralph Newberie and Robert Barker, 1599)

Hall, Charles Francis, *Life with the Esquimaux*, 2 vols. (London: Sampson Low, Son, and Marston, 1864)

Hamdani, Abbas, 'Ottoman Response to the Discovery of America and the New Route to India', *Journal of the American Oriental Society*, 101.3 (1981), 323–30

Hartman, Saidiya, 'Venus in Two Acts', *Small Axe*, 12.2 (2008), 1–14

Havard, Gilles, and Cécile Vidal, *Histoire de l'Amérique française* (Paris: Flammarion, 2019)

Hemming, John, *Red Gold: The Conquest of the Brazilian Indians* (Cambridge, MA.: Harvard University Press, 1978)

Herrera, Antonio de, *Historia general de los hechos de los castellanos en las islas i tierra firme del mar mar oceano*, 4 vols. (Madrid: Imprenta Real, 1725–30)

Heuer, Christopher P., 'Arctic Matters in Early America', in Jennifer L. Roberts (ed.), *Scale*, Terra Foundation Essays, 2 (Chicago: Terra Foundation for American Art, 2016), pp. 180–214

Houston, Stephen D., Karl A. Taube and David Stuart, *The Memory of Bones: Body, Being, and Experience among the Classic Maya* (Austin: University of Texas Press, 2006)

Jesus, Roger Lee Pessoa de, 'O segundo cerco de Diu (1546): Estudo de história política e militar' (unpublished master's dissertation, University of Coimbra, 2012)

Johnston, Mark A., *Beard Fetish in Early Modern England: Sex, Gender, and Registers of Value* (Burlington, VT.: Ashgate, 2011)

Jorge, Lídia, *A costa dos murmúrios* (Lisbon: Publicações Dom Quixote, 1988)

Kelsey, Harry, *The First Circumnavigators: Unsung Heroes of the Age of Discovery* (New Haven: Yale University Press, 2016)

Klaus, Carrie F., 'From *Désert* to *Patrie*: Marguerite de Navarre's Lessons from the New World', *L'Esprit Créateur*, 57.3 (2017), 58–66

Knecht, R. J., *The Rise and Fall of Renaissance France, 1483–1610*, 2nd edn (Oxford: Blackwell, 2001)

Kockel, Marcelo Fidelis, 'Naufrágios e outros infortúnios na história trágico-marítima da carreira da Índia (séculos XVI e XVII)' (unpublished master's dissertation, São Paulo State University Júlio de Mesquita Filho, 2014)

Krenak, Ailton, *Ideas to Postpone the End of the World*, trans. by Anthony Doyle (Toronto: House of Anansi Press, 2020)

Lança, Marco Antonio, 'São Vicente, a primeira vila do Brasil', *PosFA-UUSP*, 17 (2005), 102–15

Lane, Kris, 'Africans and Natives in the Mines of Spanish America', in Matthew Restall (ed.), *Beyond Black and Red: African-Native Relations in Colonial Latin America* (Albuquerque: University of New Mexico Press, 2005), pp. 159–84

——, *Pillaging the Empire: Global Piracy on the High Seas, 1500–1750*, 2nd edn (New York: Routledge, 2016)

Langfur, Hal (ed.), *Native Brazil: Beyond the Convert and the Cannibal, 1500–1900* (Albuquerque: University of New Mexico Press, 2014)

Las Casas, Bartolomé de, *Historia de las Indias*, ed. by Agustín Millares Carlo and Lewis Hanke (México: Fondo de Cultura Económica, 1951)

——, *An Account, Much Abbreviated, of the Destruction of the Indies, with Related Texts*, trans. by Andrew Hurley, ed. by Franklin W. Knight (Indianapolis: Hackett Publishing Company, 2003)

Léry, Jean de, *History of a Voyage to the Land of Brazil*, ed. and trans. by Janet Whatley (Berkeley: University of California Press, 1990)

Lestringant, Frank, 'Going Native in America (French-Style)', *Renaissance Studies*, 6.3–4 (1992), 325–35

López de Gómara, Francisco, *Cortés: The Life of the Conqueror by His Secretary*, ed. and trans. by Lesley Byrd Simpson (Berkeley: University of California Press, 1966)

Loureiro, Rui Manuel, 'As fontes do projecto de navegação de Fernão de Magalhães', *Abriu*, 8 (2019), 35–67

Lukach, Katharine, and Jeffrey Dobereiner, 'The Painted Body', in Nicholas Carte, Stephen D. Houston and Franco D. Rossi (eds.), *The Adorned Body: Mapping Ancient Maya Dress* (Austin: University of Texas Press, 2020), pp. 32–50

Lyon, Eugene, 'Spain's Sixteenth-Century North American Settlement Attempts: A Neglected Aspect', *Florida Historical Quarterly*, 59 (1980), 275–91

Macedo, Hélder, 'Bernardim Ribeiro: factos e presunções', in Hélder Macedo (ed.), *Menina e moça ou saudades* (Lisbon: Publicações Dom Quixote, 1990), pp. 7–49

Madeira, Angélica, 'Shipwreck Narratives: Between History and Literature – Reflections on *História Trágico-Marítima* (Tragic-Maritime History)', *Limite*, 12.2 (2018), 95–111

Magana, Edmundo, 'Some Tupi Constellations', *Ibero-Amerikanisches Archiv*, 10, n.s., 2 (1984), 189–221

Maggs, Tim, 'The Great Galleon São João: Remains from a Mid-Sixteenth Century Wreck on the Natal South Coast', *Annals of the Natal Museum*, 26.1 (1984), 173–86

Mancall, Peter C., 'The Raw and the Cold: Five English Sailors in Sixteenth-Century Nunavut', *William and Mary Quarterly*, 70.1 (2013), 3–40

Marté, Roberto (ed.), *Santo Domingo en los manuscritos de Juan Bautista Muñoz* (Santo Domingo: Fundación García Arévalo, 1981)

Martínez, José Luis (ed.), *Documentos cortesianos* (México: Fondo de Cultura Económica, 1990)

Matsuda, Matt K., 'Conquered Colonies and Iberian Ambitions', in Matt K. Matsuda, *Pacific Worlds: A History of Seas, Peoples, and Cultures* (Cambridge: Cambridge University Press, 2012), pp. 49–63

Mawson, Stephanie Joy, *Incomplete Conquests: The Limits of Spanish Empire in the Seventeenth-Century Philippines* (Ithaca, NY: Cornell University Press, 2023)

McCarthy, William J., 'Gambling on Empire: The Economic Role of Shipwreck in the Age of Discovery', *International Journal of Maritime History*, 23.2 (2011), 69–84

McDermott, James, *Martin Frobisher: Elizabethan Privateer* (New Haven: Yale University Press, 2001)

———, (ed.), *The Third Voyage of Martin Frobisher to Baffin Island, 1578* (London: The Hakluyt Society, 2001)

Mearns, David L., David Parham and Bruno Frohlich, 'A Portuguese East Indiaman from the 1502–1503 Fleet of Vasco da Gama off Al Hallaniyah Island, Oman: An Interim Report', *International Journal of Nautical Archaeology*, 45.2 (2016), 331–51

Mendes, Isabel Maria Ribeiro, 'Luís Falcão nas capitanias de Ormuz e Diu', *Boletim de Trabalhos Históricos*, 41 (1990), 15–35

Metcalf, Alida C., *Go-Betweens and the Colonization of Brazil, 1500–1600* (Austin: University of Texas Press, 2006)

Middleton, John, *The World of the Swahili: An African Mercantile Civilization* (New Haven: Yale University Press, 1992)

Mignolo, Walter, 'Crossing Gazes and the Silence of the "Indians": Theodor de Bry and Guaman Poma de Ayala', *Journal of Medieval and Early Modern Studies*, 41.1 (2011), 173–223

———, 'Epistemic Disobedience and the Decolonial Option: A Manifesto', *Transmodernity*, 1.2 (2011), 44–66

Monteiro, John M., 'The Crises and Transformations of Invaded Societies: Coastal Brazil in the Sixteenth Century', in Frank Salomon and Stuart B. Schwartz (eds.), *The Cambridge History of the Native Peoples of the Americas: South America* (Cambridge: Cambridge University Press, 1999), III.2, 973–1024

———, 'The Transformation of Indigenous São Paulo in the Sixteenth Century', in John M. Monteiro, *Blacks of the Land: Indian Slavery, Settler Society, and the Portuguese Colonial Enterprise in South America*, ed. and trans. by James Woodard and Barbara Weinstein, Cambridge Latin American Studies (Cambridge: Cambridge University Press, 2018), pp. 7–47

Moura Hue, Sheila, *Antologia de poesia portuguesa: Século XVI*, 2nd edn (Rio de Janeiro: 7 Letras, 2007)

Nelson, Jennifer, 'A Ming Chinese and Spanish Imperial Collaboration in Southeast Asia: The Boxer Codex', *Art Bulletin*, 104.4 (2022), 20–45

Newitt, M. D. D., *A History of Portuguese Overseas Expansion, 1400–1668* (London: Routledge, 2005)

Niell, Paul, 'Colonial Gothic and the Negotiation of Worlds in 16th-Century Santo Domingo, Dominican Republic', in Alice Isabella

Sullivan and Kyle G. Sweeney (eds.), *Lateness and Modernity in Medieval Architecture* (Leiden: Brill, 2023), pp. 395–422

Novaes, Adauto (ed.), *A outra margem do Ocidente* (São Paulo: Companhia das Letras, 1999)

Oberg, Michael Leroy, *The Head in Edward Nugent's Hand: Roanoke's Forgotten Indians* (Philadelphia: University of Pennsylvania Press, 2008)

——, 'Tribes and Towns: What Historians Still Get Wrong about the Roanoke Ventures', *Ethnohistory*, 67.4 (2020), 579–602

Obermeier, Franz, 'As relações entre o Brasil e a região do Rio de La Plata no século XVI nos primeiros documentos sobre Assunção (Asunción) e Santa Catarina', *Jahrbuch für Geschichte Lateinamerikas*, 43.1 (2006), 317–42

Oliveira, Fernando, *Viagem do Magalhães*, in *Obra Completa*, ed. by José Eduardo Franco and Rui Manuel Loureiro, 7 vols. (Lisbon: Fundação Calouste Gulbenkian, 2021)

Orta, Garcia da, *Coloquios dos simples, e drogas* (Goa: Joannes de Endem, 1563)

Ostapkowicz, Joanna, Fiona Brock, Alex C. Wiedenhoeft, Rick Schulting and Donatella Saviola, 'Integrating the Old World into the New: An "Idol from the West Indies"', *Antiquity*, 91 (2017), 1314–29

Oviedo, Gonzalo Fernández de, *Coronica de las Indias* (Salamanca: Juan de Junta, 1547)

Pagden, Anthony, and Sanjay Subrahmanyam, 'Roots and Branches: Ibero-British Threads across Overseas Empires', in Massimo Donattini, Giuseppe Marcocci and Stefania Pastore (eds.), *L'Europa divisa e i nuovi mondi: Per Adriano Prosperi* (Pisa: Edizioni della Normale, 2011), II, 279–301

Parry, G. J. R., 'Some Early Reactions to the Three Voyages of Martin Frobisher: The Conflict between Humanists and Protestants', *Parergon*, n.s., 6 (1988), 149–61

Parry, J. H., and Robert G. Keith (eds.), *New Iberian World: A Documentary History of the Discovery and Settlement of Latin America to the Early 17th Century* (New York: Times Books, 1984)

Pearson, M. N., *The Portuguese in India* (Cambridge: Cambridge University Press, 1987)

Pérez Montás, Eugenio, *La ciudad del Ozama: 500 años de historia urbana*, 2nd edn (Santo Domingo: Universidad Católica Santo Domingo, 1998)

Phelan, John Leddy, *The Hispanization of the Philippines: Spanish Aims and Filipino Responses, 1565–1700* (Madison: University of Wisconsin Press, 1959)

Pigafetta, Antonio, *The First Voyage around the World (1519–1522): An Account of Magellan's Expedition*, ed. and intro. by Theodore J. Cachey Jr (Toronto: University of Toronto Press, 2007)

Pinto, Mark Sebastian, 'The Forgotten Community, "the Siddis of Uttara Kannada": How the Portuguese Indian Ocean Slave Trade Produced a Community of Indians of African Descent', *Interdisciplinary Journal of Portuguese Diaspora Studies*, 8 (2019), 165–88

Pinto, Paulo Jorge de Sousa, *The Philippine History Retrieval Project*, vol. 2 (Manila: National Historical Commission of the Philippines, forthcoming 2024)

Piqueira, Gustavo, *Primeiras impressões: o nascimento da cultura impressa e sua influência na criação da imagem do Brasil* (São Paulo: Editora WMF Martins Fontes, 2021)

Polónia, Amélia and Rosa Capelão, 'Women and Gender in the Portuguese Overseas Empire: Society, Economy and Politics, 16th–17th Centuries', in Francisco Bethencourt (ed.), *Gendering the Portuguese-speaking World: From the Middle Ages to the Present* (Leiden: Brill, 2021), pp. 71–101

Ponce Vázquez, Juan José, *Islanders and Empire: Smuggling and Political Defiance in Hispaniola, 1580–1690* (Cambridge: Cambridge University Press, 2020)

Prange, Sebastian R., ' "Measuring by the Bushel": Reweighing the Indian Ocean Pepper Trade', *Historical Research*, 84.224 (2011), 212–35

Ramanujan, A. K., 'Some Thoughts on "Non-Western" Classics, with Indian Examples', *World Literature Today*, 68.2 (1994), 331–4

Ramos, Fábio Pestana, 'Os problemas enfrentados no cotidiano das navegações portuguesas da carreira da Índia: fator de abandono gradual da rota das especiarias', *Revista de História*, 137 (1997), 75–94

Real, Miguel, 'Naufrágios: o lado negro da expansão ultramarina', *Limite*, 12.2 (2018), 167–72

Renaud, Tabitha, 'Rivalry and Mutiny: The Internal Struggles of Sixteenth-Century North American Colonization Parties', *Terrae Incognitae*, 43.1 (2011), 24–38

Rezvani, Leanna Bridge, 'The *Heptaméron*'s 67th Tale: Marguerite de Navarre's Humble Heroine Confronts the *Querelle des Femmes* and Catholic Tradition', *Romance Notes*, 52.1 (2012), 43–50

———, 'Nature and Nourishment, Bodies and Beasts: The *Heptaméron*'s Portrayal of Marguerite de Roberval's Marooning', *Dalhousie French Studies*, 102 (2014), 3–7

Rodriguez, Felice Noelle, 'Juan de Salcedo Joins the Native Form of Warfare', *Journal of the Economic and Social History of the Orient*, 46.2 (2003), 143–64

Romoli, Kathleen, *Balboa of Darién: Discoverer of the Pacific* (New York: Doubleday, 1953)

Roxo, Elisangela, 'A volta do manto tupinambá', *Piauí*, 27 June 2023 <https://piaui.folha.uol.com.br/volta-do-manto-tupinamba/> [accessed 14 February 2024]

——, 'The Return of the Tupinambá Mantle', *Piauí*, 4 July 2023 <https://piaui.folha.uol.com.br/the-return-of-the-tupinamba-mantle/> [accessed 27 October 2024]

Roys, Ralph L., and Juan José Hoil, *The Book of Chilam Balam of Chumayel* (Washington: Carnegie Institution of Washington, 1933)

Sadlier, Darlene J., *Brazil Imagined: 1500 to the Present* (Austin: University of Texas Press, 2008)

Samson, Gilles, and Richard Fiset, *Chantier archéologique Cartier-Roberval, promontoire du Cap-Rouge (CeEu-4), Québec, Canada: rapport synthèse des fouilles 2007–2008* (Québec: Ministère de la Culture et des Communications/Commission de la capitale nationale du Québec, 2013) <https://www.insrcr.com/publications_insrcr> [accessed 14 February 2024]

Santos, Tiago A., Nuno Fonseca and Filipe Castro, 'Stability Characteristics of an Early XVII Century Portuguese Nau', *Proceedings of the 9th International Conference on Stability of Ships and Ocean Vehicles* (STAB 2006), Rio de Janeiro, Brazil, 25–29 September 2006, pp. 69–80

Saraiva, José H. (ed.), *Ditos portugueses dignos de memória: história íntima do século XVI* (Mem Martins: Publicações Europa América, 1979)

Schreurs, Peter, 'The Voyage of Fernão de Magalhães: Three Little-Known Eyewitness Accounts', *Philippine Quarterly of Culture and Society*, 28.1 (2000), 90–109

Schroeder, Susan, 'Introduction', in Susan Schroeder (ed.), *Native Resistance and the Pax Colonial in New Spain* (Lincoln: University of Nebraska Press, 1998), pp. xi–xxiii

Schwartz, Stuart B., 'Indian Labor and New World Plantations: European Demands and Indian Responses in Northeastern Brazil', *American Historical Review*, 83.1 (1978), 43–79

———, (ed.), *Early Brazil: A Documentary Collection to 1700* (Cambridge: Cambridge University Press, 2009)

Seed, Patricia, *Ceremonies of Possession in Europe's Conquest of the New World 1492–1640* (Cambridge: Cambridge University Press, 1995)

Seler, Eduard, *Die Ruinen von Uxmal* (Berlin: Verlag der Königl. Akademie der Wissenschaften, 1917)

Sharpe, Christina, *In the Wake: On Blackness and Being* (Durham, NC: Duke University Press, 2016)

Small, Margaret, 'From Thought to Action: Gilbert, Davis, and Dee's Theories behind the Search for the Northwest Passage', *Sixteenth Century Journal*, 44.4 (2013), 1041–58

Smith, Adam, *An Inquiry into the Nature and Causes of the Wealth of Nations*. vol. 2 (Printed for W. Strahan and T. Cadell, 1776)

Sousa Coutinho, Lopo de, *História do cerco de Diu* (Lisbon: Bibliotheca de Classicos Portuguezes, 1890)

Stabler, Arthur P., *The Legend of Marguerite de Roberval* (Pullman: Washington State University Press, 1972)

Staden, Hans, *Hans Staden's True History: An Account of Cannibal Captivity in Brazil*, ed. and trans. by Neil L. Whitehead and Michael Harbsmeier (Durham, NC: Duke University Press, 2008)

Stanley, Lord, of Alderley, *The First Voyage Round the World, by Magellan* (London: Hakluyt Society, 2010)

Stoler, Ann Laura, *Along the Archival Grain: Epistemic Anxieties and Colonial Common Sense* (Princeton: Princeton University Press, 2009)

Stone, Erin Woodruff, 'America's First Slave Revolt: Indians and African Slaves in Española, 1500–1534', *Ethnohistory*, 60.2 (2013), 195–217

———, 'Crossroads of Slavery: The African Slave Trade Meets the Indian Slave Trade', in Erin Woodruff Stoner, *Captives of Conquest: Slavery in the Early Modern Spanish Caribbean* (Philadelphia: University of Pennsylvania Press, 2021), pp. 130–55

Subrahmanyam, Sanjay, *The Career and Legend of Vasco da Gama* (Cambridge: Cambridge University Press, 1997)

———, *The Portuguese Empire in Asia, 1500–1700: A Political and Economic History* (Chichester: Wiley-Blackwell, 2012)

———, *Across the Green Sea: Histories from the Western Indian Ocean, 1440–1640* (Austin: University of Texas Press, 2024)

————, 'Written on Water: Designs and Dynamics in the Portuguese Estado da Índia', in Susan Alcock et al. (eds.), *Empires* (New York: Cambridge University Press, 2001), pp. 42–69

————, 'Holding the World in Balance: The Connected Histories of the Iberian Overseas Empires, 1500–1640', *American Historical Review*, 112.5 (2007), 1359–85

————, *Empires between Islam and Christianity, 1500–1800* (Albany: State University of New York Press, 2019)

Tavares, Rui (ed.), *Portugal: uma retrospectiva: 1603–1385* (Lisbon: Tinta-da-China, 2022)

Taylor, Dicey, Marco Biscione and Peter G. Roe, 'Epilogue: The Beaded Zemi in the Pigorini Museum', in F. Brecht et al. (eds.), *Taíno: Pre-Columbian Art and Culture from the Caribbean* (New York: Monacelli Press, 1997), pp. 158–69

Thevet, André, *André Thevet's North America: A Sixteenth-Century View*, ed. and trans. by Roger Schlesinger and Arthur P. Stabler (Kingston: McGill-Queen's University Press, 1986)

Thomas, Hugh, *The Conquest of Mexico* (London: Hutchinson, 1993)

Thomaz, Luís Filipe, 'A questão da pimenta em meados do século XVI', *A carreira da Índia e as rotas dos estreitos, Actas do VIII Seminário Internacional de História Indo-Portuguesa, Angra do Heroísmo, 7–11 de June. de 1996* (1998), 37–206

Tomlinson, Gary, *The Singing of the New World: Indigenous Voice in the Era of European Contact* (Cambridge: Cambridge University Press, 2007)

Tozzer, Alfred M., *Landa's Relación de las cosas de Yucatan: A Translation* (New York: Krauss, 1966)

Trouillot, Michel-Rolph, *Silencing the Past: Power and the Production of History* (Boston, MA: Beacon Press, 1995)

Turgeon, Laurier, 'Shell Beads and Belts in 16th- and Early 17th-Century France and North America', *Gradhiva*, 33 (2022), 40–59

Utrera, Cipriano de, *Polémica de Enriquillo*, intro. by E. Rodríguez Demorizi, Academia Dominicana de la Historia, 34 (Santo Domingo: Editora del Caribe, 1973)

Vali, Murtaza, 'Lightning Strikes: Murtaza Vali on the Art of Kidlat Tahimik', *Artforum*, 58.3 (November 2019) <https://www.artforum.com/features/murtaza-vali-on-the-art-of-kidlat-tahimik-245087/> [accessed 14 February 2024]

Velho, Alvaro, *Roteiro da primeira viagem de Vasco da Gama*, ed. by Neves Aguas (Mem Martins: Publicações Europa-América, 1987)

Velho, Alvaro, and João de Sá, *A Journal of the First Voyage of Vasco da Gama, 1497–1499*, ed. and trans. by Ernest George Ravenstein (London: Hakluyt Society, 1898)

Viveiros de Castro, Eduardo, *From the Enemy's Point of View: Humanity and Divinity in an Amazonian Society*, trans. by Catherine V. Howard (Chicago: University of Chicago Press, 1992)

———, *The Inconstancy of the Indian Soul: The Encounter of Catholics and Cannibals in 16th-Century Brazil*, trans. by Gregory Duff Morton (Chicago: Prickly Paradigm Press, 2011)

Voigt, Lisa, 'The "True History" of Captivity Narratives in the Iberian Empires', in Lisa Voigt, *Writing Captivity in the Early Modern Atlantic: Circulations of Knowledge and Authority in the Iberian and English Imperial Worlds* (Chapel Hill: University of North Carolina Press, 2008), pp. 40–98

The Voyages of Jacques Cartier, intro. by Ramsay Cook (Toronto: University of Toronto Press, 1993)

Welch, Sidney R., *South Africa under John III, 1521–1557* (Cape Town: Juta & Co., 1948)

Whitehead, Neil L., 'Hans Staden and the Cultural Politics of Cannibalism', *Hispanic American Historical Review*, 80.4 (2000), 721–51

———, 'The Ethnographic Lens in the New World: Staden, de Bry, and the Representation of the Tupi in Brazil', in Walter Melion and Lee Palmer Wandel (eds.), *Early Modern Eyes*, Intersections, 13 (Leiden: Brill, 2010), pp. 81–104

Wintroub, Michael, 'Information: Pilgrimage in a Church of Poems', in Michael Wintroub, *The Voyage of Thought: Navigating Knowledge across the Sixteenth-Century World* (Cambridge: Cambridge University Press, 2017), pp. 8–66

Zvereva, Alexandra, *Les Clouet de Catherine de Médicis: Chefs-d'œuvre graphiques du Musée Condé* (Paris: Somogy Éditions d'Art, 2002)

Websites and Databases

Journey without Return: An Inventory of Spanish Shipwrecks off the Coasts of the United States and Bahamas <https://www.shipwrecks.es/> [accessed 12 July 2024]

Património de influência portuguessa <https://hpip.org/pt> [accessed 12 July 2024]

Prices, Wages and Rents in Portugal 1300–1910 <http://pwr-portugal.ics.ul.pt/> [accessed 12 July 2024]

Acknowledgements

It takes many people to make a book. What follows records my thanks to some of the many people who have helped me along the journey of making this one.

Without Ben Clark, I would not have managed to share these stories with a wider readership. He's supported me throughout and encouragingly laughed at my jokes along the way.

I am immeasurably grateful to everyone at Penguin/Viking who helped bring this project to fruition, especially to Connor Brown and Trisha Mendiratta for their insights and patient assistance of many kinds.

Kit Shepherd read everything with astonishing attention to detail and Igor Reyner fashioned a bibliography out of several messy folders.

I often think what my career would have been like if I had not had Patrick and Geraldine as my college colleagues: it is such a joy to work with two people who think and write about culture so carefully and creatively. I am also grateful to my university colleagues for their longstanding support and encouragement: thank you Cláudia, Claire, Georgia, Gui, Luísa, Phillip and Tom.

Francesca, Jenny and Flash have offered solidarity on several fronts and joined me on many miles of walks. Emma suggested the title to me when I was coming up with the initial ideas for this book. Bea listened to me talk about this project and asked questions about it in more places around the world than anyone else. Rowan read each chapter, helped me to embrace writing my own voice, and often sat encouragingly opposite me and my piles of books in a library carrel that I will forever associate with some of the characters of *Wreckers*.

Finally, this book is dedicated to my family who have always been there for me in their idiosyncratically Park-ish ways.

Index